INSIDE JOB

A LIFE OF TEACHING

by
Robert S. Boone, Ph.D.

THE PUDDIN'HEAD PRESS
2003

Additional copies of this book may be ordered by writing to:

The Puddin'head Press
PO Box 477889
Chicago IL 60647
708-656-4900

Cover Design: Wildenradt Design Associates
Back Cover Photography: Susanne Poling
Editor: John Manos

First Edition

ISBN# 0-9724339-1-0

To My Wife
Sue

TABLE OF CONTENTS

INTRODUCTION

PART 1
IN THE SCHOOLS

PART 2
OUT OF THE SCHOOLS

INTRODUCTION

Any teacher's life is a journey. A voyage of discovery. A teacher wakes each morning to new terrain, a new bend in the path, a new fork in the trail. The territory, though often similar, is never the same. There are the peaks and valleys of any career, of course, but there are also the exact and exacting bluffs and hollows, gullies and hummocks of working with students each day. And yes, intriguing views and spectacular vistas as well. Some wayfarers travel with the teacher for a moment; others share the journey for a long time. And some, though they may only appear ephemerally along the path, leave a deep and lasting imprint.

Inside Job: A Life of Teaching is the record of Bob Boone's journey. Bob's odyssey as a teacher has been especially interesting and particularly instructive. He is the founder and director of Young Chicago Authors, a nonprofit organization whose mission is to encourage self-expression and literacy among Chicago's youth through writing and performance. The organization has burgeoned in the last decade from a scholarship program for select students to an outreach program that influences hundreds of young writers each year. Young Chicago Authors currently provides creative writing courses and performance forums, free to youth, as well as services that aid educators in promoting creative writing within the schools. Where did the idea for Young Chicago Authors originate? How was it pioneered?

The answers lie in the story of Bob's journey as a teacher.

That journey began, most likely, in the Pioneer Room at Crow Island School in Winnetka Illinois, where Bob and his grammar school classmates learned by doing. *Inside Job*, though, starts on Staten Island where Bob's eighth graders presented a singular version of Dickens' *Christmas Carol*. His next sojourn was in Frankfurt, Germany where he learned that how people see themselves and each other affects everyone's understanding. At Northwestern University, Bob met Wally Douglas who helped him alter the educational maxim from Teacher-Stuff-Student into Teacher-Student-Stuff, a concept Bob already had an intuitive sense of, but something all of us in schools need to be reminded of intermittently. Bob moved on to Highland Park High School in suburban Chicago where he practiced what Douglas preached. And while there, Bob discovered, too, that he needed sometimes to go outside the walls of traditional public education to get the *Inside Job* done. Traveling at night and sometimes in the dark was necessary as well.

Bob next found his way to instruction for standardized tests, first the General Education Diploma (GED) exam and then the SAT and ACT–the paradox being, of course, that at times those necessary gates provided the best way to reach some of those students that had already left standard educational settings. By the time Bob reached Columbia College in Chicago (he had in the year before his arrival on Staten Island earned his masters degree at that other Columbia in New York), he saw himself as a *freelance* teacher. And what he did best was get students who aren't supposed to be writers to write: future NBA stars at Athletes For a Better Education, for example, and children from Cabrini Green, the Chicago housing project described in the media as a "war zone".

Young Chicago Authors, built from these experiences, first found a home in the conference room of the Monadnock Building in Chicago's Loop. The program now resides on West Division Street in offices decorated with photographs and art depicting both Bob's own voyage and the treks of the many young writers with whom he has worked. The YCA grads are well met–Antevia and Tenaya, Juan and Koz, Carol and Liz, Vicki and Jesus, and the others. But, in fact, the rovers and roamers one meets all along Bob's path over the years are vivid and colorful, sometimes eccentric and always memorable. There are Drew and Dotty on Staten Island and Zsa Zsa and Ingrid in Frankfurt. Wally at Northwestern, of course. Thelma and Hack and Robert in Highland Park. At AFBE, Chick and MR. MAGIC.

Bob's title, *Inside Job*, works in part because it's an insider's account of a life spent in teaching and in part because it suggests something almost criminal–the breaking of rules that is sometimes necessary to make the Teacher-Student-Stuff idea work. But the title works best because the book is really about people locating the writing voices that are within them. It's about Bob finding his voice for this book and about all those students in disparate settings from Frankfurt to Division Street discovering their voices and realizing that, whatever their subsequent occupations, they are writers.

Just as a writer writes, a teacher teaches. In fact, one really only learns to teach by teaching. But writing about teaching–not so much the theoretical contracts but the actual classroom moments, the descriptions of the territory rather than the explanations of the map–are still helpful. Part of understanding involves learning from the experience of others who have been traveling along the path. I've shared Bob's journey since those Teacher-Student-Stuff moments at Northwestern. Those readers about to embark and those just starting on their journeys will, of course, benefit from *Inside Job*. But so will the rest of us. Those that have come to their first real bend, those trying to find the safest crossing, those attempting to locate the clearest pass, and, yes, those of us already far down the final slope–all of us will benefit from sharing Bob's passage.

Jay Amberg
December, 2002

IN THE SCHOOLS

THE HEADMASTER

On a Saturday morning in the spring of 1964, Sue and I each drop a nickel into the machine and board the *Gold Star Mother,* the ferry that will take us from Manhattan to Staten Island. In the fall, we'll start teaching on Staten Island, and we need to find a place to live. Before sitting down on an outside bench, I buy a hot dog heaped with sauerkraut. It's small and slightly gray. It looks tired and doesn't taste too good. I seem to recall that a few years ago, a Belgian tourist had encountered a human knuckle inside one of these ferry wieners. I lob the rest over the side just as we chug past the Statue of Liberty.

Staten Island, the joke goes, got its name when Peter Stuyvesant, sitting in a small boat in New York Harbor, squinted through the fog at a large hunk of land to the south and asked, "Is staten island?" I've already heard this joke several times and expect to hear it some more, and before long I'll start telling it.

Our future boss is waiting for us in the parking lot of the ferry terminal. His name is Henry Morrison, and he is the headmaster of the Staten Island Academy. He is leaning against an old green Chevy and smoking. Instead of the sport coat with the leather elbow patches that he wore so comfortably at our interviews, today he's wearing a faded green flannel shirt, jeans, and old tennis shoes. His hair is barely combed. He is thin, almost fragile.

At our interview, he had been pleasantly rambling. When I talked, he listened carefully. I told him I had not been an honors student in high school, but that I had always had an idea that I might want to teach. In college, I didn't break any records, but I kept thinking of myself more as a teacher than a scholar. My work at Columbia Teachers College convinced me all the more that I should be in the classroom. "I'm glad to hear that," he had said, "I'm not looking for intellectuals."

Along the street behind him loom old factories and warehouses. These spooky buildings, the hulking ferries, and the smoky air drifting across the water from New Jersey give the scene a gritty urban feeling. "Welcome to our lovely island," he says. He gestures to what's behind him and nods wryly. "It's a good day for apartment hunting. I'm really glad you came out today."

I'm sure he means it. When he hired Sue and me, he filled two teaching positions at once. Rather than cranky radicals or scowling misfits, we must look like the well-adjusted suburban types that we are. And he's probably pleased that we are practical young people who take care of matters early. We won't be showing up in the fall without a place to live.

On the way to his house, Henry pulls up in front of a liquor store and disappears inside. A few minutes later he's back, lugging a case of whiskey. "Some school people are coming by tomorrow," he wheezes as he pushes the case next to where I am sitting in the back seat.

We head up Todt Hill past large houses set back in the woods. It's hard to believe that this is New York City. At the very top of the hill stands an old mansion that is now the elementary school for the Staten Island Academy. It's a massive, red brick building with sturdy, white colonial pillars. I have been told that the high school will be moved up near here in a few years, but for now the building, known as Dongan Hall, is surrounded by large athletic fields. On the edge of one of the fields sits a small half-timbered cottage-like place where Henry and his wife Janet live.

Janet Morrison greets us at the door. She is taller and sturdier than her husband. She leads us into a simple living room filled with stuffed bookshelves. On the table are tuna fish sandwiches, chips and iced tea. We serve ourselves while she pours a bourbon for Henry, who has folded himself into a large chair by the fireplace. Through the window on the lawn we can see a round, red-haired youngster raking. "That's Dennis," Henry smiles. "He's been driving his teachers crazy so I thought I'd have him spend the day working here. Maybe I can figure out what's going on. And maybe not." He shrugs and sips on his drink.

I like the guy. He's not afraid to have a drink in front of us. He drives a crappy car. He wears ordinary clothes. He wants us to call him by his first name. He speaks frankly and not in some phony educationese. He asks Dennis to rake his lawn. He's going to let us borrow his car so we can hunt for a place to live. He's not one of those public school principals who moved up from the coaching staff or from driver's education to be the boss. I already know that he graduated from Colgate, earned an M.A. from Trinity and taught in several Eastern prep schools. William F. Buckley is one of his former students. This is the kind of guy I can respect. After all, I'm going to be a new teacher. I want my boss to know what he's doing. I want him to have a sense of what good teaching is. Henry strikes me as someone like that.

After lunch, I take the wheel of Henry's car, while Sue, a much better navigator, sits next to me with a map of the island and a newspaper in her lap. The two of us check out apartments in New Dorp, Dongan Hills, Tottenville, and several other little villages that make up Staten Island. Compared to our Greenwich Village neighborhood, most of Staten Island below the hills seems unapologetically plain. We find a little place we like in West Brighton—ten minutes down the hill from the school and around the corner from a Chihuahua stud service.

Later that afternoon we sit on chairs on the lawn recently mowed and raked by Dennis, drink gin and tonics and eat chips and dip. We describe our place in West Brighton. Henry tells us that lots of teachers live "down" there, but not many students. "That's not quite right," Janet laughs, and then, for some reason, we all laugh.

After several more drinks, Henry takes over the conversation. He tells us that the school is good now but will become even more "highly competitive." Teachers like us will make it that way. We are the kind of "nifty" people he wants. He obviously likes words like *nifty* and *highly competitive*. He's showing off for us, but I also really believe that he has a clear vision of what his school can become.

On the way to the ferry, he leans back and talks while Janet drives. He wants us to know that we'll like where we'll live and that he and Janet have many friends from that part of the island. We shake hands in front of the ferry terminal. "We'll see you in the fall, and maybe you'll decide to stay here for a long while. Maybe raise a family here. That would really be nifty." His wife leads him back to the car, and with nickels in hand, we walk toward the ferry.

The memory of Henry sticks with me as I complete my M.A., and it is still with me later that summer as Sue and I drive back to Chicago and I begin to think about the 5th and 6th graders I will be teaching. In my imagination, I can hear Henry's New England accent, see his slightly stooped angular body, his messy hair, his slightly shaking hands. He is always nearby, looking over my shoulder, sending me notes, quietly advising me, listening attentively, explaining a subtle rule of grammar, sticking a novel in my mailbox. He is smoking, of course, and his breath smells slightly of bourbon.

The night before my first day of teaching, I stack my grad-school books in a bookcase near my desk. There are methods books, linguistics books, novels and collections of short stories. There are books by John Dewey and James Conant and several books of criticism. Last year I lost myself in these books; this year I may never open them. I write down a simple plan for tomorrow's half-day of school.

The next morning, I walk up the creaking steps to the third floor of Dongan Hall. It's an old building, once the home of FDR's Secretary of State. That man's children probably slid down the long banister. I wear a brown sport coat, a red tie, dark pants, and loafers. The third floor has four large classrooms. If they are converted bedrooms, the bedrooms were immense. The central hallway is lighted by a large window. Sprinklers hang from the high ceiling. It feels like exactly what it is: a mansion of pre-income-tax opulence made over into a school.

As I head for my room, I'm excited. Downstairs, Sue is greeting her 1st graders. And I'm up here, ready to become a teacher. For the first time in my life I carry a briefcase, a gift to myself from E. J. Korvettes. I have two pens, one already well chewed. Chewing pens is a family habit. By noon the second pen should likewise be well gnawed.

Some teachers are on the third floor already. Ada Sanchez, the French teacher, is sitting at her desk in a room on the left. I can see flowers along her window ledge and a neatly arranged bookshelf. I make a mental note not to spill coffee on her desk. A compact little lady with gray hair and good posture, she also speaks fluent Spanish. She was born into a wealthy Castilian family outside of Madrid. I have been warned not to ask if she is Mexican or Puerto Rican. She's friendly, but doesn't smile much. "Good morning, Bob," she calls out. "All set to go?" I tell her I am and wonder what she thinks of all the teachers like me who come here for a few years and then move on while she stays and stays and stays. She probably imagines each class as a bus and the teacher as the driver—steering, accelerating, turning, braking and finally hopping off for another to replace him.

Does this Ada Sanchez know what little driving experience I have? I have a post-graduate degree from Columbia Teachers College, so I have spent time thinking about teaching and talking with real teachers, but I have no classroom experience except for one time last spring (at my request) when I came out to Staten Island to teach for one hour. That day I read Edgar Allen Poe's "The Black Cat" aloud with the class and then rattled off a dozen leading questions about character and conflict. The teacher I was replacing slouched in the back and read *The Ginger Man.* I wanted to ask how he enjoyed Donleavy's writing. But I didn't. When the class was over, he said I did fine and shook my hand. By 3:00 PM I was back on the ferry heading to Manhattan. So much for my student teaching.

But I think I know what's expected of me. The main thing seems to be: Keep 'em quiet. Keep 'em busy. Show up on time. Give 'em plenty of homework. Fill the grade book with marks. I was surprised to discover that we would be giving letter grades to these kids. I learned this yesterday at the elementary school faculty meeting. Henry had welcomed us and then introduced the lower-school principal, Alan Stone, who is also the math/social studies teacher. Stone's a big guy in his fifties with lots of white hair and a gruff voice. He looks like a large W.C. Fields. While Henry looked on uncomfortably, Stone talked about running "a tight ship." Henry excused himself as Stone began to talk about the day-to-day business of the school, finishing off with one more rant about tight ships. After the meeting, Stone took me aside to tell me that Anderson, the teacher I am replacing, couldn't keep the kids quiet. He hoped I could do a better job.

The other key word, of emphatic importance, is "prepare." If I do a good job, the kids will be "prepared" for the next grade as they move on toward high school and eventually college. If they are not "prepared," I will have done a bad job. My job is to keep track of what the next year's teachers expect my kids to know. It's not really what we talked about at Columbia, but "prepare" is a useful term to hang on to.

But it's an odd word. Do we prepare kids the same way we prepare a meal or prepare our income-tax report? I assume that as the year develops, I will keep adding to my sense of what the students need in order to be prepared. In the meantime, we'll read books, study grammar, and write papers. Isn't that what kids do in English?

I'd be worried if I were walking through the hall of some blackboard-jungle school with greasy-haired guys in leather jackets snuggling up with their smirking slutty girlfriends. I'd be downright terrified if I were about to face a class of AP high school seniors who already knew all about Milton, "The Waste Land" and the objective correlative. But I've got small people in my future. We'll meet in a building that used to be someone's house. How dangerous could these kids be? How complicated is the material? What could ever happen that I could not handle? Several teachers have told me that what really matters is to stay ahead of the kids. Just get to where they're going before they get there.

I write my name on the board, erase it, write it again, fiddle with the stuff in my briefcase and wait for my 5th graders to show up, and before long two blond-haired boys walk through the door. We shake hands and introduce ourselves. One is named Ricky, the other Mark. Ricky is easily a foot taller than his friend. They wear plaid sport coats and clip-on ties. They move to the back of the room. I ask if they are Mets fans and find out that they are. More kids walk in, and soon all eighteen desks are filled with little people. One girl is so short that her feet do not touch the floor when she sits at her desk. Next to her sits a short boy named Pierre, who, I have been warned, suffers from epilepsy. They all look at me matter-of-factly as if I belong in front of the room. No one stands up and calls me an impostor.

I pause, take a deep breath and become a teacher.

"I'm Mr. Boone," I say. I have never been a "Mister" before. I point at my badly written name on the board. "I'm your English teacher." I take roll, mispronouncing several names. They really howl when I pronounce the name "Harry" as "Hairy." That's my Midwestern accent, I tell them, but when a boy in the back row keeps on laughing, I send him a stern look and he covers his mouth. We will be studying language, I tell them, and reading books like *Rascal* and *The Call of the Wild.* We also will study mythology and write lots and lots of papers. I make a list on the board of what we will cover. This all comes out easily. I am much more organized and confident than I expected. "Tomorrow I will give you the assignments for the first few weeks." My voice is just like a teacher's. How did that happen?

With fifteen minutes to go, I'm done talking, but before I have time to panic, Peter, a roundish boy in a green sport coat, asks me why I came to Staten Island. He's one of those kids with an open face and ill-fitting glasses that it is impossible not to like on sight. I tell him why Sue and I came here, and my answer prompts a random chat with the kids, who all seem eager to talk.

"My wife and I are interested in Staten Island," I tell them. "What are some things to do?" I feel as if I've just started a conversation with agreeable strangers at a bar or on a train. They act as if all they want to do is yak it up.

"Go to the Tibetan Museum."

"The zoo has a great snake house."

"What about restaurants?" I ask, just to keep things moving. How many 5th graders are going to be gourmands?

"Gene's is good."

Bookstores? "There aren't any."

Then Tommy, a slender boy with a sly cast to his face, asks me if I know why the southernmost bridge over to New Jersey is called the "Outerbridge

8

Crossing."

"I suppose because it's the last bridge. The outer bridge."

"Wrong," they all laugh. "It was named after a guy named Outerbridge. They couldn't call it the Outerbridge Bridge."

Nick tells me I'd better take the ferry to Brooklyn soon. "When the bridge is done, that ferry will close down. All they'll have is the ferry to Manhattan."

"What do we do at recess?" I ask.

"We have a catch," says Beth. She's a large girl with sandy hair and braces. She has already learned to slip a palm in front of her mouth when she laughs.

"You mean 'play catch'?" I ask incredulously.

"We New Yorkers say have a catch; you guys from Chicago can say it the way you want."

They keep asking questions. Am I related to Daniel Boone? Did I know their former teacher? Could we take a trip to Asbury Park? Why do I chew pens? This is my first lesson in how acutely observant my students will always be.

I think about their ideas while I wait for the 6th graders. Through the window I can see the athletic fields. Henry's house is partially visible on the other side of the soccer field. In the woods somewhere out there is the grave of one of the minor Vanderbilts. Nearby is an Augustinian seminary. Todt Hill is the highest point on the eastern seaboard, and I am by far the tallest person here on the third floor, so what does that make me? *Todt* means death in German. I hope that's not significant.

The 6th graders are a little bigger and noisier but just as agreeable as the 5th graders. One boy has a red bow tie. I recognize Dennis, the boy who mowed Henry's lawn. I keep playing the teacher role—even firing off a frown at two chattering girls in the back. A few minutes and I seem to have their respect. I tell the

6th graders that they will study grammar and read *The Arabian Nights, The Adventures of Tom Sawyer, Gulliver's Travels, The Diary of Anne Frank* and *The Odyssey.* I make a list for them, and then I ask them questions. Like the 5th graders they seem to enjoy this bantering. I am pleased by how easy it is to start a conversation with these kids.

I see Henry in the hall after school. He asks how my day went, but when I start to answer, he tells me that last night he heard David Brinkley say "between you and I." I shake my head and frown mournfully at the misuse of this pronoun. I walk out of the building feeling confident..

The next morning I see Henry in the hall again. He asks how I'm doing, but when I start to tell him, he excuses himself and hurries off to greet a parent. Mary Ann, the 4th-grade teacher, walks up and tells me not to take it personally. It happens all the time. I tell her he must be very busy. "Are you kidding?" she laughs.

At recess this second day, Fred and Ricky ask me to teach them how to punt a football. I tell them what I know: Drop it straight down. Kick the ball on the inside of the foot to make it spiral. Kick so high that the other foot leaves the ground. I imagine a picture from an old college program of a grinning punter—one leg high, toe pointed, arms outstretched. I demonstrate, and the ball sails off in a perfect spiral, landing fifty yards away. I have never kicked a ball that far. Everyone on the playground looks over at me. Who is this guy? Someone throws it back. I politely refuse to kick again, but the kids insist. This time the ball shoots off the side of my foot and nails a small girl in the ear. She's not pleased.

Toward the end of recess, Pierre has a minor seizure. He's on the ground shaking, and the kids are there stretching him out while Nick slaps his legs. This is just what Stone told me would happen. By the time I get there, Pierre's on his feet smiling. He straightens his shirt and adjusts his tie, pushes his blond hair away from his forehead, and casually moves away. I expected an epileptic fit to be more dramatic than that.

I have decided to concentrate on reading for the first few weeks. I had made list of different plans of attack, but until the second day I had never really decided. It was almost as if I was waiting to see what I would do. The 5th graders will read mythology, and the 6th graders will read *The Adventures of Tom Sawyer*. I know the subjects. I'm confident I can fill the time productively. How can I go wrong with reading? At some point I will add more writing and grammar, and then I can keep the whole thing going until June.

The choice seems right. The kids read at home and in study halls. In class we read aloud and stop to discuss anything that seems important at the time—a new word, a funny passage, odd behavior. I give little quizzes and bigger ones and finally tests. I want to make sure they are able to comprehend the stories at a literal level. Who was Injun Joe? Who was Muff Potter? When do people realize that Injun Joe killed the doctor? Where did they find Injun Joe's body? What is a Real Barlow? What did the schoolmaster wear on his head? Why did people think Tom was dead? Who was Hera? What is a Titan? When did Orpheus look back? Where did Paris take Helen? Why did Cronus eat his kids?

The new teacher in me wants to see that grade book filled. But the reader in me wants the kids to enjoy the stories as much as I do. My best teachers in high school and college left me with a deep affection for reading. I can't resist terms like conflict and characterization, but I certainly don't want to get into literary analysis with 5th and 6th graders. Whether I'm being scholarly or not, the kids respond enthusiastically to the stories, but I think their enthusiasm has more to do with the books than with me. One time Ronny asks if we could stop talking so he could read by himself.

One day a 6th grader asks me about theme. Do all stories have morals? No, I tell her, they don't. She studies me as if I too am a story with a central theme. Her older brother said they did, she argues. "I want you to enjoy the stories," I tell her. "Worry about the morals later on." She shrugs noncommittally.

The teachers' room at Staten Island Academy isn't the kind of inviolate sanctuary that can be found in many schools—it's simply one of the smaller rooms in the mansion, with a single door and just one window facing the grounds. It's comfortable enough. It's always dense with cigarette smoke. Occasionally I see Sue here. She's often exhausted from teaching the little kids, an artist trying to adapt to a life of teaching 1st graders. Sometimes I pass the lunchroom and see her sitting in a little, tiny chair along with her kids. In class, she's finding more and more ways to use her art.

In the teachers' room one afternoon, Henry walks up while I am mimeographing a mythology quiz. He nods and asks if he can borrow a copy of the quiz. Later I find it left on top of the radiator near the door.

In class we're always on the lookout for puns. Peter tells me that the man outside mowing the lawn has a "sod job." Peter's face lights up whenever he thinks of a pun, glowing almost as brightly as his red hair. I tell him he has no sense of "humus." Katrina's puns are usually more sophisticated than mine. She says that an unopened package in the hall gives us "Crate Expectations." Several of the kids tell me I'm a "Boone" to mankind. One day I ask the kids to use "abhor" in a sentence, and Eric says that a house with hate in it could be called an "abhor house." How had he ever thought of that? Fred points out that an old plant on the windowsill is a "has bean." And a boat that left the dock was "out to launch," and that a person who is not hanged might think "no noose is good noose."

All the joking around relaxes the atmosphere

and makes it easier to learn. It gives the class a feeling of belonging. It also shows the kids how much they have inside of themselves already. They gain respect for their own spontaneity. I gain even more.

After a loud joke one afternoon, I notice Henry squinting through the window in the door. When he sees me, he nods and hurries away. This happens a few more times in the next few weeks, but he never says anything. An older colleague tells me that Henry's usually had a couple of bourbons before he makes these little "inspection tours." Anyway, I'm told, I shouldn't worry about it because Henry has no idea what's going on. It's clear by now that most people at the school don't take him seriously. Still, I expected to have more contact with him, and when I do, maybe I'll find the thoughtful schoolmaster I met last spring at the ferry.

I also have started a writing unit. I figure writing a lot is better than writing a little, so I have them write a lot. They write book reports. They write summaries of what they have read. They write about the characters in the stories. I respond initially by telling then what I like and what needs more work. But I also talk about organization, mechanics, and spelling. I have to concentrate to make sure they can read my lousy handwriting.

Stone gives me a ride home one day. I'm sure he's going to ask about some of the noise coming out of my classroom, and I'm ready to defend myself. Instead he asks me why I didn't teach at college. Shouldn't I have stayed in school for a Ph.D.? I tell him my M.A. is from a teachers' college and that I want to teach younger kids. I also tell him I was only a fair student in high school. In college I did well only in my major. I've struggled in school like most other people. He seems pleased and tells me that he was a terrible student. We stop for shot and a beer at a bar down the road, next door to the Chihuahua stud service.

My friends at Columbia want to know about ten and eleven-year-olds. They are all teaching high school and can't quite imagine doing what I am doing. I tell them that my students are much more mature than I had anticipated. I'm really not sure what they can't do. My advisor is pleased that I like the younger pupils. "You might be in the right place," he tells me.

At the moment I do feel I'm in the right place. I had never considered teaching younger kids, but they seem perfect for a person like me. There are so many things I can't do—dance, sing, swim, speak foreign languages, play chess, write neatly. I am not really a scholar. I like books. I like to write. I can do several things at the same time. 5th grade seems like a safe spot for me.

I get along with the other lower-school teachers, who are mostly women. They approve of my teaching but are suspicious of the new grammar. They gripe about Henry's lack of backbone, lack of memory, lack of self-control, but I still like what I remember about him. Stone, to most of these teachers, is a semi-harmless oaf. Over time, I also get to know the upper-school teachers. They complain more openly about Henry. They complain about low pay and rude students. Some feel guilty because this is a private school.

For parents' night I wear a new sport coat and a blue tie. I have even polished my shoes. Very snappy, I think, a real, professional teacher. The classrooms are jammed with adults. My room reeks of perfume. The plan is for Mom to squeeze into the school desk while Dad crouches nearby. I talk about the books their children have read and the papers they have written. I tell them that the new grammar describes the language more accurately and that it gives me more choices for activities. But still I have included the old grammar so kids will know parts of speech and how to diagram a sentence. I am fearful of one of the parents who teaches English at NYU.

But he says nothing. I try to look organized and thorough for all the business executives in the room. I'm nervous, but I speak well enough. Several parents come up afterwards to say how much their kids like my class. They have sent their kids to a private school for greater personal contact, and they think they have found it.

I expect this kind of parental interest. These parents—whether they are Manhattan business people or NYU professors, whether they are Barry Goldwater Republicans or old-fashioned New York liberals—expect to play a key role in their kids' education. When I teach in other schools in other communities, this might not be the case. Henry, I'm told, sucks up to these people all the time. This is odd because Henry and the parents don't seem that much alike. My sense is that the parents welcome creative teaching if the teacher seems serious. As it turns out, progressive education will do much better in the rich suburbs than in the inner city.

Afterwards I go with Stone to a local bar known as Pop's Last Chance. I feel relieved because no one asked me tough questions. The parents seem pleased with what the kids are doing. Stone crows about dodging the questions "the asshole parents" asked. Schools don't need parents around. All they do is "fuck things up." I can tell he likes me better now that he knows I'm not some effete Ivy League superstar. He tells me about a time he and his Navy buddies were beaten up in a small Southern town by a bunch of rednecks. He also talks bitterly about Henry who has "fucked up the discipline." Henry would not have lasted a minute in the Navy. This is the first time he's been so openly critical of Henry. Before we drive home, he tells me I'm doing a pretty good job of running a tight ship—much better than my predecessor—but there's still too much noise coming out of my room. Some field trips are coming up, and it will be my job to keep the kids quiet on the bus.

I can usually keep my classes quiet, but not always. The kids know that I am not really a tough person, so threats don't work. Sometimes they laugh too much and things come apart. But, because of Stone, I did emphasize discipline right away. Besides, I like a quiet classroom with no shouting and no interruptions. Nick is my biggest problem. He can be noisy and rude. He can be a bully. He's big and handsome and even Katrina has a crush on him. Shouldn't a girl as smart as Katrina be able to see through Nick? Nick and I talk a lot about his behavior. He understands why I want him to be quiet. He understands why this material is important, but in most classes he either talks or lets his mind slip away.

By Thanksgiving I know a lot about the kids. I know Pierre asks irrelevant questions and I also know that his father died last year. Eric and Katrina want to be doctors, just like their parents. Ricky loves music; Chip's parents want him to go to Princeton; Greg does not like me; Bobby's house is big and friendly; Ronny knows all about the Civil War. Most seem to like sports. They are up to date on recent fads like the "Name Game." They travel to Manhattan frequently. Not all are from wealthy families, but they are all living comfortably. Yet they don't strike me as spoiled rich kids.

The kids spend part of the week before Thanksgiving taking standardized English and math tests. The smart kids do well, the not-so-smart kids do not do as well. The English scores are higher than the math scores. No one pays that much attention, but a few people do congratulate me as if I were responsible for this. It occurs to me often that the people who say I'm doing a good job are either wrong or insincere. They often really mean I am doing a good job because the kids are quiet or busy.

Also in November I meet individually with the parents. Even if I intend to say something critical, I end up saying that I have seen improvement or certainly potential. I show them tests and papers, and I speculate on how their children will do in high school. Pierre's mom asks about her son's epilepsy. Another mother asks if her son cries. Tony's mom is afraid that her boy might hurt the smaller boys. She tells me her husband's ancestors came here to help build the New York subway system. She wants us to come over in the spring to use the swimming pool. Liz's mother says that my family can stay at their club when they come to visit.

In December, I run out of energy. It is as if I have hit a wall, like a long-distance runner. Suddenly nothing is more important—absolutely nothing—than getting through the next few weeks and leaving for a while. I am not laughing as much. The little voices are penetrating. The kids don't seem to listen to me as well. Katrina yawns while I am explaining noun clauses. A parent calls to ask if I'm aware I have made several spelling errors in my comments on his daughter's paper. I'm turning into a bore. Pierre has three fits in one day. Nick gives Ricky a bloody nose. Someone pees on the radiator. I find myself saying things like, "You'd better learn this or you'll be sorry when you get to high school." I can't get rid of a cold. I lose things. At the end of the day I am as anxious as they are to hit the road.

I smoke because I am tired, and I am tired because I smoke. I smoke whenever I have the chance, but so does everyone else. If I stay late to grade papers, I smoke right at my desk. When we take the kids on the bus down the hill to the Moravian church to play basketball at the gym, I smoke in the bus. Everyone smokes.

The day before vacation many of the kids bring presents to the teachers. By nine o'clock my desk is piled with books, scarves, gloves, wine and aftershave lotion. Bobby, who has not brought me anything, suddenly excuses himself and runs out of the room. I look out the window and see him sprinting across the field to his house. A few minutes later he is back with a half-filled bottle of vodka wrapped in yesterday's *Staten Island Advance.*

In January, after trips to Nashville to visit Sue's parents and Chicago to visit mine, things fall back into place. Now I know not to be surprised when I run out of energy. I look for a place to grade papers during free periods. I consider the attic, a very large closet, the kitchen and an unused boiler room. I finally decide on the kitchen. In the morning Mrs. Bux, the head cook, and her crew are in this kitchen, cooking up shepherd's pie and other meals for the kids. In the afternoon the kitchen is warm and empty. I can sit and grade papers at a long table near the stove by a wall covered with hanging utensils. One afternoon, Henry wanders in, and we chat for a moment. He looks confused and unhappy. I have heard that he has had to cancel a play at the high school because of questionable language. At issue was the word "chamberpot." Evidently a parent had complained about it. The teachers say this is just one of many times he has given in to pressure from the parents. I start to tell him about the papers I am grading, but he excuses himself and walks back out the door.

Finally, in April, Henry asks me to meet him after school in the library to discuss my teaching. Should I be worried? No one takes him seriously, but still, he's the boss. Lately, I have been testing new waters. The 6th graders are writing original stories. The 5th graders are working on memory pieces. Both classes did a reading of *Alice's Adventures in Wonderland* for the smaller kids. Henry might see this as frivolous stuff that I picked up in teachers' college. How will this prepare the kids for next year? How is this really leading them down the road to college? I'm ready with answers about the importance of creative expression, but I can't draw upon much experience to support my points.

The library used to be the family living room.

There's a fireplace along one wall and large windows looking out onto the grounds. I sit at one of the long wooden tables and write an *Oliver Twist* quiz for my 6th graders. Earlier that week Ronny had said that Oliver didn't say "I want some more." He said "I want Samoa," and that means he's a land-grabber. Henry is late. I look up, and he's walking by. I call out and with a surprised look he makes a sharp turn and sits down across from me. He's smoking. For some reason we shake hands. He borrows a piece of paper and gets ready to write. How do I like the little kids? I love them. Is Stone too gruff? We get along fine, I tell him. Do the parents bother me? Not really. I expected private-school parents to be concerned. Do I understand why some of the teachers don't like the parents? I do, but they don't bother me. Would I ever want to teach in the high school? Sure. We pause for a while. He has run out of questions. I think I can smell bourbon. He lights another cigarette, and we start to talk about college. I ask him how many Staten Island students go to Big Ten schools.

"Well," he coughs and blows out smoke and grinds his cigarette out in a coffee cup, "if the truth be known, we prefer for our kids here to shoot higher than the Big Ten." Then, just as he is about to list the schools he does prefer, he stops talking. His Adam's apple moves up and down. His jaw drops. His hands shake. He reaches into his shirt pocket for another smoke. He has just remembered that Sue and I both graduated from a Big Ten school, the University of Wisconsin. I start to make a joke out of it, but he's on his feet mumbling about a meeting and then out the door. I can hear him rushing upstairs to his office.

For a while, I keep the Big Ten story a secret. But finally I tell another teacher what happened. Word spreads fast. They all nod knowingly. Can't I see that all he really cares about is how things look? Now he's embarrassed because of how he looks to Boone.

I finally have to admit to myself that I was

simply wrong about Henry. The Henry I thought I understood last spring is not the Henry who runs the school. Last year I thought that he was guided by a vision of an old-fashioned prep-school instructor committed to excellence. He might bend a little to the parents, but in his heart he was an educator, pure and simple. Now I see him as totally under the spell of what he imagines outsiders want him to do. I don't think he's a total phony; he's just weak, and booze makes him weaker.

But as Sue and I get ready to go spend a couple of months in Europe, I feel good about the year. Teaching captured my life so thoroughly that Henry's odd behavior made no difference. The parents thank me for making school fun, though several wonder why I was such an easy grader. Stone doesn't like the easy grades or some of the noise from my class, but he finds the time to say I had done a pretty good job. He clearly sees me as a male buddy in a building full of women. The other teachers look at me as part of the team. I am especially pleased because I have found so many different ways to keep kids involved.

The final faculty meeting of the year is held in the lunchroom. Stone thanks us for keeping a reasonably tight ship. He hopes next year we won't go back to the Museum of Modern Art. ("It all looks like scrambled eggs to me," he says.) Henry tells us that next year the Staten Island Academy will be even more competitive than ever and that he has hired more nifty teachers like all of us. We have some scholarship money to encourage some of the kids "down the hill" to get a fine education at our school. He figures even more of our kids will go to highly competitive schools like Yale, Brown, and—he looks right at me—the University of Wisconsin.

CHRISTMAS PERIL

"Bob! Oh, Bob, I need to talk to you." It is the chirpy voice of Betty, our buoyant music teacher. She is wearing a red and white dress with a smiling Santa on the front. "I need your help." After myself and Stone, Betty is the third-tallest teacher at the Staten Island Academy. Although I often see her large form hurrying from place to place, I don't know Betty well. I do know that the kids "go" to her at least once each week for chorus. At Christmas vacation they "go" to her more—often during class—to get ready for our pageant.

We have stopped next to Ron's biology lab. The faint smell of a Bunsen burner and formaldehyde reaches my nose. The hallway is crowded, boys as always wearing sport coats and ties, girls in dresses. Vacation is only a month away. The voices around us seem louder and more strident than usual.

"Bob, I've got a problem. We have way too many 7th and 8th graders in this year's Christmas Pageant. Some of them—the boys especially—have a lot of energy, but I just can't get them to cooperate. You do such a good job with them."

She begins to praise me. I am so good with "rambunctious" kids. They relate to me so well. I am just a natural with this age group. It's so good for them to work with a man. It's a pity more young people don't go into teaching. There's more to life than money. Would I—her tone turns a little more insistent as she looks at me imploringly—consider taking them off her hands and doing a play instead? "We have the scripts for *A Christmas Carol* all ready for you. A few years ago, Mr. Anderson tried, but I think you can do a better job." Even though the "tried" and the "better job" parts worry me, I let her shovel on more praise. I take it all in, fully aware of her reasons for the glowing remarks but unable to stop letting the flattery work me over. I do not remind her that I teach mostly 5th and 6th graders and, with my schedule trimmed slightly, a few high school kids in a section of senior English. Not 7th and 8th graders. I do not mention that I have seen some of my former 6th graders now as 7th graders, and the change has not been pretty. I don't add that I have no experience in theater at all, that it would be impossible to find anyone less qualified. My only acting part in my entire life was as an orphan whose letter to Santa got lost. That was when I was in 5th grade myself, when the best actor in the class came down with chicken pox and I was pressed into service as part of an overall shift of parts.

But the bell is about to ring. I don't want destroy this edifice Betty has constructed of me. I like thinking of myself as the kind of guy who can deal with the problem kids. Ignoring many clanging mental alarms, I open my mouth, and out it pops: "Yes."

Betty jumps up and down, setting the Santa Claus bells on her sweater a-jingle. She squeals the good news to Principal Stone on his way to the teachers' room for a cigar. He rolls his eyes and shudders.

By lunchtime that day word has already leaked out that we are going to have a Christmas play and that I will be directing it. Two teachers walk by my table and touch me sympathetically on the shoulder. That afternoon I find a list of "actors" in my mailbox. Betty's initials, along with a smiley face, are at the bottom. Most of the 7th graders on the list I can remember from my 6th grade class the year before; each of the boys has in his own way shown the potential to be dangerous in a group. The 8th graders I do not know personally, but I have heard their names at faculty meetings.

Already I am starting to lose my nerve. This is the first time I have really felt any serious doubt as a teacher, but it's there. I cannot deny it. It is the fear of public failure. But there is no turning back. Betty has already placed an announcement on the board. The only good news—and it is indeed good news—is that Drew Van Winkle, a colleague who has become a good friend, has volunteered to help me out. Drew brings a lot to the table: Marine experience in the Korean War, a touch of acting, a lively temper, and an excellent sense of humor.

The next day in my mailbox on pink paper is a short note from Betty: "No time to lose." She follows up that reminder with a list of rehearsal dates. We have barely three weeks to put the thing together. Earlier in the day, I read a chapter of *The Call of the Wild* with the 5th graders. As usual, they responded with gusto. I'm still a big hit with my official classes. I wonder if the same rapport is possible with the 7th and 8th graders.

That afternoon we have our first meeting with the cast. Twenty of us pack into a small classroom in the corner of the building. It's a hot, dark place normally used—on the rare occasions that it is used at all—for conferences. The students jabber while Drew and I explain that, because we have so little time, we will ask for volunteers for the different parts and "if necessary" do some assigning. I have never read anything about directing a student play, but I'm sure this is not the ideal way to begin.

Donald, an 8th grader with an insincere smile, offers to play Ebenezer Scrooge. Donald is certainly bright enough to memorize the part, but he is far from trustworthy, and he despises authority. Many teachers have described his yawning smirk. I appoint Alex to be the prompter. The smartest kid in the school and one of the most agreeable, Alex should be more than equal to the task of helping actors who have forgotten lines.

The rest of the casting is equally suspect. The student who will play Bob Crachit stutters. The girl playing Mrs. Crachit wears braces and has a habit of giggling. Tiny Tim is much larger than his parents. A Jewish boy whose parents may not be wild about their son playing this role will play Marley's ghost. A kid everyone hates will play Scrooge's likable nephew. The only girl with any real acting talent is given the part of the newspaper boy. She has one line. 7th graders who are likely to seize any opportunity to show the 8th graders that they too can be insufferably obnoxious play the various ghosts.

One of these 7th graders I remember well from last year. Nick howls at anything that sounds remotely dirty. And laughing, for Nick, means collapsing and then banging his head, fists, and feet on the floor. With Nick you have to steer clear of words like "pussy" and "balls," no matter what the context. "Erection" is definitely out. Science teachers have to be wary of "sperm whale," "woodpecker," and "titmouse." Naturally, "intercourse" is out of the question. And God help anyone whose nickname is Dick. Nick is first to notice that Crachit could be pronounced "Crochit." He even finds a way to make Ebenezer Scrooge sound like "Ebenezer Screw." Last year, he provided some comic relief. This year he has to be considered trouble.

Once the casting is completed, we have three weeks to rehearse. We will meet after school every day for two hours. Because Betty's singers practice in the auditorium, we have to use a classroom. And because these kids are so hard on classrooms, we end up in the rarely used small room where we first met. It has a heating system that cannot be regulated. We must open all of the windows to keep the temperature below 80. The windows are heavy and often come crashing down.

I come to rehearsals with good memories of my regular classes, which continue to run smoothly. When I talk, the students listen. When others talk, we all listen. The kids might be getting excited about

Christmas, but they have not stopped doing their work. Other teachers, including even Stone, have complimented me for "keeping a lid" on things. I find myself wishing I could do the same with the rehearsal sessions, but I can't.

A typical rehearsal involves serious shouting. When Drew and I enter the room, the kids are shouting. We must shout to make them stop shouting. But because they never really did stop shouting, we have to shout even the most basic instructions. When we finally shout our way into actual rehearsal, something always goes wrong—a fart, a burp, a forgotten line, a crashing window—and then the kids explode and fall down, and we get mad and start shouting all over again.

We hit the low point early, at least, as far as rehearsals are concerned. On the third day, after we shout the kids into semi-silence, Drew starts to demonstrate how the first ghost scene should be played. Most of the cast looks amused as Drew, pretending to be Jacob Marley, bends over and drags an imaginary chain across the room. Off in the corner slouches Donald, smirking and yawning. In his hand is a rusty metal rod that he has probably pulled out of the trash. Drew, in a credible British accent, begins to recite Marley's lines just as Donald begins to beat the rod on the floor. Drew stops speaking and Donald stops pounding. Drew starts up, and so does Donald. "Donald," Drew finally calls over, "Stop that. OK?" Donald stops for just a second and then starts scraping the rod along the radiator and sending a twanging sound around the room. "Donald," Drew advances towards him. Donald scrambles to the corner, but Drew grabs the rod and starts to pull. Donald holds on as Drew tugs harder.

Then, as we all knew he would, Donald abruptly lets go of the rod, sending Drew careering across the room and crashing into the desks pushed into the corner to make room for the actors. Donald hits the floor howling. Drew stands up and gets ready to charge, but suddenly his glare melts into a frown. He sprints back across the room to where Donald is bent over holding his hand and wailing. Evidently, when Drew wrenched the rusty, jagged rod free, he tore open Donald's hand. A student standing nearby peeks over Donald's shoulder and gags. "You can see the bone! Mr. Van Winkle, he'll never play the piano again!" Drew is there talking softly, insisting that Donald show him the wound. Finally with a pitiful whimper, the boy opens his hand revealing a pink, smooth palm. No blood. No bone.

An hour later, Drew and I are at Pop's Last Chance throwing down beers and wondering why we can control our own classes but not these kids.

For some reason, after the hand incident, things get a little better, and by the beginning of the third week, the kids can navigate the first act without too many blunders. But only the first act. We decide to concentrate on that, figuring success in one area will lead to success in another. Besides, we have asked the kids to memorize their parts for the second act and assume that they are progressing on their own. To our dismay, it is not until a full rehearsal three or four days before the performance that we learn that no one knows any of the Act II lines. Our last two rehearsals are frantic attempts to get the last act to work. At the end of the last rehearsal, we implore the kids to learn their parts "once and for all" over the weekend. My euphoria that this will soon be over is stronger than my fear of disaster.

By this time, Betty has become more involved. She arranges for the costumes, fixes up the stage, and assigns a few teachers to help us out the night of the play. I feel edgy, but at least it will soon be behind me. Having never directed a play, I have no idea how poorly prepared we are. I reckon that at the very worst, the kids will stumble through their lines with a little help from Alex.

And who knows? Maybe these young people will put on a magnificent performance. The audience will gasp at Scrooge's cruelty, agonize over Tiny Tim's condition, tremble in the presence of death, and exalt at Scrooge's redemption. Maybe this will set a new standard of excellence—or maybe not.

The day of the play I schedule in-class essays for two of my regular classes and films for the other three. In the hall between periods, teachers nod and mouth, "Good luck." One crosses his fingers. Another offers to sell me a plane ticket to Rome. Drew turns tight-lipped and surly. Could Korea have been any tenser than this?

I've never tasted battery acid, but by early afternoon, my mouth tastes of what I imagine the flavor of battery fluid to be. One hour before show time we all meet in a classroom near the auditorium. I tell the cast one last time how things should work. "When you're not on stage, don't get in the way. But listen for your cue." Drew then reminds us all that people will be watching. He says he believes they can all do a good job. "Just don't quit on yourselves." With that we crowd together like a football team and cheer.

The gym doubles as the theater. Folding chairs have been brought in. The basketball hoops have been raised; wrestling mats have been pushed to the sides. It smells of wax and perspiration. Once we herd the cast inside, the kids stand around quietly and wait for their time to come. For the play itself, a student will be in charge of entries and exits while Drew and I will stay far out of sight. We head for a storage room located literally beneath the stage. Our other choice is to sit with the audience, which is simply out of the question. The storage room is filled with old scripts and lots of broken things. It must have flooded once because some of the books that are stacked in rows are also stuck together. It smells a little of gas. But it's out of sight, which is what matters most to Drew and me.

The evening begins with Betty's choral group performing a Christmas medley with a few Hanukkah songs added. The chorus—almost all girls—sings splendidly. For the last number, "We Wish You a Merry Christmas," the entire audience joins in. From our hideout beneath the stage, Drew and I can hear most of this, and we can hear Betty's bright staccato voice thanking the audience and then announcing that the play is about to begin. Drew stares up at the ceiling and moves his lips. I light another Marlboro.

When Donald and the actors walk on to begin the first scene in Scrooge's counting house, the crowd applauds encouragingly. Not bad, I think. The people must like what they see. Then we hear muffled dialogue with several loud, "Bah, humbugs," and I can imagine Scrooge griping that he has to give his workers time off for Christmas. Then the laughter starts up from the audience. We have no idea what the laughter is about. I sit fitfully smoking as the laughter grows, dies down and then builds to a foot-pounding hysteria at the close of the first act. I smoke some more. Drew stares at his knees. He looks as if he could vomit at any moment.

Throughout the second act, the laughter is more or less continuous, though never quite as loud as it was at the end of Act I. But still we don't know what is causing the hilarity in the audience. How could a play featuring a mean old miser and a dying crippled boy make people laugh? And finally we are laughing too.

Then it's over. The crowd is now stomping its approval. Nick runs down to find us and drags us up on the stage where Donald presents us with "Certificates of Appreciation." As Drew and I stumble out to accept the awards, I notice irrelevantly that the gym odors have been replaced by the smell of perfume worn by the mothers and grandmothers in the audience. Henry joins us and calls for one more round of applause. This time they all rise to their feet.

In the car on the way to the cast party, Sue tells me what happened. This explanation takes quite a while because she has to stop often to laugh. Part of the problem, she explains, was missed lines. Even Donald had breakdowns. Thus, Alex was called upon to prompt from the very beginning. By the second act he simply remained standing up by the front of the stage with a glass of water next to him.

Along with the speaking problems were physical mishaps, mostly because the kids had never really worked on this stage. They often stood in front of each other or way too far apart. They collided with each other. Scrooge rolled out of his bed. The Ghost of Christmas Present tripped and fell, knocking off his wig. Tiny Tim delivered his famous "God bless us one and all" from offstage.

But Marley's ghost got the biggest laugh of all. His scene involved dragging a chain across the stage while the terrified Scrooge looked on from his bed. Halfway across the stage, though, Marley stopped and tugged at his chain. Nothing happened. It was snagged somehow in the heating grate. He pulled even harder, tearing loose the grate and sending up a cloud of dust. A grandmother sitting in the front row thought the auditorium had caught on fire and sprang to her feet, at which point Henry raced to the front to assure everyone that there was no fire.

The cast party is held at a big house near the school. Everyone cheers when Sue and I walk in. I ask for an extra-large vodka martini. Drew and I find our hands being pumped and our backs slapped. One father, a big fan of Charlie Chaplin, claims this is the funniest thing he has ever seen. And he means it. Some parents apparently think we planned this as a farce and want to know how we got the idea to catch the chain in the heating grate. Only Betty seems unhappy with the performance. She has only herself to blame for this fiasco. And us, of course.

A few days later we fly to Nashville for the first

part of Christmas vacation; then we move on to Chicago and finally back to Staten Island to start teaching all over again. Thankfully, the play soon is behind us—a humorous memory, a small piece of school lore, a priceless illustration of how one small decision can thoroughly disrupt the lives of well-intentioned people.

When school sessions resume, my classes go especially well. I feel energized and in control. But the memory of our total loss of control with the play will not quite go away, nor should it. Within the catastrophe, though, I have discovered something. Colleagues behave with a certain cautious sympathy, as though I may be mortified, and perhaps I should be. But I'm not. The rehearsals were anarchy. The play was a disaster, unintentionally hilarious for the audience. So what? The kids seemed to have a good time, and the audience certainly had a good laugh. If my clueless directing debut turns out to be the worst mistake I make as a teacher, I think I'll be able to view myself as an unqualified success. Drew and I pass in the hall and share a wince or two. We had been good friends before; now this seals the deal. Not a bad bargain, overall.

TWO RAYS

It's a gorgeous April Saturday as I drive from our cozy little apartment—not to play tennis, not to visit the zoo or the Tibetan Museum or the polluted ponds of Staten Island—but to go to school to teach a make-up for a February snow day. It's such a beautiful morning that the tidy bungalows along our street seem like quaint cottages, the houses on the hill like mansions. The Academy itself, already a mansion by design and in appearance, on this lovely day could be a grand country estate surrounded by its fields of grass and stately trees.

The front door to the school is locked, so I walk along the side of the building, trailing a hand against the weathered bricks, to an unlocked open window. I raise it, wedge it up with a broken baseball bat left there for that purpose, and climb into the cafeteria. I reach back outside for my pile of teaching materials, drop the bat to the ground and close the window, and walk into the unlighted dining room.

Before I can get my bearings, a muffled voice greets me. "What the fuck are you doing here? It's Saturday, for Christ's sake." It's the slurred, perpetually aggrieved growl of our janitor, Ray Paulson, muffled because he is collapsed face down at one of the tables. Nearby are his bucket and mop and what at a passing glance appears to be an empty bottle of Thunderbird. I am not surprised.

"Make-up for the snow days, Ray. I've got a special class for the 6th graders." I try hard not to sound too cheery. "This is for the one we missed last February." Like me, Ray started working at SIA at the beginning of the last school year. Whenever he looks at something that is not right in front of him, instead of turning his head, he shifts his eyes. "Classic prison behavior," according to a colleague, who knows nothing about it. But while Ray may be shifty-eyed, generally mean, and often hung over, he mops, polishes, and straightens out capably enough to keep his job.

He raises his head and deepens his scowl. He has black hair and a broad forehead with a scar. He always brings to my mind a snake handler. "It sounds like one of scumbag Stone's ideas." He breaks off into a long phlegmy cough. "You know what that guy is?" I shake my head. "That guy's a prick with ears." I'm puzzled by the figure of speech, but I don't say anything. Then, with a discontented grunt, Ray collapses back into his arms. Somewhere in the building poking her broom into cobwebby corners and furiously smoking will be Ray's wife, a stumpy little creature with a wheeze. She hates Stone too, but she hates Pam, Stone's secretary, even more. "If Stone's ass ever fell off," she wheezed at me one time in the parking lot, "Pam's nose would be in it."

I wish Ray a happy Saturday. There is no indication that he heard me. I stop to unlock the front doors and skip-step up the stairs to the third floor. My footsteps as I climb the old wooden stairs send creaks and groans through the empty building. At the top of the stairs, before walking into the classroom, I look out the window at the end of the hall to make sure the softball diamond has been raked. It is a truly lovely day, one of those hopeful spring mornings that make anyone other than Ray glad to be alive.

I stack the materials I've been carrying on one side of the top of the desk and place the wastebasket up on the other side. I scrunch up a few old attendance bulletins into a ball, back up to the far windows and arch a long set shot into the wastebasket. I follow that with a delicate little jumper from behind Ricky's desk. After a long skyhook from the bulletin board filled with Beatles photos, I start to announce. "Boone pushes the ball down the court.

From a standing dribble, he fakes left and moves right—nothing but net." It is right after I nail an impossibly long one from the doorway, gleefully declaring, "Swisheroo for two," that I sense other human beings staring at me from the classroom across the hall. It's Ada Sanchez. With her is a parent there for a conference.

"Are you alone, Bob?" Ada calls out haltingly. I have moved back into the room and placed the wastebasket on the floor.

"We're all alone, Ada." I mumble as I partially close the door and shudder. She's seen me play basketball before, but what's this parent, whose daughter will be my student next year, thinking about this person playing an imaginary basketball game with himself? Maybe she'll conclude that I'm on the same level as the kids and see it as a good thing.

Today, I have decided to give the kids a large helping of what I have been feeding them all year—*new* grammar. It has become quite the thing. There are many versions—structural, transformational, tagmemic—but every variation assumes that traditional Latin grammar does not accurately describe the language we use. More importantly—at least for me—the new approach demands more activity from the kids. The "old" grammar might call for diagramming a sentence with a subject, helping verb, action verb, prepositional phrase, indirect object, and direct object. The new grammar asks students to make up sentences that fit a given pattern. In general, the new grammar books are livelier because the authors breezily believe it should be fun for kids to learn about their language.

My first year, I smuggled in exercises from the new grammar. But this year we use a book that actually incorporates many of the new approaches. I have already started to wonder how important this will be to me later on. Am I addressing the big questions that we hurled around in graduate school? What do we teach? How do we teach? What is the role of the school in society? Now, in my second year of teaching, I am deeply interested in this new grammar, and no one tells me not to be. So far, the approach seems like a success to me. It certainly proves that kids already carry around a rich trove of knowledge about their own language, and my job is to get it out.

Noise radiates from below. Up the stairs storm twenty-one 6th graders. I beat them to the door. "Leave your mitts out in the hall. We'll be playing softball after class." The room fills with kids wearing shorts and t-shirts like water flowing into a tub.

I love teaching these 6th graders. They can read good stuff like *The Adventures of Tom Sawyer* and groan at bad puns. From my miserable experience directing 7th and 8th graders in the Christmas play, I know what horrible things will soon happen to these pleasant little people. But for the moment they feel like my family.

"Before we start, I want you to write down what we'll be doing until the end of school." I scribble a weekly calendar on the board. "This week we'll finish *Tom Sawyer* and then write an in-class essay. Then we are going to finish the mythology book. The last book of the year will be *Rascal*. It's about a boy with a pet raccoon. You'll have a chance to write your own animal stories." I speak with my back half-turned. They are all writing something. The girls, as always, have their little assignment notebooks. The boys may be writing on their arms. "Then at the end of the year, we'll review the grammar for one final biggy."

Is all this previewing really necessary? The school likes me to do this avoid "surprises." The kids seem to appreciate it, even though I often change the plan. But in truth I'm doing this for myself. The new teacher in me is making sure the bases are covered, making sure I look organized. In the front row sits Katrina, certainly one of the smartest students and among the wisest as well. She was a prize student last year. Katrina smiles up at me in a knowing way. "Don't worry, Mr. Boone," she probably feels like saying, "We know you're the teacher."

Quickie time. First we play hangman. The word is "agitate," and the winner is Karen. Then we play "I'm Thinking Of. . ." The answer is Paul McCartney, and the winner is Ricky. Then, at the urging of the others, Alex, for what seems the fiftieth time of the year, reads "The Cremation of Sam McGee." This time he stands on top of my desk to perform.

Now that everyone is loose, it's time to start the lesson for the day. "We've been doing a lot with sentence patterns," I sit down on the edge of the desk. "Right now you should be able to name every pattern possible in a simple sentence. Today, I'm going to give you a sheet filled with different patterns. Make up a story that follows the pattern. Make it as ridiculous as possible. Funny is good. I'll mimeograph the good ones." By now I am passing out the sheets. "Make sure your group has both boys and girls. Pick a person with good handwriting to be the recorder."

"Not someone who writes like you, Mr. Boone." My bad handwriting is legendary.

"No, Katrina, not someone who writes like me."

I glance over at Ray Hoffman, who is sitting in the back row. Ray, by far the biggest kid in the class, is a recent transfer from public school. Earlier in the year, I spent a lot of time trying to bring him into the regular orbit of the class, but in spite of my efforts, he seemed doomed to become the "big dumb guy" who lurks on the fringe of an otherwise focused student group. But lately he has done all of his homework and has actually participated in class discussions. He likes Tom Sawyer. But today he frowns and grimaces as he slides his desk over to join a group. I walk over and ask if he understands. He glances up with a pained look and nods.

Ten minutes later the groups are humming away.

Twenty minutes later, if anything, they are even more involved. Only Ray seems less than totally engaged. He is looking out the window. Once he starts to raise his hand but he drops it back on the desk.

Forty minutes into it they are still working, except for Ray, who now just stares at his hands.

After an hour, I call them together to share the stories. Bobby's group has written a story about a sea captain who can't swim. Pierre's group has written a myth explaining why we have dandruff. Karen's people have a story about a man-eating amoeba named Maurice. Each performance is followed by applause and laughter. I collect all they've done. It will be no problem typing this up and returning it Monday.

The room has a Zen-like relaxed feeling as if something important has just been completed. Warm spring air wafts in through the open windows. The class has worked out just the way I imagined. I assumed the kids would know the patterns, that they would enjoy making up their own stories, and that they would like to do this in groups. I know that I am lucky to have such a cooperative collection of students. At the moment I am quite pleased with myself for choosing to teach younger kids, for getting involved with the new grammar, for finding a creative way to handle it. I will be doing more and more with creative writing because I know what the kids are capable of doing. All of these positive thoughts are rushing through my head as I tell the kids to get ready for softball.

Then Ray throws up.

Just as the kids are starting to move towards the door, I hear a splatter followed by a shout, then a louder splash and a stampede of kids past me. No force on earth could stop them. "He puked. Ugh, Ray puked! You can see carrots!" They are gagging as they push past me out the door. Soon they are slamming their way down the stairs. A few slide on the banister. Through the window I can hear their shouts from outside.

Ray stands in the back alone. From that very spot I had buried the long set shot into the wastebasket. The floor and the desks and the wall and even the chalk tray of the back-wall blackboard are sprayed with vomit. His shoes and pants are spattered as well. He stands, forlorn, with his hands jammed in his pockets. His jaw is twitching. "I'm sorry, Mr. Boone. I should have gone to the washroom."

I put my hand on his shoulder. I give him a handkerchief. I feel terrible for him.

"It's all right," I say. "Wait here, Ray. I'll get a mop, and we'll clean this up together. Don't worry about it. Okay? It happens all the time. When I was older than you, I threw up all over a stranger at Midway Airport." I trot down the stairs and toward the storage room where there should be an extra mop and bucket. On the way I stop at the principal's office, where Stone is sitting at his desk reading *The Sporting News*. I stick my head into the office. "Ray threw up." I am panting. "I need a bucket and some mops and sponges. I'll take care of it."

Instead of nodding, shrugging, raising his eyebrows, or any of the other reactions I expected, Stone throws down the paper with a snort. "That filthy son of a bitch!" He starts to rise. He looks even larger and more threatening than usual. "Ray puked right here in my school? That's it. That's fucking it. That low-life will never walk into this building again." He's on his feet now.

For a second I stand in utter bewilderment. Then I realize he is talking about Ray Paulson, our janitor. "No, no, no." I move into the doorway prepared to block him. "Ray *Hoffman* threw up. It happened at the end of class." Stone sits down again and shakes his large buffalo head. Clearly he is disappointed.

Later, Ray Hoffman and I walk down the stairs together. "Let's go play ball. The kids need you out there. You go change into gym clothes and meet us on the diamond." He nods and disappears down the hall. I walk out onto the field where the kids are waiting. Ray wants to play, I tell them. "Let's make him feel good."

We are sitting in a group along the third base line. The bushes behind are just starting to form buds, but through the screen of green lace I can still see Henry's house in the back. Mark is holding a sheet of paper listing the two teams. He is eager to announce the batting orders. I look over at Katrina, who is smiling at me and shaking her head ever so slightly. How can this 6th grader have sharper insights than I do?

Then there is a shout and onto the field trots Ray Hoffman. We all cheer.

AMOS

Today I am sitting on an old couch in the "regular" teachers' room because the janitors are painting the attic nook, where we male teachers have created our own work area. On my left, furiously grading senior math quizzes is Rachel, wife of a rabbi and by all accounts our most serious teacher. In 1963 she stood in a huge crowd in Washington, D.C., and heard Martin Luther King deliver his extraordinary "I have a dream" speech. She has demonstrated for the Rosenbergs. Her "Leave Vietnam Now" letter was published in the *Times*. As a teacher, Rachel is energy personified, and the kids love her. All of this frenetic activity seems especially incredible considering that she had polio as a child and still wears a brace on her left leg.

On my right sits Daisy, our only black teacher. She and her husband Amos, a doctor at the Public Health Hospital, moved to Staten Island from Alaska. Within weeks they had moved into the school community, attending soccer games and faculty parties. She gives me a ride to school on Wednesdays. Henry is so impressed with her teaching that we wonder if he might refer to her as a "Nifty Negress."

With the period about to end, Rachel stops grading and begins to chat. "You know," she says, "I'd like all of you to come to our place in Manhattan." She starts to put her papers into her old leather briefcase, which looks like something Emma Goldman might have carried. "Just because I live on the Upper West Side doesn't mean we can't all get together." We agree. Nods and noises of assent emanate from all directions. Daisy mentions that at her old school in Alaska, the faculty got together mostly to eat caribou.

We all smile. Rachel, a vegetarian, groans.

Just as I start to make a move to leave, Rachel walks up to where Daisy is sitting. "Let's make plans right now," she says. "Come out this Sunday. You and Remus can take the ferry and drive up the Hudson and be at our place in no time. You can even drive over and take a look at Columbia. It's really quite lovely in the fall."

I stop, frozen with astonishment. Did she say "Remus" when she meant "Amos?" Daisy is staring with offended suspicion, but Rachel rattles on, oblivious. "Or, you and Remus can drive over the Goethals Bridge, hop on the Jersey Turnpike and take the expressway to the Lincoln Tunnel. That's the ugly way, but it's even faster." She nods hopefully.

"Amos." Daisy says softly. I look pleadingly over at Rachel, but she keeps on going.

"Then, of course, you could drive over the Verazanno Bridge into Brooklyn and take the Battery Tunnel or the Brooklyn Bridge to the FDR. Remus can figure it out. He is a doctor, after all." She smiles at her little joke.

Daisy has risen to her feet and is glaring down at Rachel as she moves across the room, yet Rachel remains in some kind of unconscious fog.

Looking around the room, Rachel is unaware of Daisy's rising anger. "We'd like to take you to one of the local places. Does Remus like Italian food?"

"Amos!" Daisy's voice fills the room. Now she is standing over by the coffee pot surrounded by Styrofoam cups. "My husband's name is *Amos.*" And with that she marches out of the room.

Rachel stares at me, looking baffled. "What's with her? She seemed furious. Did you hear the door slam?"

I tell her: "You just called her husband 'Remus.' His name is *Amos!*" And then she realizes. This embodiment of New York liberalism has casually referred to a black woman's husband as "Remus."

She might as well have called him "Rastus" or "Sambo." To Daisy, it isn't a simple matter of getting the name wrong. It isn't a small thing to Rachel, either. Rachel rises, horrified, and limps out the door. She has left her books behind. The bell has rung, so the hall will be crowded. In seconds she catches up to Daisy and apologizes. They hug and laugh, and that is it. They will get together on Sunday.

I have a good time telling and retelling the "Amos" story to the guys in the attic. It's obvious to all of us why this is so funny, but we laugh anyway. Things like this just don't happen that often, and we want to savor the memory. Two people say, "I've got to remember that," meaning, of course, that they plan to pass the story along.

The only person with a different reaction is Dr. Aubin, a retired professor from Rutgers who teaches for us part time. By now he's heard me tell the Remus story several times. He laughs, but just as we are about to leave for classes, he makes fresh observation. "You know, this could have been sad. Really sad. It's lucky both ladies reacted well and made good choices. Rachel could have done nothing and hoped that time would heal, but instead she ran to apologize. Daisy could have chosen not to accept her apology. But both did the right thing." He does wonder, though, if there might be some lingering hurt. Rachel has to be thinking about how this could have happened. Daisy has ask herself how she is really regarded by the other teachers. "This thing might not be as simple as it looks."

We all nod nervously as we move to the door. "But, anyway," he concludes, looking right at me, "you got a good story out of it."

ALEX'S DAY

It's the winter of 1966, and I am standing in my sneakers in the gym of PS 29. I'm holding a clipboard and watching my 6th graders lose a basketball game to the public school kids. My team is hopelessly outclassed. The score is 45 to 29. This is not a bad score. Last year we lost to them 58 to 6.

With only a few minutes remaining on the clock, I call time out. I want to make sure the subs get one last opportunity to play. This means Alex will get his chance. Alex is the smartest kid in the 6th grade this year. He is also the smallest and the frailest. He wears the thickest glasses. Someday he'll follow his father into the medical field and probably make a name for himself as a surgeon or cancer researcher. This afternoon he'll play point guard against kids from the public school.

I remind him not to forget to dribble and to be on the lookout for an open teammate. And when he does make the pass, he should cut right to the basket. He nods nervously and sprints onto the gym floor. The referee hands him the ball and he starts to dribble his way up the court. "One hand on the ball at a time," I shout. He slaps at the ball awkwardly. Across the way, the parents of the public school kids are laughing. The ref ignores an obvious double dribble as Alex crosses over the centerline. The public school kids, sensing the situation, have decided not to press.

He stops and adjusts his glasses and squints up at the clock. Under the basket, our bigger kids are holding up their arms and shouting for the ball. Our other guard stands near Alex. He too is pleading for the ball. Then Alex starts dribbling again—another violation, but no one blows a whistle.

He stops close to where I am standing, and a

PS 29 player charges up to block the way. He is a big kid who looks like he might shave. He waves his arms and moves between Alex and the basket. Alex should pass to the other guard, but he looks frozen with fear. Suddenly I can hear the boy guarding him start to whisper as he keeps jumping and waving his arms. "Kid, give me the ball. Give me the ball now." The whispered litany becomes a constant. Alex looks helplessly at the scoreboard, takes an illegal step to the right and holds out the ball. The big kid snatches it, tears down the court, and sinks a final basket just as the horn goes off.

Game over.

We all shake hands and then give a big cheer: "Two-four-six-eight, who do we appreciate: PS 29! PS 29!" Ordinarily, this kind of cheer is delivered by the winning team, a form of pseudo-gloating that obviates more-naked expressions of contempt. But we all raise our voices to show our sportsmanship and fighting spirit.

We hike down through the long, shiny hall to the parking lot. Alex has run ahead. He'll probably curl up in the back of the bus and try to ignore the taunting. He might even bury his nose in a schoolbook. I'm not going to scream at him as Stone would. But I want to do more than console him. In my year-and-a-half of teaching, I have faced many situations outside the classroom. I'd like the kids to discover for themselves why some actions are preferable to others, but often I will step in to tell kids what I think. "Don't hurt people." "Don't gossip." "Don't butt in line." "Don't bother others." "Don't destroy property." "Don't pee on the radiator." Up until now, applying a school rule or a rule of common sense could solve all of these kinds of problems. I was doing what other teachers did and what my own teachers had done.

Clearly the Alex incident calls for me to do something. By the time we get to the bus, I know exactly what I should do to help this kid, who could be in tears. I will tell him not to get too down on himself. I will tell him not to quit basketball. The fact that he's such a good student makes it even more important for him to be one of the boys. I will tell him that the kids from PS 29 might seem tough, but they are really OK people. I will remind him that softball is coming up. I'll let the others know that I won't tolerate much teasing.

When I get to the back of the bus, instead of a shattered Alex in the grip of agony, I find a grinning Alex yucking it up with his teammates, one of whom asks why he gave away the ball. "Simple," Alex crows, "I'm a coward." We all laugh, and I go back to the front of the bus.

The next day, on the playground before school, I find Alex standing by himself. I ask if he's all right. He says that he is. I tell him I felt bad when he surrendered the ball.

He shrugs and smiles, "Hey, Mr. Boone, it doesn't matter. I'm terrible a player anyway, and I *am* a coward."

Then it suddenly occurs to me what I should say. "Alex," I lower my voice. "This is all I want you to know. I don't think you want to be known as a coward. No matter what you do in life, you don't want to be thought of as a pushover. It's hard to think clearly when these things happen, but next time, don't give in so easily. Try to be brave."

He turns and looks out at the road. I think I hear a soft sigh. Maybe I have reached him. He looks back up at me once again. "But, Mr. Boone, wasn't it brave of me to admit that I was a coward?" And with that he hurries off, leaving me time to decide which words should appear on today's *Odyssey* quiz.

DRIGGS

Sue and I have relocated to Germany—West Germany—where we are teaching at a private school where Drew once taught. He was returning to the school, and he talked us into joining him. It was a good time to leave. The Staten Island Academy, now inclusive of primary and secondary grades, was becoming a little bit mean-spirited. I had no trouble imagining myself staying there, but as a young teacher, I wanted something else—some sense of adventure, of new vistas opening before us. Sue and I love to travel, and we have a new baby who we think will like the experience. Fanny is just a year old, but nonetheless we think she'll enjoy Germany. We certainly expect to. Our assignment is for two years— the standard contract, after which we must pay German income tax.

And it feels good to be here working at the Frankfurt International School—even though some of my students will be 8th graders, who my experiences with the Christmas play fiasco taught me to dread. I'm looking forward to new kids, new colleagues and new books. I'm looking forward to weekend trips to Amsterdam, Munich and Paris. When this cast gets off my arm (broken in an embarrassing Wiffle ball accident), I will start playing volleyball on Wednesday evenings.

Most of the students at our school are children of American businessmen working for companies like Honeywell or Chase Manhattan. Generally, they live here for two years and then return to the suburbs of Minneapolis, Chicago or some similar place. A few students are Army kids whose parents have decided to take them out of Frankfurt American High School. Several are children of diplomats: Nina is from

Sweden; Chantel is from France; Lillian is from the Netherlands. Hilla was born in Israel and has lived all over the world. And we have a number of German youngsters—many of whom flunked out of the German schools—who see our school as a second chance.

Because the school has no dining room, teachers and students eat together in the classrooms. Some people don't like this, but I do. The unusual arrangement offers a good chance to learn about the kids. Hal is a member of a German Boy Scout troop. Cindy misses Boston. David has an eccentric uncle from England who's always showing up unannounced at their house. Loren's family is in the oil business. Michael's father is a minister in the Church of Christ. He grew up in Nashville near my wife's home. Liz likes to read; Jim likes to hike. Paul wants to try out for the Olympic ski team. Susan tells me to visit the small castles in the area, to take our daughter to the small zoo in Kronburg, to walk through Sachenhausen where they sell delicious apple wine. Bob tells me where to buy used books. He says that when we eat at the Zum Lowen in Bad Hamburg, we should order wild boar with cream sauce. I learn about good places to hike, to eat American food, to swim. I learn about "Gunsmoke," "Johnny Dollar," "Suspense," and the other shows that play on Armed Forces radio. I learn where I can buy the military newspaper *Stars and Stripes*, so I can keep up on the American football scores.

I learn that buses are a big deal at the school. Virtually all of the students ride to school on one of the thirty Mercedes buses that pick them up from all over the Frankfurt area. Some ride the bus for more than an hour each way. The buses are big and clean. The drivers tend to be surly. Because the kids live far apart, school becomes their place to be together. They seem happy to be here because this is where they see their friends.

I share the story of my *Christmas Carol* theatrical nightmare. I explain how I got my foot stuck in a wastebasket my first week of teaching. I describe Big Ten football weekends in Madison, Wisconsin. I show them the scar where I got my finger caught in a beer can. I tell them about meeting Sue on the porch of a fraternity house. I tell them about having a mild case of polio in 8th grade. I explain what it was like to attend New Trier High School, which had more than 4,000 students when I attended. I tell them about a friend of my brother's who woke up with a python swallowing his leg. I describe standing nose-to-nose on a New York subway car with a man who had a dollar bill pasted to his head.

David describes his favorite tortures and about foods not to eat. "Stay away from blood sausage— *blutwurst*—and pigs' trotters." David doesn't know that the full gamut of German foods is offered all over Chicago and is no surprise to me. Ricky suspects his German neighbor was a member of the SS. Liz tells me how her uncle died in Vietnam. Jim gives me directions for getting to a gypsy camp on the outskirts of the city. Boris invites me to watch American basketball downtown.

I like lunch.

My classroom and the eight other upper-school classrooms share a central courtyard. At 11:00 every morning, I stand in the courtyard with the other teachers, and we supervise recess. We stand out there even when it's raining. When it's not raining, the air still smells moist. The paving stones are slippery. We puff away on Stuyvesant Cigarettes, mutter dirty things to each other, and banter with the kids. The group usually includes Clive, a language teacher from Bristol, England, Bill, a short stubby American history teacher, Dee, a biology teacher, and Caine, an English teacher who grew up down the street from where Joe Namath was born. My friend Drew is here too.

Some students stop to joke with us. "Nice socks, Mr. Boone. I hear you broke your arm throwing a Wiffle ball. That's not exactly manly, is it?"

"If you had seen my screw ball, Maguire, you'd know how manly I am. It was utterly unhittable." Unfortunately, I threw it so often that day on the Jersey shore, my arm snapped.

"Mr. Fenner," another student says to Clive, "when are you going to sell that piece of English crap? How can you drive something called a Mini? Come on man, buy a real car."

"You mean like a Buick?"

"You can buy one from my dad's place near the Army base."

Clive strikes back. "Stevens, we've been here one month, and your locker already looks like it's been colonized by lepers. Things are living in there. And, Moore, I thought you were going to write an angry letter to the paper about the lack of AP classes. Losing your nerve?" The kids that don't banter with us stand in small groups while others, usually new to the school, walk around alone. The girls wear short skirts and boots; the boys slouch and wear shirts that hang out. Some are growing their hair longish, Beatles style. They all poke each other and run off, ready to be caught. Lothar and Arianne stand very close. He touches her nose. She holds onto his belt. Freshmen sneak a look at them and titter.

We know it's time to go back to class when a dozen or so German women dressed in gray appear on the road and push their way through the kids. These ladies are built low to the ground. Their thick, gnarled faces contrast perfectly with the smiles and smirks of the American kids. These are the cleaning ladies (*putzfrauen*). They have arrived together on the trolley (the s*trassenbahn*) from Frankfurt and are heading to the basement for buckets, mops and other cleaning supplies. "Isn't it terrible?" Dee says. "I can't tell them apart."

My classroom has large windows that look out at the original building of the school, a half-timbered structure that was once a hunting lodge. Behind this is a forest that stretches all the way up to the Taunus Mountains. During the war, to escape the bombing, many families moved into the woods. The room smells of pine. The floor is covered with slightly buckling linoleum. Every morning at 7:30 Herr Oertel, one of our janitors, leaves a case of milk in the doorway. Last week, Ricky tripped on it and spilled milk all over the room. While he and I were cleaning it up, he invited me to his Bar Mitzvah. "How about that, Mr. Boone? A Bar Mitzvah in Germany!" I don't mention that prior to the late 1930s, German Bar Mitzvahs were as commonplace as rain in Frankfurt. I know what he's getting at. On the bulletin board is a picture of Truman Capote. Along the wall are samples of student writing.

Today the students are finishing off a short story unit. I have enjoyed this tremendously, and I think the kids have too. The textbook includes such stories as "The Most Dangerous Game," "The Ransom of Red Chief," "Flight," and "The Lottery." In one of the shortest meetings I have ever attended Nancy, the department chair, told us that that our job was to motivate the kids. Pure and simple. Don't worry about covering material. She assumes that we like to read. She assumes that we know how to use words like *plot, conflict* and *character*. She assumes that the teachers can agree on what books to read and when. But she is clever. Practically every day she gives us a sample of student writing that she likes. Most are literary essays from her senior class. She praises clearly written thesis statements, a good use of evidence, clear and correct writing. She expects her students to know how to use the accepted literary terms—especially as they relate to character. But she also includes poetry and forms of personal writing.

Today my 8th graders will discuss "The Chaser," by John Collier. It's about a young man who buys an inexpensive love potion from an old man in Chinatown. The old man, who also sells costly poisons, assures the young man that this potion will work beyond his wildest dreams. The young man is ecstatic: Now his fickle wife will care only about him. Nothing other than loving him will matter to her. She will be his love slave. What he can't see, of course, is that his wife's unfailing attention will drive him nuts, and one day he'll be back to buy the poison. The story ends with the old man saying, "Au Revoir."

When I talk about fiction, I like to talk about character and story rather than theme. My classes might end up speculating about what this "might prove" about the human condition, but if we don't, so what? This is English, not philosophy. In high school I had a teacher who turned every story into a philosophical statement and turned lot of people away from reading. She spent more than a week picking apart "To Build a Fire." At Columbia the "theme question" came up repeatedly. Younger teachers wanted to know if good reading meant spotting theme. Older teachers warned us not to be symbol hunters. Teachers pointed out that anthologies are often organized according to themes ("Man in Search of Himself," "Spiritual Values," "Struggles" and so on, all emphasized with the requisite capital letters). I know that I like books with great characters, with compelling plots. I like books that take place in unfamiliar settings. I like books that are funny. But books with profound ideas are not necessarily what I need. They're also not especially intriguing to young readers.

But today I'm going below the surface. I want my 8th graders to understand what's implied: Too much undisguised love can be a bad thing, and we don't always know what we want.

I begin, as I have lately, by asking the class to jot down answers to several questions.

"What did the story make you feel?"

"Describe the main character. Why is he there?"

"What's his wife like?"

"What all does the old man sell?"

"What will the potion do for Alan?"

"Why does the old man say 'au revoir'?"

This gives them all a chance to think for themselves. Occasionally, I collect these responses, but I never grade them.

They all write eagerly, and no one dives into it more than Zsa Zsa, a noisy, red-haired girl who lives in Bad Hamburg. Zsa Zsa's right hand moves back and forth across the page while her left hand is already raised. The only one not writing is John Driggs, a tall, bony young man with a gigantic snarl of curly black hair and a spotted and torn trench coat. While the others write feverishly, Driggs smiles peacefully out the window, lightly tapping his chewed pen on the desk. He is an American but has lived his whole life in Frankfurt. He speaks German better than he speaks English. He walks fast and talks to himself. Everyone likes Driggs.

"Driggs, did you read the story?" I know he didn't. He knows I know he didn't. But I ask anyway.

He raises his eyebrows and shakes his head. "I left it on the Strassenbahn, Mr. Boone." He widens his smile. I can see his braces.

"The new book I gave you last week?" He had left his other book out in the rain. He had stuck it back into his book bag. Now everything he turns in is streaked with mud.

I'm about to hand him another copy of the story when the assistant principal for the lower school sticks his head into the room and asks in a north-country British accent, "Can I borrow Driggs? We have a plumbing problem in the girls' loo."

"What's a 'Lou'?" Francie shouts.

"That's what the English people call a bathroom," Zsa Zsa calls out.

Driggs, it seems, is indispensable within our cloistered society. He can fix anything in the school, from broken projectors to leaky toilets. His locker is packed with wrenches, wire, oil and tape. He even has a plumber's snake, which he'll probably use today. Frequently, I pass him in the hall talking to a janitor about something technical. He's been spotted on the roof and under the headmaster's car. Once during a test, a bus driver pounded on the window, and Driggs ran out to fix his carburetor. Today Driggs hurries out of the room while the rest of the kids continue to answer questions about "The Chaser." Zsa Zsa, absolutely inflamed with ideas, is now crouching in her chair, her feet on the seat.

I ask Zsa Zsa to put down her hand, and then I begin the discussion. "What's probably going to happen to the young man's marriage after he slips his wife the love potion?" More than half the kids have hands in the air. I call on one who does not.

"Dan, what do you think?" Dan, the president of the 8th grade and all-around good guy, knows that the man sells poisons as well as love potions. He can see why the young man is so excited to have his girl passionately devoted to him. Who wouldn't? But the end is not clear to him. As far as Dan is concerned, the story is about a guy who buys a love potion.

Zsa Zsa knows there's more to it. She is on her feet, hand stretched upward, a pleading look distorting her face. I ease her back in her seat and ask Dan if he understands that "au revoir" means "see you again."

I ask, "Why did he say that and not good-bye? Why might the young man want to come back? What would he come back for?" He stares and shrugs. Zsa Zsa is again rising to her feet. Once again I push her down as if she were a giant doll in a jack-in-the-box.

I tell them all to put down their hands. I want Dan to figure out the answer. I go back through the story. "The young man comes for the potion. He finds out the man also sells poisons. But the poisons are far more costly than the love potion. He finds out that the potion will make his wife care only about him for the rest of her life." (I raise my voice with "life.")

With that, Dan leans forward and speaks. "He's going to come back to get the poison so he can kill her because she'll drive him crazy by hanging all over him."

I reach over and shake his hand. "Good job." I tell him. "Great job. Can you see that what you have said was not actually written into the story, but it's there?" He nods.

"Why is 'The Chaser' a good title?" I ask the entire class.

"Because," Zsa Zsa can no longer hold back, "the guy's girlfriend might have chased after other people before, but now she will be chasing after him." Good answer.

"When do people call a drink a chaser?" I ask, figuring no one will know.

But David does. "That's what you call a weak drink that you gulp down after drinking something stronger." I'm impressed.

"Good work, David. I hope you're not speaking from experience." We share a good-natured guffaw.

And then Dan speaks up. "The poison will be like the chaser for the love potion. It's something he'll use afterwards."

"Great comment, Dan." That gets him another handshake.

We have ten minutes left. Just enough time to read the story aloud once more. "Notice," I say in my best teacher's voice, "that we know more than the character. That's called dramatic irony. Zsa Zsa, would you like to read?" She's on her feet.

Just as her voice starts to fill the room, through the door marches Driggs with a toilet plunger carried rifle-style on his shoulder. Shoulder arms for a plumber. Full of pride, he takes his seat. I hand him a book and tell him to read along. It looks as if he's added a new stain to his trench coat. The plunger is at his side.

Zsa Zsa finishes, and the room grows quiet. I have just enough time to ask Driggs what he thinks, now that he knows what the story's about. He tells me he's a bad reader; he tests below average, and he's in a special reading class, but I know he can read when he tries. He summarizes the plot quickly.

"Good work. What else is going on here? Is this the end or what?"

He half-smiles, somehow manages to run his hand through his steel-wool hair, and rattles off several sentences in German just as the bell rings.

Another student translates his remarks. Driggs said, "Too much love can be a bad thing." I praise his analysis, but he's supremely indifferent. His own "achievement" was unimpressive from his point of view, hopelessly inferior to solving a plumbing problem. I feel a sudden rush of inadequacy—Driggs obviously reached this conclusion on his own, irrespective of all of my "teacher" prodding. I also recognize that my weak German is going to hamper some of my teaching. Driggs—Mister Fix-it—is obviously able to act out of character. The question is, can I? He then answers my question before I can ask it. "I can talk about things in English, but I talk about ideas in German." With that, he's out the door before I can tell him he's forgotten the toilet plunger.

AN EXCHANGE

"Stay close," I call out weakly as my sophomores sprint ahead of me down the road. "We don't have to be at the *Gymnasium* until 9:30." If anything, they are picking up speed. "How'd I sound, Marty?" I shout at the disappearing back of a blond girl.

"Stick to English, Mr. Boone," she calls back over her shoulder. "Just say 'high school,' not G*ymnasium*. Your German stinks." She exaggerates my Midwestern nasal way of saying it.

The lone sophomore who has not run ahead is Jim, who marches beside me. Jim and I both started at the Frankfurt International School in the fall of 1967—he as a freshman, and I as a teacher. He laughs easily and tries new things. He doesn't sit in the back of the class and mutter. He isn't a bully, a wimp, or a suck-up.

Lately Jim hasn't been smiling. Last week he flunked a test on *Lord of the Flies*. A day later, I returned his research paper ungraded. ("You've got to prove something. Don't just summarize what you found at the library.") Then last weekend at the school dance a teacher caught him in the woods drinking beer. A few days earlier an anonymous letter had turned up on the principal's desk. It accused Jim and other sophomores of buying pot from local GIs.

Jim starts the conversation. "How's the family, Mr. Boone?" I eye him suspiciously and keep walking. "Your daughter sure speaks German just like a native. How old is she?" He knows she's three years old, so he doesn't wait for my answer. "Are we going to read any more stories by Stephen Crane? I really like the 'Blue Hotel'." He stays away from *Lord of the Flies*. "You know," he intones thoughtfully (was he actually stroking his chin?), "I'm really looking forward to meeting these German kids today. It's important for us to make contact with people from the local culture. How did you set this up, anyway?" By now the rest of the sophomores are out of sight.

"Jim, cut the crap, OK? And don't look hurt. I know you've had a bad week, but don't..."

"Don't what?" He looks genuinely pained.

"You know what I mean." I can't quite bring myself to tell him to quit trying to sound like an adult.

"But I do want to know how you arranged this thing. I've heard that our school has never visited a German high school."

"Weren't you in class the day I made the announcement?"

"I wasn't there that day. Remember? I was..."

"With the principal. I forgot." So I hurry through the story. Last winter two German high school students—Dieter and Horst—came by our apartment for a chat. For the next two hours, they sat in our living room drinking coffee and firing off questions in perfect English. What kind of school is the Frankfurt International School? (Private, American curriculum, parents of most of the kids work in the area, not to be confused with the Army schools.) How do I like teaching in Germany? (Very much, good kids, loose curriculum, great chances to travel.) What do I think about the war in Vietnam? (I hate it.) What about American literature? (I like Ralph Ellison. I do not like Eugene O'Neill.) They asked many questions about my students. Do they miss the States? Do they feel they have enough rights? What do they think about drugs and sex? Each time I shook my head and shrugged, it became clearer that the kids from the two schools should get together.

As I talk, Jim emits several "uh-huhs" while stifling several yawns. When I stop, he tells me what a great job I'm doing and abruptly trots off down the road, leaving me alone to enjoy a German rarity—a sunny day. I grew up in Chicago, like Frankfurt a no-nonsense, hard-working city distant from the coast of a continent and subject to a lot of overcast days. You would think I would not be perturbed by Frankfurt's lousy weather, but I never have grown accustomed to it.

I wave to our bus drivers standing in the shadow of the many Mercedes coaches. Many of these guys are supposed to have fought in the war. Maybe so. They're about the right age and several limp proudly. Today they wave back. I feel a lift.

At the corner where the school driveway meets the road to Frankfurt is the Waldlust, a small hotel set back in the woods. My colleagues and I often drink here after school. Right now it is just 9:00 AM, and the waiters are sponging off the cafe tables and opening the Cinzano umbrellas. Behind the Waldlust, in the lush garden area, are cages for two pet pigs—Fritz and Julianna. This happens to be my daughter's favorite place in all of Germany. It is here that she fine-tuned her astonishing ensemble of pig noises. When she isn't snorting, she jabbers at them in German. Fritz is her favorite.

I turn right on the road to Frankfurt and pass Camp King, a small American base. My department chairman lives here with her husband, an Army captain. Two of our younger teachers are engaged to soldiers stationed here. Teachers from our school can use the base nursery and movie theater, but we must pay with American dollars. A few Saturdays ago eight of us from the school played volleyball against the Camp King team. We lost, but it was close. Even though the Americans still have a huge presence in West Germany, and even though the war in Vietnam is growing and becoming an ever-bigger issue, especially for military personnel, this camp always feels slow and relaxed. Today the guard at the gate is reading an "Archie" comic book.

I have been told that in 1944 from this very

spot outside of Camp King, you could see Frankfurt ablaze. Now, almost twenty-five years after the war ended, many large Frankfurt buildings, including the opera, remain bombed-out shells. Like Ricky's astonishment at conducting his Bar Mitzvah in Germany, the scars of the Nazi era and of World War II are very real and all around me.

I turn left and follow a narrow street up a hill into a village called Oberhoestadt. I could be anywhere in Germany. The houses are mostly light stucco. All have fences. The Mercedes, BMWs, Volkswagens and other cars parked along the street sparkle in the sunlight. These cars will all be locked, just as the gates in front of the houses will be locked, and just as about everything else in Germany is locked—sometimes even the refrigerators and telephones. For me, the most telling aspect of whatever culture shock exists between Germany and the United States is my penchant for disorder colliding with the German focus on a certain adherence to agreed rules. In the last two years, I have collected tickets for leaving my car unlocked. *My car.* One was a real whopper for leaving the keys in the ignition!

Locks and stucco houses and limps and scowls—all these things German have filled my mind lately because it has been decided that today the kids will address the issue of stereotypes. How do German and American students see each other? How are they "supposed" to see each other? Where did they get these notions? I had wanted a free form, open discussion, but Herr Shroeder, the teacher from the German school, wanted something a bit more structured, and I acceded to his desires.

Something odd happened the next day when I told the kids to start thinking about stereotypes. "For instance," I asked innocently enough, "what are Germans 'supposed' to be like?" This was an example, not a question. My remark was essentially rhetorical. I expected no response. But instead of nodding, this class of American kids turned into Germans. Loren was driving an imaginary car while scowling and pointing at his head. Bob was pretending to be pushing ahead in line. Ingrid was eating with her elbows thrust out and her mouth practically touching the imaginary food. Others saluted Nazi style. The bell rang, and they stayed in character. I tried to seize the moment. "Think about what you're doing. Isn't that the point? Think about what you are doing."

"We're having fun; that's what we're doing," Liz called back as she goose-stepped out of the room. And they were. This really proved only two things: that my students, as always, could turn my teacherly guidance into a joke, and that these American kids knew what Germans were "supposed" to be like, not how they acted with individual Germans. But still I was astonished at just how much they understood the German stereotype. Where did they learn these ideas, and why is it that we latch onto them so enthusiastically?

I was just as guilty as the kids. I fully understood that all stereotypes are a caricature of a range of common characteristics, yet I delighted when Germans acted "in character." I loved telling friends about my pushing fight with a German bus driver at the airport. He was furious because I was in the wrong lane. ("You are not where you are supposed to be!") Everyone knew that when we first met our German neighbor, he was shooting gas pellets into the ground to kill mice. These made for good stories, which I expect to tell for the rest of my life. Still, as a teacher, it is perplexing that what people seem to learn first is the generally perceived characteristic, not the subtle differences.

What I have also noticed is that the longtime teachers at our school turn these comic characteristics into something much worse. These veterans speak with utter confidence about "all Germans." All Germans, according to them, are, narrow-minded, humorless, single-minded, pushy bossy, servile, conforming. Even their good qualities are construed as bad: They are too clean, too organized, too serious, too hard-working. Sue and I hear many times, "It's not surprising they would follow Hitler. Man, they love to take and give orders." What makes this all the more weird is that these German-haters are often married to Germans. They live in the Germany community. They tell their anti-German stories with Germans in the room.

So maybe Herr Schroeder is onto something. In a situation where two cultures must co-exist, why not explore the individual perceptions?

My sophomores are waiting for me in front of the school. Naturally I notice how American they look with their quasi-long hair, shirttails out and general sloppiness. And they're loud and silly. They don't look like serious young scholars.

Except for the absence of an American flag, the *Oberhoestadt Gymnasium* looks very much like Any School, USA. The structure has one story and is spread out. The windows are large and decorated with drawings. There are plantings along the outside of the building. Inside it looks like any American school except that the teachers all wear blue sport coats and gray turtlenecks. As far as that goes, if everyone in both countries had the same fashion sense, it could be any school in the United States. There are even lockers. The teachers all dress in a boring, cautious way that nods at fashion but misses being stylish.

Herr Schroeder greets us in the hall. I introduce him to my kids as "my German counterpart." They wave hellos and keep on jabbering. Schroeder frowns. The kids keep talking. Then with a nod he strides off down the hall, and we follow.

The discussion room is large and airy and distinctive for what it lacks—no posters, no bulletin boards, no piles of student stuff. The German students sit at one table; our kids sit facing them. It's like a Cold War conference of adversaries. Herr Schroeder and I sit at the end. Dieter and Horst wave at me. Other kids wave familiar greeting to one another. Of course, some would know each other. Herr Schroeder stands up to welcome us and to explain the "ground rules." He seems pleased to know that word. We will speak only in English. We will talk about "the perceptions we have of each other's culture." Comments should be short. He will keep track of the responses.

Silence.

A German girl in a red sweater finally asks, "Where are you all from in the states?"

Pause. Lengthy.

"Texas," "Vermont," "Twin Cities," "New York City." It occurs to me that a response like "the Twin Cities" is going to be baffling to our German counterparts.

Silence. A few Germans nod.

Bob says that he's lived in Germany all of his life. "This is where I'm from." He rattles off something in German, and all the kids laugh. I laugh too without knowing why.

More silence.

Then Loren stands up. "What do you German kids really think of Americans?" He points his finger like a politician. "Be honest now. My neighbors think we're a bunch of rich slobs. What do you all think?" He sits down and smiles over at a couple of German kids he seems to know.

Dieter shouts from the German side. "And what do you think of us? Are we as serious as we're supposed to be? Do we love work? Do we like everything in order?"

"Let's start with what we're supposed to be like," says Loren, who is showing unusual initiative. The German kids call out words while Schroeder writes the responses on the board. "All Americans are rich." "They all wear good shoes." "They're wasteful and friendly." "They act free and happy." "They all drive big cars." "They drive dirty cars." "They're all optimistic." It's clear that using the word "supposed" frees the kids to speak comfortably. They are not responsible; this is what other people have said.

What are Germans "supposed" to be like? The shouting picks up again. "Smart." "Serious." "Bad drivers." "Serious expressions." "Super organized." "Strict." "Hard workers." The German kids join in talking about themselves. One girl talks about crossing the street. "We wait in line like robots, even if no cars are there." Her trick is to go to the head of the line and then march across the street. "And the other people in line all follow like ducks."

Then the talk switches back to Americans. Liz tells an ugly-American story about a tourist who can't keep his voice down in church and another who lights his cigarette at the eternal flame—using the eternal flame as his lighter.

The stories keep coming. Bob tells about taking a boat across the Main River from Rudesheim to Weissbaden. By mistake the attendant on the Rudesheim side had taken the "hin" (over) part of the ticket instead of the "zuruck" (return). On the other side Bob could not get back because the ticket said "hin," and the attendant on that side would not accept it. So Bob borrowed a pen from the attendant and crossed out "hin" and wrote "zuruck." The attendant took the ticket and let him return. Several Germans tell stories about dumb Americans who did not know the language. I squirm uncomfortably. When Schroeder leaves the room, they all start jabbering in German.

Schroeder comes back, and we start to pull it all together. When I ask, "So what? What does this all prove?" Several say it just proves that we know a lot about what the others are supposed to be. I can't argue with that. "You didn't learn these ideas in textbooks," I comment. "Where did they come from?"

No one really answers. I'm not sure I know.

Schroeder takes over. He reviews the concept of stereotyping. It's inevitable that we generalize, but we must always test general statements. If they don't hold up, we must reject them. He speaks in English, but occasionally he will jump into German to repeat his point to his class. "And what if we take it too far? What if we all think in that general way without questions? What will happen?" We can feel it coming. "This thinking makes it possible for a Hitler to arise. It makes it possible for the KKK to murder black people in America."

No one's about to disagree. But it's time to leave anyway.

Schroeder and I shake hands in front of the school. Because there is not much time left in the school year, this meeting will not occur again until the fall. I will be back in the States, but my replacement will follow up.

On the way home, I feel especially good because things have gone smoothly—no fights, no embarrassing pauses. I feel good because I had made the whole thing happen. It was my idea, my planning, my follow-through that made this happen.

The next day the students and I talk about the trip. Did they have fun? Yes. Should we do it again? Sure. How would they like to plan the next one? Good idea. Then I ask the question we should have asked yesterday. "You guys know all of these stereotypes, but do you believe them? Do you expect Germans to behave the way they are supposed to?"

The answers are mixed. Some say never. Some say they might expect certain behavior, but that's about it. If the person acts in character or not, it doesn't really matter. Jim says that, even if you treat someone as a group person, your idea changes the longer you know him. I ask about those Americans who have lived here a long time and seem to be even guiltier of stereotyping. "They're old," Ingrid says.

"They don't have anything better to do." More stereotyping.

I ask again how we learn these generalities. They're not in textbooks. Is it that we always learn the general quality first? I tell them that I've noticed that people try to look smart by being able to fire off these broad statements. I remembered a British guy in Harry's Bar in Paris back in 1962. Instead of seeing him as the leech that he was, I was impressed because he spoke so broadly and confidently about all French and all Americans.

"This really bothers you, doesn't it?' asks Ingrid.

"I guess it does," I say. "But it bores me too. I think I prefer the particular things."

I ask them to write a true story that has "something" to do with how people see each other as members of groups. "Make it very specific."

The next day the papers arrive. Liz writes about a girl in a school who acted like a snob, and the kids were so mean that she tried to kill herself. They didn't realize that she was painfully shy, not a snobbish person. I like that she has written about a different kind of group.

Jim writes about making friends with his neighbors, two of who were in the group from the German school we had visited. At first they don't feel comfortable together—probably because of what they assumed about each other. Then one day they found out what they should have known all along: They all liked to drink beer. In fact, Jim added, when he got caught drinking in the woods, he was with these German kids.

I try to tell myself that Jim hasn't missed the point.

POLICE DOGS AND 2001

With the end of our stay in Frankfurt approaching, for one last time I fill my classroom walls and windows with selections of student creativity:

a short story about a girl who gets pregnant and moves back home with her mother;

want ads written by Holden Caulfield;

letters to Ann Landers from Macbeth and his wife;

original cartoons;

profiles of famous people;

arguments for and against the Vietnam war;

true stories about great triumphs;

coincidences.

Lately, I've come to recognize that I am going to miss Germany a lot. I'll miss that round little man from the house across the street who hangs from the second-floor window and yells at my daughter, "Fanny, Fanny! Aye-yi-yi! Aye-yi-yi!" I'll miss the little bag of *brotchen* (rolls) delivered every morning outside our gate and the 2,000-year-old linden tree in the middle of our village, next to the restaurant that prepares rump steak and onions. I'll miss the Sunday drives with Sue and Fanny up to the top of the Taunus where we have breakfast. I'll miss the little muddy roads that run past farms and the view from our kitchen window of a field with cows grazing. I'll miss hiking through the dark woods with Fanny on my shoulders. I'll miss driving to Frankfurt on Sundays to get a London newspaper at the train station where we watch the "guest" workers—Greeks, Turks, Italians—walk around in suits, flirt with the ladies, and smoke smelly cigarettes. I'll miss the sound of the *strassenbahn*. I'll miss listening to American football on Armed Forces Network. I'll missing hearing Herr

65

Shaeffer, the local gas station owner, describe cleaning the colonel's swimming pool in Brooklyn where he was a prisoner of war in the early 1940s.

But now, before I leave, I still have a job to do: accommodate Michael. He has seen *2001: A Space Odyssey* three times, and that's all he can talk about. More than once he has interrupted a class discussion to proclaim belligerently that "Stanley Kubrick is a much greater artist than Shakespeare because he knows what the future will be like." Bob or Ingrid will usually pick up the argument. I'll try to steer things back to *Macbeth*, but I soon crumble, and the debate is on. The problem is that only a few students have seen the movie, so we plan one final field trip to watch the film at a theater in Frankfurt.

On a holiday morning in June, we meet at school, take the *strassenbahn* to the city to see the movie, then we go to Wimpy's for lunch. Later we go to a park, sit in a circle and argue. After that, we walk around the city for a while until the kids head for home on various trams and buses. A pleasant day.

Afterward I walk to the apartment of one of our teachers, an American woman named Nina. She has invited several teachers for dinner. "Some of you are about to leave, and we've never done anything together. Hans and I would love to have you come over." Hans is her husband. He is a native of Frankfurt and reputed to hate Americans, or at least people from the school. Hans is relentlessly unpleasant. A thick man with a broad forehead, his typical expression is an angry frown. Various examples of his rude behavior are legendary among my colleagues. As far as I can tell, everyone dislikes Hans, especially the other German teachers who wonder how a nice American girl could have ended up married to this monster.

To get to the apartment, I climb several flights of creaky stairs. The living room is cramped and gloomy. Nina and the guests are sitting in a circle in the middle of the room. The talking seems animated and happy. I spot Hans in the corner and decide to start up a conversation. I tell him that earlier that day I took my class to a movie in downtown Frankfurt and now have walked over here to meet Sue and the other guests at his apartment.

"Which movie?" he grunts.

"*2001: A Space Odyssey*," I answer hopefully. "The kids in my class had been arguing about it so I thought I'd give them all a chance to see it."

No comment. He fixes a glower on his wife, who is joking with the other teachers. She's had a little too much Rhine wine. Then without saying anything, Hans pushes past me, through the conversation group, and out the door. We can hear the stairs creaking as he hurries away. All talking ceases until finally Nina says, "Nice friendly German, isn't he?" We all laugh.

In a while, after it's obvious that Hans is not returning anytime soon, Nina gets up to prepare dinner while the rest of us keep up the chatter. The year's essentially over. Very soon there will be a few more papers to grade. A test or two. That's all. We're excited. Someone tells a joke about people from the west country of England. Drew tells a joke about a chef in Alaska. Drew's wife complains about the principal at the Frankfurt International School. It strikes me again that within days this will be completely irrelevant to me.

Nina calls us for dinner, and we all sit around a long table in their dining room. Hans' place remains empty. Nina apologizes and mumbles something about work stress. She serves the *ripchen* and potatoes, and I dig in. Good food. I start to tell the group about the field trip to see *A Space Odyssey* when something large and furry brushes past my leg. It's a large dog—a German shepherd, or Alsatian, as they call them here—that is immediately followed by another. They rub past my legs with quiet growls.

Then into the room strides a beaming Hans dragging along two men dressed in long black robes with large wooden crosses hanging from their necks. They must be street ministers. "I found these gentlemen and their dogs outside and invited them up. I said they could eat with us. Isn't that the Christian thing to do?" I am reminded of Michael's aggressive, challenging way of introducing his opinions about Stanley Kubrick. Michael does it with more charm.

The ministers apologize. Hans finds chairs and squeezes them in. The dogs stay below the table, bumping legs. Nervous about the dogs, we all sit very still. Nina stands dumbfounded and then ladles small helpings of what is left onto their plates. Sue gladly shares her food, and then we all do the same.

The minister who sits next to me is from Ohio. He and his colleague, along with other ministers, are on a mission to provide spiritual counseling for the GIs stationed in West Germany. I can't precisely determine their affiliation. They seem to be Protestants, but they are dressed vaguely like Roman Catholic priests. They have been here for two months and plan to return soon to the United States. He tells me his brother was at the last Super Bowl where he saw Joe Namath lead the Jets to victory over the Colts.

Hans circles the table jabbering happily as the rest of us—dogs and humans—try to make the evening come to an end.

Driving back in Drew's van, we can't stop laughing. This will be the greatest Hans story ever. This will define what a horrible person he is. "That'll teach her to marry a German," says one of the ladies, who is in fact a German herself. Drew laughs so hard that he almost drives off the road.

Our apartment is half-filled with boxes about to be shipped back to Chicago. I pay the baby-sitter and drive her home. The next day I return to school for the beginning of final exams. The memory of Hans and the ministers and the dogs stays in my mind for a while—but not for long. I have the school year to finish, and soon my family and I will be off to Yugoslavia where we'll camp for three weeks before flying back to Chicago, where I will enter the Ph.D. program at Northwestern University.

WALLY

Warm, fragrant autumn air floods courtyards and lawns. People move trance-like with vacant smiles, if they move at all. Most are sprawled staring at the sky or at each other or at nothing at all. They wear tie-dyed shirts, headbands, love beads, short shorts and lots of denim. A few have dogs. Several throw Frisbees. A few hundred yards to the east, dozens of sailboats cut through Lake Michigan, bluer today than the sky. Da Nang, napalm, Woodstock, the Black Panthers, Charles Manson, the Cubs, bra burning and the Beatles seem far, far away.

I sit on the lawn, take in the sights, and daydream. I have just written letters to old teacher friends, and I'm bursting with school memories. I am leading twenty-five 5th graders into New York's Museum of Natural History. I am pacing the sidelines of a soccer match. I am explaining the new grammar to a group of skeptical parents. I am sitting on a couch sipping a martini at the headmaster's house. I am drinking a beer at a bar called Pop's Last Chance. I am skiing into a tree on the Tyrol, breaking up a fight between two girls in the parking lot, mopping up vomit. I am eating an apple pastry covered with cream and grading papers about the movie, *2001: A Space Odyssey*. I am driving the 5th-grade comedians Ricky and Jeffrey home ("Did you take a bath?" "No, is one missing?"). I am sitting in our kitchen half-asleep, staring at a pile of ungraded essays.

I shake off the memories when I look at my watch—1:00 p.m. Time for class.

Inside Evans Hall it's as if I've entered a different dimension. The room is as cold and damp as a medieval castle. The windows are so skinny and the ivy so thick that barely any light can fight its way through. I take a seat next to eleven other Ph.D. candidates. Our desks are bolted to the floor.

The course we are about to begin is called "Educational Issues." The teacher is Dr. Wallace W. Douglas, but we've been told to call him "Wally." Because he is our advisor, we already have met him, but we have never seen him teach. As we wait for him to show up, we talk. Dan tells us that he ran into a former student who is now at sophomore at Northwestern. "She wanted me to speak at a peace rally. When I said wouldn't, she called me a 'fucking pig' and stormed off without saying good-bye." He smiles and shrugs. Dick, back from a stint with the Peace Corps in Tanzania, tells us about a former corps member who strangled his wife while two native boys looked on from behind a tree. He thought he had gestured for them to leave, but they read the sign as "Come here." Thanks to their testimony, the husband was convicted and hanged. Evelyn shows us a magazine written and illustrated by one of her 7th graders from the city. Art describes several summer workshops. I tell them about Driggs, the boy who could fix anything. I'll save my description of the *A Christmas Carol* disaster for another day.

We are all "teachers on leave," so we have absolutely no need for our dress-up clothes: No ties and coats for the fellas; no skirts for the gals. Strangers squinting into this gloomy cavern would see twelve of the plainest individuals on earth. Or more likely, they would not see us as individuals at all, but as undifferentiated clumps of unfashion. I wear faded Bermuda shorts and a multi-spotted yellow golf shirt that once belonged to my dad. Dick is decked out in a faded work shirt, maroon sweatpants patched with Duct Tape, and loafers with no socks. Dan sports a plaid shirt, striped shorts, and wingtips with no laces and liberally spotted with something white.

I am actually enjoying this new life. It's comforting to be part of a small group of invisible people who have so much in common. Most of us are in our late twenties. We drive Volkswagens or other economy cars, live in rented space, and belong to baby-sitting pools. We're too old for Vietnam. We know some people who are there. We hate the war but have no plans to do much about it. Had we been around the summer before, we might have joined the demonstrators who tangled with Daley's police. Or, we might not have.

No teacher yet, so I go out for a quick smoke and find the lawns even more crowded. A couple, sharing the same cigarette, bends toward each other. A girl is lying on top of her boyfriend. A boy is lying on top of his girlfriend. A tall fellow with a scraggly beard is selling *The Seed*, Chicago's alternative newspaper. A man in a turban is sleeping. Two skinny boys with dark glasses and pasty skin are playing chess. One is wearing a yarmulke.

When I get back inside, Dan is talking about Wally. "Will he be as much of a prick as a teacher as he is as an advisor?" I wonder the same thing. My first day on campus I talked to Mike Flanigan, Douglas' assistant. We became instant friends. Flanigan asked good questions, listened to my answers. He has a good sense of humor. Wally, on the other hand, was another story, basically a total opposite. He yawned during my description of teaching in New York and Europe. He winced when I said I tried to be relevant. He wasn't in the least surprised that I knew quite a bit about his work with Coleridge and later with educational theory. With the other new graduate students, he was just as rude. And, while Flanigan keeps telling us not to worry, we still wonder if we are giving all this time and money for a program run by a mean old man.

Then suddenly into the room wearing a gray suit and blue tie walks Wally. Considering how long we've been waiting for him to appear—long enough for me to go outside and smoke a cigarette—his arrival shouldn't seem abrupt, but it does. There is something perpetually startling about Wally. Maybe it's his way of moving, quick and purposeful but distracted at the same time. He is carrying a worn leather briefcase and is shadowed by three older graduate students. They take seats behind us in back of the room as he begins to struggle with his briefcase. He is a fragile little guy with pink skin and trembling hands. As I look down at him tugging at the papers in his briefcase, he looks especially frail. I have already learned that he can't drive a car or ride a bike.

Finally he produces a handful of papers that he starts to read. "These," he snorts to no one in particular, "are required book lists from local high schools." He begins reading aloud, then stops to chortle, and then reads some more. "I see here that New Trier is requiring Shakespeare, Conrad, Hemingway and the other dead white men." He smiles at his own humor. "Evanston High School is no better." The trio in the back chuckles knowingly. The rest of us sit silently.

Next, still without any words of welcome or introduction, he walks to the board, picks up a small piece of chalk and stands with his back to us. He writes three words: Teacher, stuff, learner. He promptly erases the words and writes them again in caps: TEACHER, STUFF, LEARNER. His back is turned to us. From that angle he looks terribly small and vulnerable. His hair is sparse enough and certainly gray enough that he could be a very old man, though he is only in his early sixties.

Next, he turns from the board and heads toward us, but then he turns around and goes right back. He stares some more at the words, erases them, and quickly rewrites them in a new order: TEACHER, LEARNER, STUFF. After that he turns and walks up to where we are sitting and looks right at me. "Bill," it would take him a while to learn my name, "Bill, how should teachers regard stuff?" He gestures awkwardly behind him to the writing on the board. I sit stupidly. What is he up to? All I can do is meekly smile and slowly shake my head.

"Stuff. How do you define stuff?"

"Stuff?"

"Stuff."

"Stuff?"

"Yes, stuff." He has closed and folded his arms and now looks like Jack Benny. "By 'stuff,' I mean what you taught." He looks up at the row of acolytes in the back and rolls his eyes dramatically.

I've never been asked such a vague question in my life. "I guess—if I understand you—at the schools where I have worked the kids are all heading for college, so the 'stuff' we taught was going to help get them there." He cringes. The back-row cheering section snickers. I feel as if I'm back in high school Spanish with Señor Almaguer shaking his head while I lose another battle to the subjunctive.

"You decided that."

"We decided that." I sharpen the edge of my tone. "We were the teachers."

"I see." He moves on to Dick, then Dan, then Evelyn. The same question. The same answers. The same sarcastic snorts and frowns. The same knowing chuckles from the yahoos behind us. I'd like to choke the guy behind me with the hee-haw laugh. Finally Art, who knows Wally from summer workshops, speaks up but in an apologetic voice. "The stuff is on the inside. Teachers should open up their students, not fill them with what we think they should learn." He looks at us and shrugs.

And that's all Wally needs. He's off and running. Yes, he says, all of the schools still fill kids with what they want kids to learn. They see the job of teaching as pouring in when it should be motivating and inspiring. Either the kids know already or they have the capacity to learn on their own. "That's what it's all about."

When he is done, he stops and then delivers his little speech all over again. When he finishes this second time, he tugs a yellow legal pad out of his briefcase. "Sign your name and write down what might be the subject of your reports. You're going to do most of the work in this class." When the pad reaches me, I jot down "Creative Writing." When the pad gets back to Wally, he sticks it back into his briefcase and walks out with the older grad students trotting adoringly behind him.

And we sit stunned. Was that supposed to be teaching? Does he think we have never heard that a teacher's first job is to motivate? Isn't this guy supposed to be a great educator? And what's with the morons in the back? Dan breaks the silence: "Wally Douglas has convinced me to get away from college teaching as fast as I can. That was an embarrassment." He leaves and we follow, smiling and shrugging to each other.

And that was it. Except that on the way home I am consumed with thought about my past teaching. When did I reach inside? When did I lecture? And all I can think about are my own learning experiences.

A few days later, I'm back on the lawn. Just like the last time, college kids are all around me. If anything, there are even more Frisbee tossers. A girl lying near me is openly smoking a joint. The odor of the marijuana wafts past me. Someone with a guitar is playing something I don't recognize. My dress is even plainer—or more eccentric, depending on your view— than it was last week. I'm wearing brown Bermuda shorts, a faded blue sweatshirt and old sneakers. I feel more like a teacher than ever. Do people think "Teacher" when they look at me?

I'm still trying to make sense of Wally's first class last week. Like everyone else, my initial reaction was outrage. No one likes to be bullied and humiliated. On the way home I had ranted and raved in the car. But later in the week I had begun to laugh about the incident. I was amused enough by the story to tell it to several people. Those who knew Wally all nodded knowingly.

I had also been astounded that Wally—this prominent English literature scholar—had made such a big deal about such an obvious point. Don't we all know this? Isn't it general knowledge that a good teacher is one who elicits kids' discoveries for themselves? Good teachers help their kids believe in themselves. We all know that. And, of course, much of the current educational reform—much of it coming from England—is all about that. The classroom is now open. The dais has disappeared.

But this compact little notion will not go away. And I find myself on a tended lawn, at an expensive school surrounded by hip college kids, thinking and thinking and thinking about what happened last week.

WALLY REDUX

It's a glistening May Saturday morning in Evanston, and I feel like walking. I park my car on the north end of the Northwestern campus near an athletic field full of Frisbee players and head south down Sheridan Road. Across the way is the Patton Gymnasium. In the late 1920s, my father-in-law swam backstroke for the Northwestern team in the pool at this gym. He won the NCAA championship but couldn't afford to go to the Olympic trials. Last fall, when he came to visit us, we went to a football game and later walked through the campus where he had a chance to see hippies passing out antiwar pamphlets. He found the whole scene bewildering.

Classes have resumed after the student strike that followed the Kent State shootings in May, and the sidewalk is clogged with students in shorts and smiles. Two boys with long hair, beads, and sandals are walking next to me and arguing about the Cubs. The shorter of the pair says the Cubs will never get over last year's mortifying flop. His buddy thinks the Mets will sink and the Cubs will rise. "They're just too good. Too good." I pass the tennis center. Every court is filled with several groups waiting to play. Dashing around the far court and whacking awkward backhands is my professor for Modern British Literature. Last week he returned my long paper on Orwell. "Good ideas, good plan, good research, needs tightening."

A tall fellow with a shovel-shaped red beard and bare feet walks up and sells me a copy of *The Seed*. He has pink eyes and shaky hands and reeks of cannabis. He's wearing a button that reads "Nixon pull out. Your father should have." I stop at an announcement board to study the names of antiwar speakers coming to the campus this weekend. Underneath the announcement is one for a "Bra Burning Festival" at Belmont Harbor. A group of high school seniors following a student tour leader passes me. At the corner of Sheridan Road and Chicago Avenue, I skirt the stacks of the iron fence that the students used to erect a barricade to block traffic to protest the Kent State killings and the war in general.

Nearby two young black guys with large Afros and scowls are standing by a table with stacks of mimeographed books entitled, "We All Killed Fred Hampton." Last winter Hampton and several other Black Panthers had been shot and killed by the Cook County Sheriff's police. The Panthers were asleep in their beds at the time. The *Chicago Tribune* published a front-page photo of some countersunk nail holes in the interior door trim and claimed they were the result of shotgun pellets fired by the dead men. One of the men with the books is in my modern literature class. He asks me if I've started to study for the final.

I'm on my way to see my advisor, Wally. We have end-of-the-year school business to go over, but first I must tell him that I'm not coming back to Northwestern next year because I've taken a job at a local high school. I'll finish my degree in the evenings and during the summers, but my days as a full-time graduate student are over.

Since that uncomfortable day last autumn in Evans Hall, I have improved my relationship with Wally. I've taken three of his classes and worked with him on several department projects. We've eaten together. We've drunk martinis together. He's come to our apartment and polished off meals cooked by Sue. He loves her cooking. I've grown to enjoy his nasty humor. I think he likes me and actually seems interested in my experience teaching in Germany. He has some regard for my intellect, though his favorite "Boone story" is of the time when, on a cold day in December, I used a coat hanger to get into a car with the keys locked inside. The car belonged to the chairman of the English department.

But most telling of all, I have never been able to stop thinking about the simple point Wally made last fall—teachers inspire; teachers don't impose. I think about this point when I recall my own teaching. I think about it when I make plans for the future. I'm still astonished at how much this obvious little piece of philosophy has influenced the way I regard teaching. I'm astonished at my own astonishment.

At first I was actually embarrassed that this "breakthrough" was so obvious. But now I've decided that I needed long enough to have my own experiences make these ideas feel right. I look back at my own failures and successes and see that they had a lot to do with my effort to help kids learn for themselves. Now all of these words and slogans have a special meaning. The teacher does not impose. The teacher inspires, facilitates, opens up. The material is not fixed and absolute. Instead of being a formless object to be shaped by the school machine, the student is an individual growing organism. The school's duty is to help the student grow to whatever his or her full potential may be.

So simple. So obvious. So often repeated, but so important. What it all adds up to for me is MOTIVATION. The teacher's job is always to find ways to help students want to make discoveries on their own.

But while I've have come like Wally a lot, I'm still a little nervous about the meeting. He might take my leaving personally. He might accuse me of breaking a promise. He might say I have lowered my standards just when I started to raise them. I feel ready for him, but I'll be glad when this is behind me. I just want to make sure that I say what I mean—everything that I mean. And I want to make sure that I say it convincingly.

The English Curriculum Center is a solid two-story red brick building near the campus on Chicago Avenue. It was built to be some rich Evanstonian's home. As the university spread out, the building was taken over by the School of Education. For the past nine months I have spent a hefty chunk my life in this building. I do department work, write papers and read books in a small office in the back. I meet with others from the English Education program in the small library. Last month ten of us sat around the table and wrote a letter to the president of the university supporting the student strike. Every Friday we meet there to evaluate a teacher training program we are running for nuns at a Catholic school near Humboldt Park. I keep food in the refrigerator in the kitchen in the back. I keep a suit and tie in the closet. It's right next to my baseball glove. We have a department softball team as well as a touch football team. We used to go out the back door to the Traffic Institute, which had an old-fashioned coke machine. But last month antiwar demonstrators blew up the building.

My official reason for meeting with Wally today is to discuss my Independent Study. Back in January, I decided that my graduate school classes—as good as they were—wouldn't cover all of the books I wanted to read. Wally helped me make the list of fifteen books. Some were classics like Dewey's *The Child and the Curriculum* and *Summerhill*. But most were books by contemporary writers like John Holt and Jimmy Britain.

This morning I find Wally slouched behind his desk scowling and smirking at a student paper. He's wearing a coat and tie. "I hope that's not one of my papers, Wally." I slip into a chair opposite him.

"It's not," he grumbles. "But at least this person knows footnote form." He gives me a hard stare. A new pile of books has been added to the piles behind him. Most of these look to be volumes about the teaching of English in Great Britain. The wall to his left has books from his earlier life as a pure scholar.

There are books about Wordsworth and Coleridge and the other Romantics. Wally wrote several of these books. The books on his right are education texts and books of theory. These are from his new life.

We take a stab at small talk. How are my courses going? ("Fine. I'm really enjoying the Orwell class.") Am I going to sign up for a literature class this summer taught by a visiting British professor? ("I am.") He asks about Sue. ("She's starting to make quilts and doing a lot of gardening.") He asks about my daughter Fanny. ("She'll be starting nursery school. She likes to go on bike rides and to draw.") When I tell him I've been playing golf and tennis, he winces. When I tell him we're about to go camping in Wisconsin, he is so appalled that his jaw drops.

I ask about his upcoming trip. He'll be taking part in a workshop in Leicester. He'll be delivering a series of talks in Bristol. He'll stay with old friends in London and then go to a conference in Bath. He's also on a committee to evaluate modern secondary schooling outside of London. He adds a small shudder to this bit of news.

Then I take a deep breath. "Wally." I raise my voice just a little and sit up. I look over his shoulder and out the window. An old Greek named George is cutting the grass with a hand mower. "Wally, I'll be leaving Northwestern after the summer. I've taken a job at Highland Park High School."

A long pause. He clears his throat and looks down at his tiny red hands. "When did you decide this?" He emphasizes *this*. He sounds genuinely surprised.

"Last night."

He raises his eyes in his characteristic Jack Benny style and pulls at his tie. He pushes the papers away.

"An opportunity came along, Wally, and I don't think I should pass it up. It's that simple."

"But what about this program? You must like it.

You spend all of your life here at the Curriculum Center. You've even been watching the Cub games here on TV. You and the teachers drink beer here at night. You keep a bike in the back. You brought Fanny here to work." I am amazed that he is so aware of my habits.

"I love it here," I answer. "I've made great friends. I'll have terrific memories, but I really want to get back into the classroom." I go on to say that I want to try some of the things we've been talking about at Northwestern. I tell him that his program has shown me that I have the potential to be a good teacher. I know better than ever how to let kids learn on their own. I have a much better idea of what I want my students to become. I can see what it means to be creative. I babble on. I feel nervous but relieved that I have told him all of this. "And I'll finish. I've got evenings and summers to get my degree, and I will."

"Highland Park's a great school. Jerry, the department chairman, is in this same program here at Northwestern."

"Jerry's a good guy. We talked about ways we can work some of the new ideas into the program there. The curriculum is quite traditional, but there's room to try some new things. The school is near our apartment. It's suburban but fairly mixed. The city of Highland Park has a great liberal tradition. I want to go back to high school teaching, and this looked like a great chance so I took it. Besides, I need the money."

"You can finish on your own," Wally says at length. "A lot of teacher types come here for a year and then leave, but I do think you'll finish." I'm pleased that he doesn't consider me a "teacher type."

That makes me feel good, but I've got more to say. "I've really liked being on a campus this year. But I think by next year I might get tired of all of this."

"All of what?" The eyebrows are raised again.

"All the politics. I hate the war as much as anyone, but I'm sick of talking about it. I'm sick of the noise and the demonstrations. I'm sick of these little rich kids pretending to be revolutionaries. I'll sign petitions. I'll take part in the strike. I'll vote for antiwar candidates. But that's not where I want to make a stand. I'd much rather be in a classroom full of kids."

"You've been reading too much Orwell."

"You're probably right. It's hard to walk past these rich little radicals with their long hair and not hear Orwell laughing."

Wally nods and half smiles. He doesn't quite agree, but he doesn't want to argue about it. He hates the war. He made sure his department supported the strike. But he's too old and too frail to do much active protesting. "You'll be more comfortable back in the classroom," he says.

Then abruptly—in true Wally style—he changes the subject. "Time to talk about the Independent Study." A few weeks ago he called to say that I had earned an "A" in the class. He wanted this meeting to be more than a "mindless evaluation." I would turn in my notes, but we would talk about my reactions to what I read. "I want to hear what you made of all this stuff."

One at a time I hand him individual responses for each book. Each includes a summary and quotes. I have evaluated each in terms of the "Teacher-Learner-Stuff" model that Wally uses. Again a simple approach. This little model gives me a tool for thinking and talking about schools.

Finally, I tell him that I'd like to explain how I see all of this in terms of my teaching next year at Highland Park High School.

"Sounds interesting."

"As I see it, the Highland Park senior writing program may be narrow in some ways, but the kids can choose their own subjects. They don't have to write about literature the way they do at a lot of high schools. This will give me a chance to help them find subjects that they find interesting and to make clear statements that they can prove." I'm getting excited. "I'll be able to use small groups for the kids to help each other come up with good subjects for writing. I'll bring in models from . . ."

Suddenly he's waving his little hands like a traffic cop. "All right. All right. I get the idea. Let's go somewhere for a drink. Let's talk about the books tomorrow."

Tomorrow, for the books, never comes.

TOUGH QUESTIONS, EASY ANSWERS

End of the day. I lean against the gray wall in the main lobby, set my foot on my briefcase and wait for my student to show up. Flowing past me is a turbulent river of people—hundreds and hundreds of people. Last month, as a brand-new Highland Park High School teacher, all I could have said about the boys in this crowd was that most had long dark hair and looked like hippies, jocks or nerds according to their persuasion, and that the girls, who also had long dark hair, wore jeans, short skirts, or overalls and who sorted out into equivalent categories. The adults—even the thick-necked specimens—wore coats and skinny ties if they were male, dresses if they were female. A month ago I wouldn't have known where they were coming from or where they were heading. A month ago this was Any School, USA.

But now that I'm a one-month veteran, I already know what to call things and where to find things. The room on my left is the Instructional Materials Center (IMC), as the library is now called. The bookstore across the way is operated by Pat Pasquesi, one of the dozens of Pasquesis associated with HPHS. Pat attended HPHS in the 1940s, fought in the Second World War, and returned to run the bookstore. He has already shown me his WWII scrapbook. Down the hall is the cafeteria; take a right from there, and you're in the glass corridor where the tough kids from less-affluent Highwood and Fort Sheridan hang out. Last year one of these guys hurled a freshman through the plate glass window out into the courtyard. Upstairs are the classrooms. I use four of them because as a new teacher, instead of having my own room, I am a "rover." The first week I spilled coffee over the desk of the school's second-oldest teacher. "You need to follow the rules too, Bob," I was told in a frosty way.

The heavy guy puffing past me on his way to the gym area is Rex, the locker-room attendant. The lady in a blue uniform walking next to him is Sylvia, his wife. She is a hall guard, and kids torment her. The scruffy bald fellow hurrying into the library is Fred, a long-term biology teacher and a part-time Chicago cab driver. The stocky scowling guy storming past Fred out of the IMC is Steve, the audio/visual director. At a new-teacher orientation meeting in his studio he had ordered one of the gabby newcomers to "shut up." People say he's not as bad-tempered as he seems. A month into the job, I have no evidence to support that statement. The kid with the ring in his nose, cattle-style, is Walter. The oafish boy on Walter's right is Adam, whose father, a rabbi, once bowled a 300 game. The two kids in fatigue jackets are from Fort Sheridan. The week before one had been busted in a drug raid west of the school at the Chicago & Northwestern railroad tracks.

Roberta is the tall girl leading the other determined-looking girls into the IMC for a meeting of the social service club. She and her male counterparts represent the "typical" Highland Park students. When outsiders think about HPHS, they imagine people like Roberta, who is from a wealthy, intellectual Jewish family. Kids like Roberta know where they want to go in life, and they know how to get there. Or at least it seems that way. Walking behind them is Richard. He comes from a family with tradition. There is a Roman numeral III after his full name. His great, great something or other was the highest-ranking Jewish officer in the Confederate army.

The frowning teacher carrying a huge stack of books is Evelyn, the senior-level chair. Students move aside to give her room. She runs the show as far as I am concerned. I am now teaching writing the way she wants us all to teach writing. Form? *Expository.*

Length? *Medium.* Thesis? *Tight and focused.* Emphasis? *Evidence, evidence, evidence.* "Your students," she told us at the first meeting, "should support their thesis with three sub-points; each sub-point should have three details. We call it the 3/3." She seems pleased with my work so far.

Up saunters a grinning Jerry. He is a tall and awkward-looking senior. He is wearing jeans and a sweatshirt—the same outfit he wore yesterday and will most certainly wear tomorrow. He is carrying a stack of sheet music; he is almost always carrying music or a book on music theory. Often he carries a clarinet case, but he plays many instruments. "Thanks for waiting, Mr. Boone. I really need to get that book about Hitchcock." Jerry speaks in a low voice. He has a long angular face. Give him a few years, a beard, and a tall hat, and you'll have a young Abe Lincoln. "I don't usually take rides from teachers," he announces as we head for the door past a group of pompon girls in blue and white sweaters. "You're not a pervert, are you?"

"Give me time." I reach over and pat him on the shoulder. "Give me time," I say again. We walk out of the building and down the sidewalk to the teachers' parking lot. My car is a middle-aged light blue Opal sporting acne-like rust.

"You really have a shitty car. Don't you ever clean it?" Jerry beams as he looks around at books, newspapers, magazines, wrappers, tennis balls and other junk in the backseat. "Not like one of the gas guzzlers my parents and their friends drive."

"You should have seen my first car, "I tell him. "It was a 1958 Simca. Sue and I bought it from a Lebanese theological student from the Bronx. It broke down seven times between New York and Chicago. We spent one night in John Updike's hometown getting it fixed. My father had to tow us home from the Chicago Skyway. You want a piece of shit? That was a piece of shit." We pull out of the parking lot past the assorted economy cars and head south. "I talked to the reference lady at the public library. She'll let me sign out the book on Hitchcock if I can prove that I'm a card-carrying teacher. Then you can get the quotes you need to finish the paper. Lose the book, and you'll have librarians hounding you for the rest of your life."

He nods and reaches for a cigarette. "Can I ask you a question?" His low voice sounds even lower.

"Why not?"

"I was wondering," he offers me a smoke, "how you like the way they teach writing here. I mean, do you buy all the crap that goes along with it?" He is talking, of course, about the expository form that requires our 3/3 system. "I mean, isn't it rough for a young teacher like you to follow something so strict?"

Jerry is not the first kid to question the program. So far I have always deflected criticism, whether it comes in class or after. As a new teacher I am not about to publicly criticize the established curriculum. But now, when the questions come from a mature kid riding in my car smoking a Marlboro, I feel I must give a better answer.

In fact, I have rehearsed this in my mind. "I knew what I was getting into at Highland Park. The senior writing program has quite a reputation. This is serious stuff. These are serious people. You have to write a whole lot, but you can pick your subjects. Look, you're doing a paper on Alfred Hitchcock. A lot of the other people are writing about their jobs and hobbies. It's just that you all have to follow a strict form when you do it." I have already given a little speech like this to Wally and to friends at Northwestern.

Jerry won't let up. "I know, but what about all this stuff with 3s? You need to have three supporting arguments—not two. And each of these needs three details. I mean, come on."

I shrug and smile. What am I supposed to say? He's right. But why don't I feel guilty? I do believe my own words: The program is much more creative than one might think. But I also just feel good. I like being back in a school. I like its size. I'm pleased that I can do the job they expect. I am pleased I relate so well with the kids. I don't feel like a sell-out. But how long will I feel this way?

"I don't always count to three," I answer. "I have plenty of chances to help you find a subject you want to write. You can go into your own experience for support. But, sure, I'd like more choices. I'd like to give you more choices."

We drive past McDonald's and into downtown Highland Park. It's a relatively rich suburb of Chicago, about twenty miles or so north of the Loop. Twenty-five thousand people live here. The downtown has a couple of brand-name stores like the Gap and Lord & Taylor, but mostly it's lots of smaller shops that all seem busy. The streets are crowded. The downtown merchants were hurt but not killed by the malls that were built west of the highway. Big cars are parked along the streets. Well-dressed people walk the sidewalks. It's prosperous but not charming in the New Englandy kind of way that is affected in some of the other North Shore suburbs. But Highland Park is not glitzy or new, either. To the east of the downtown area are the big houses that can be found all along the North Shore lakefront. To the north is Highwood, a small town serving Fort Sheridan. Unlike Highland Park, Highwood has bars and clubs. Most of the Highwood families are Italian in origin, or Mexican. Unlike the Highland Park kids, few children of Highwood go on to college.

"What's Evelyn like?" Jerry asks.

"You mean my level chairman? My real boss? The jeffa?"

"She sounds scary to me. Evelyn is a scary name."

Again teacher ethics take over: Never talk about other teachers with a student. But Jerry is dying to hear something, and I wouldn't have minded sharing my feelings about this person, who was so devoted to a system I couldn't quite buy. "I don't like talking about teachers, Jerry. Give me time. Man, I've only been here for five weeks."

He nods and goes on to other subjects. What do I think of Neil Postman, Jonathan Kozol, John Holt, and all the other open educators? "They're my heroes," I answer. What do I think about the open classroom, self-directed study, free schools? "They sound great to me. That's what I studied at Northwestern." I pause and grin. "And I know what you're thinking, asshole, but I am not about to start a revolution."

He smiles as he flips his cigarette out the window into the library parking lot. He could have added, "Don't be defensive, Mr. Boone," but he was too much of a gentleman.

We check out the book. The head reserve librarian hisses, "We usually don't do this sort of thing." On the way home we stop for a coke at Shelton's, an old diner and the closest thing to a blue-collar restaurant that can be found in Highland Park. I drop Jerry off at a big house near the lake. In the driveway are two large clean Lincolns, one green, the other black. "Next time," I tell him, "don't ask me to think so much. Remember, I am a potential pervert."

"I was just curious about what you must be thinking. All of you young teachers must feel restricted." Then he heads for the house—probably to practice music.

Jerry is on target, of course. Had I followed strictly what I learned at Northwestern, I would be agonizing under Evelyn's restrictions. But the fact is that I'm not bothered at all. I like most of the other teachers, including Evelyn. Even her 3/3 system has an internal sense. The idea is that most questions can be easily developed as an "either/or" format, with just two alternate views, but coming up with three options requires some thought. And I'm enjoying myself otherwise. I play touch football for the NU graduate education team; last week I caught a game-winning touchdown pass. My classes are a delight. Maybe I am uncomfortable with the 3/3 stricture, but I can help the kids find subjects worth exploring, and that's what I do. I read stories, tell stories, ask for stories. I emphasize content over form. In other words, I am able to look inside the kids, to inspire what is there already. The trouble is that when it comes out, the kids must fit it into a rigid form.

How quickly tiny compromises are made. I'm not really doing what I studied at NU, but I'm not bothered by it. Good feelings take over. Part of the pleasure comes from simply being back in a school—teaching is stimulating, a joy. I'm lucky I enjoy being around kids. Yet I'm aware that I'm in something of an in-between time. How long will this euphoria last? Once it burns off, will I still be so happy? What will November be like? Can I continue to play both sides so well?

Meanwhile, I must go home to Sue, Fanny and our new baby, Sarah, who was born last month.

VIRGINIA SLIMS

Here she comes. Down the sidewalk and through the crowd she strides. Here she comes. She is tanned and tall and wears a loose fitting flowing red and white dress with a blue scarf. A sleek, black leather briefcase swings from her right hand. Her eyes look ahead, and she is not quite smiling, but she doesn't need to smile because her walk and her posture tell us just how deliciously happy she feels. Her left arm stretches out to the side and in her left hand—her ring-free left hand—thrusting proudly upwards, not hiding guiltily in her palm, is a long, slim cigarette.

Where is she walking so confidently? Maybe she's going to meet a contractor to discuss the skyscraper she has just designed. Maybe she's heading for a board meeting of a Fortune 500 company. Maybe she will meet her lover. But wherever she is going, it is a place that matters. The people she passes could not look more ordinary—defeated men in business suits, older women clutching packages, dumpy cops, scowling shopkeepers, swollen children. All that these drab creatures can do is stare appreciatively—almost reverently—as this supremely confident creature flows by, just as all we can do is stare awestruck from our seats in the crowded auditorium—so crowded I was forced to turn people away.

And then the music picks up, and we all start singing: "You've come a long way, Baby." I look behind me, and standing in the back is Evelyn. She is singing too, and so is Mark, the dean of discipline standing next to her. Mark is not thinking about student discipline issues; he is thinking about a song about cigarettes.

Anyone peeking into this room on any other day would doubtless find it half-filled with half-awake half-adults half-watching a film about cell division or Egypt. Or maybe they would catch a lecturer holding forth on a phase of the Renaissance. But today that person would stare into a small auditorium utterly packed with students and teachers and other adults mesmerized by a film about the creation of the Virginia Slims advertising campaign.

For the past month, two other teachers and I have been conducting a propaganda seminar after school. We started with a film about Goebbels and German propaganda. Then we moved onto films about the Soviet Union. One of the students got his hands on some John Birch Society films. Then we stretched our definition into advertising. Last week I showed the Clio awards. All these films stirred up so much interest that we began to show them during free periods and lunch periods.

But nothing we had shown brought in such crowds and created such total attention as today's film. No one in the audience said anything as the film began with a scene in a conference room filled with cigar-chomping ad men discussing the notion of a new cigarette that could "seize the Women's Liberation Movement." It showed the process of considering and then rejecting and finally choosing a product name and strategy that would do the job. The product: Virginia Slims. The slogan: "You've come a long way, Baby."

The huge applause is interrupted by the bell, and away through the doors scrambles the happy crowd, the girls striding proudly with their heads held high. Many pass by the projector to say something to me. "Nice job, Mr. Boone." "I didn't do anything." "Nice job, Mr. Boone" "I didn't do anything." "Thanks, a lot, Mr. Boone. That really was really, really something."

And indeed it was something, but what, exactly, was it? For the rest of the week, I ask anyone available to explain just why a film like this would have such an improbably powerful impact. What had this opened up? I could have predicted a good response, but nothing like this. What had happened? I ask the question in class, in the teachers' lounge, of friends, of other students at Northwestern, of my wife, of strangers. The answers all made sense—I guess:

"It was a change. How many cigarette films do we see in school?"

"Kids like to see what's going on behind the scenes."

"Music, camera work, great-looking people."

"Highland Park kids are really into the media. Of course they would like something like this."

"It was the group thing."

"The girls liked it because it made such a big deal about the women's movement."

"It proves that propaganda works."

Then gradually the excitement wears off, and I stop asking the question. We show propaganda films about China. My classes with the traditional writing program continue, but I am feeling the pinch more and more as the kids keep trying to express themselves in other forms. A teacher dies. The husband of another teacher dies. We have a rash of false fire alarms. A boy is seriously beaten at a party.

But as other matters reclaim my life, I still can't quite forget the hushed excitement of that auditorium. What, I wonder, does this have to do with my conviction that a teacher's job is to inspire and motivate? What had I exposed? And what was I to make of the fact that so many kids—different from each other in so many ways—responded to the film in the same way?

SENIOR OPTIONS

A teacher from England once told me about a librarian at his school who despised faculty meetings so much that on meeting days she had her boyfriend drive his van up onto the lawn of the school, right up to the window of the room where the meeting was taking place. He would then honk his horn (or "Hoot his hooter," as my friend said) until his girlfriend emerged from the building. And then off they'd drive to the nearest pub. The boyfriend was a large angry guy, and no one dared tell him not to drive his van on the lawn and honk his horn.

I know how that librarian feels. When I picture myself at meetings, I am half asleep, my mind a numb concoction of things I have to do (grade papers, prepare a lesson, pay taxes) or would like to be doing (playing golf, riding a bike, reading a book). The other teachers, whom I can barely make out through the smoke, are scribbling on note pads and yawning unapologetically. The room is hot. My mouth tastes foul from a mixture of caffeine and nicotine. The person running the meeting is saying what we know already or what could have been communicated in a simple note.

But at today's meeting for senior English teachers in Hazel's room I'll have to stay awake. Hazel keeps a comfortable room with straight rows, flowers on the windowsills, a rug in the back with beanbag chairs, an events' calendar that is up to date and a word for the day. Today's word is "Machiavellian." She has taught English here for many years and obviously feels comfortable in the senior setting. She writes poetry, attends all the student productions, serves on faculty committees, and follows the curriculum faithfully. I have been told that years will pass before I get my own room. I envy Hazel.

In a few minutes the meeting will be underway, and Evelyn, the senior-level chairman, will be marching through the agenda. She'll sum up this year, talk about the National Honor Society, take a look at next year's calendar, and then—and this is why I am sitting here alone—she will probably ask me to explain why I did what I did two weeks ago.

Up until May, I had been a loyal English teacher. While I found the 3/3 expository form tight, I could work with it. My students could select subjects they found engaging. These were subjects like photography, Ken Kesey, film history, LSD, advertising, Herman Hesse, Janis Joplin, astrology. At the beginning of the process, I could help my students decide what it was they thought they could prove about their subject. And I could show them at the end how successful they had been in proving a point.

In a few years, I will have the opportunity to teach other classes. I can get involved in the literary magazine and the newspaper. I can set up independent study programs. I plan to run the propaganda seminar again and to show films after school and on weekends. But, for the moment, I am quite content to individualize as much as I can inside a system that seems to be working for most of the students. After all, I could have stayed at Northwestern and kept studying. I could have found work in an alternative school in the city. But I didn't.

Then along came Peter's story.

Peter, a big, good-natured, goofy kid, told me he was going to write about his Bar Mitzvah. He wanted to show how the experience changed him. He'd discuss the lessons he learned about his religion, about ceremonies in general, and about his own ability to face challenges. He would take the particulars from the experience and shape them into his paper. Why not? It sounded like a fine subject to me. He would not be the first kid from Highland Park to write about his

Bar Mitzvah. Others had written about it as a learning experience; several had talked about its similarities to other rites of passage. I had received several papers that were critical of the money and hoopla surrounding these events. But I was sure that he would find enough particular memories to compose into a standard expository paper.

But that's not what happened, as I found out when Peter stood in front of the class and read the paper. Instead of using his experiences as evidence, he used them to illustrate a story—a simple old story that was organized according to time. He described his initial meeting with the Rabbi, his Hebrew classes, even his meeting with a caterer. Much of his story had to do with his Uncle Abe from New Jersey, a quirky fellow who showed up at family gatherings bent on making his younger relatives laugh at times when they weren't supposed to. By the time the service was underway, Abe had not been seen, but as Peter began reading the scriptures, "I looked up and there in the back row was Uncle Abe wearing a Groucho Marx nose and glasses." A few minutes later, Uncle Abe, now in a Chicago Bears jersey, had a sneezing fit in the second row. Peter ended his story at the party with Uncle Abe placing third in the limbo contest.

From hearing Peter's remarks in class, I knew he was funny guy, but I had never seen him perform. He paused at the right times, lowered his voice, raised it. He employed several different accents that ranged from the Rabbi's deep, inspirational tones to Aunt Alma's shrill complaining. He showed a wonderful sense of detail: The buffet table had a small mountain of shrimp, slabs of rare beef, and a bad-tempered carver; the band featured a stoned drummer. Peter bowed when he finished, and we all applauded.

I had planned to have Barb read her paper about umpiring Little League baseball, but instead I led a freewheeling discussion with the rest of the class. It seemed everyone had a Bar Mitzvah story, a

Bas Mitzvah story, or some other memory of a family ritual. Many of these comments were about things going not quite the way they were supposed to—someone forgets his lines or an aunt gets drunk. Many were about people acting in character—a nervous Jewish mother, a senile great grandmother.

"Mr. Boone, what did you do? Are you Catholic?"

"No, I was confirmed in the Episcopal Church in 8th grade, and you don't want to hear about it." All I could recall was memorizing the Apostles' Creed, listening to the minister telling us that the sacrament is an outward sign of something on the inside, and joking with my buddies about the wine we would get to sip. Had we known then that the minister was carrying on an affair with someone from the congregation, we might have paid more attention to him, especially when he went through the Ten Commandments.

"Come on, Mr. Boone. You must have a good wedding or funeral story."

"I really don't." They did not need to know that at my wedding one of my ushers got himself thrown in jail twice. I decided to save that one.

After class Peter and I stood by the desk. I told him how much I liked his story. Then I asked if he had the "other" version.

"The other version?"

"The expository one where you show how this experience changed you."

"No," he said. "This is it. I thought about it, and this is how I want to do it. You never give us a chance to write stories."

"You could turn this in to *Oliphant*, the literary magazine," I responded defensively. "Or submit this to me as extra credit. You could save it for next year at the University of Illinois."

He shook his head. "Nope, I'm turning this in as a regular old English assignment. I'm a senior, anyway. Take it or leave it."

I paused and thought about it. "Fair enough," I finally said. "I'll evaluate it as a piece of narrative writing." And then—I'm not sure why—we shook hands.

Word can spread fast in a school. Earlier that year one of our teachers proposed to one of our students in the parking lot before school, and by lunch everyone knew about it. When I was a junior in high school, everyone knew that Giff Stoddard had been hit in the head with a shot put even before the ambulance arrived. News of fights, car accidents, pranks, lovers' quarrels, temper tantrums, and all the other good stuff seeps into every corner of the building faster than flooding water can cross the floor. But who could have guessed that my decision to stray from the senior English curriculum would be considered news? These kids were seniors. They have better things to worry about. Why in God's name were they talking about English class?

But they were.

The next week I received narratives about canoe trips, beer parties, baby-sitting, summer jobs. A girl told about getting caught in quicksand at a campsite in Iowa. The paper was twelve pages long. She even made up a sound ("Brooooooop") to describe the noise of her body popping free as a jeep pulled her out while she held onto a rope. I accepted them, explaining that this was a one-time chance, but I knew expository writing was done for the year. Writing true stories was much more fun and much easier than struggling with an academic writing form.

Other teachers started getting these papers. Joe thought it was a good idea and encouraged them. Hazel told her kids that narratives would count only as extra credit, but she remained pleasant around me. She wanted a copy of the Bar Mitzvah paper to read to her classes. Evelyn, never a grinner, seemed to scowl at me whenever she had a chance. She walked by my lunch table twice and sat by herself. Finally I stopped her in the hall and told her how this all had happened. She nodded and said I could talk about it at the meeting.

So today, I'll have to 'fess up. I'll tell them how it happened, why it happened, and that it won't happen like this again. But I'm going to suggest that we make room in the curriculum for narrative papers. I'll point out that by allowing kids to complete these narratives, they are getting down all of the details that they could use for an expository paper. In that sense these are extended brainstorming exercises. I'll talk about Herb and Susan and a few other kids who showed an eagerness to write that I had never seen before.

Joe walks in and takes a seat next to me. Even though it's late in the year, he still is wearing a blue suit and a red tie. The only time I saw him in school without a suit was the day he brought his dogs for a special assembly. He's a breeder of Cairn terriers. Hazel walks in next. She crosses the room to spray her flowers and goes to the board to change the word for the day to "Pundit."

Evelyn, ashtray in hand, walks in, sits downs, nods and without any attempt at small talk begins the meeting. "I think," she ventures, her voice a little higher than usual, and she's looking at her hands, "I've decided we need to scrap the senior program and move to an options system. I've been thinking about this for a long time, and, with your approval, of course, this is what I believe we should do."

Silence. Pure. Unadulterated. Hazel, Joe, and I sit in utter disbelief staring at someone who has just said something so unexpected that we cannot even begin to respond. This woman, whose purpose in life has seemed to revolve around maintaining a system she created, has just decided to scrap it. This is news. How could she be this far ahead of us?

Evelyn continues. "We'll keep the writing class as one of the options, but add new courses. Joe, why don't you plan an Interviewing and Investigating class?" He starts to answer, but Evelyn plows on. "Bob, do you think you could take what you've been doing with film on weekends and in the Propaganda Seminar and make up a media course? And I'd also like you to design an Independent Reading course. Hazel, would you put together a British Literature class and a Modern Literature class? And I'll do some work on the writing curriculum.

"Anything else?" she wants to know.

"How about creative writing?" I ask.

"Do it."

In most schools, the creation of a new course takes months of planning. It may begin with a proposal, followed by a summer workshop, and finally a trial run with a few select classes. Then, and only then, will it make its way into the curriculum. But Evelyn knows it needn't take that long.

Just a few minutes ago we were members of a traditional English department. Now we are not. "Evelyn," Hazel asks, "What happened?" All Hazel can do is shake her head and smile. "Why didn't you tell us?"

"I wasn't sure until today that I would go through with it."

"But you did," Joe says.

Evelyn goes on. "I don't pay much attention to what the kids say they like and dislike. But this year I could feel they wanted more. Look at how much they enjoyed writing narratives. I know Joe likes to use interviewing techniques. I've talked to people who have run option programs like this, and they can work. Something was going to happen, so we might as well be in charge of the change. Do you understand?"

We do.

"Should we do it?"

One big nod from all of us.

"Then," she says reaching for a legal pad, "let's spend the rest of the time writing down some of our ideas."

And that's what we do. I start slowly by making a list of what my course will cover (communication theory, film TV, advertising, non-verbal communication, semantics), and then I pick up the pace as the plan for the course pours out of me. And soon it's there on paper, an immediate future I had never imagined.

COMMUNICATIONS

Rick and Suzie sit back-to-back on the floor of the classroom. Rick, the starting quarterback on the football team, has his legs stretched out while Suzie's legs are crossed in a modified yoga pose. He's wearing a dark blue football jersey, (game day tomorrow) and she's wearing designer overalls. In front of each is a pile of blocks—red ones, blue ones, orange ones, yellow ones—all of different shapes, but each set is identical. I look down from where I am sitting on the desk and wonder if these Highland Park High School kids ever imagined they would be playing with blocks when they were high school seniors.

Like the other senior English teachers, I feel confident and energetic. After all, we're teaching classes that we designed ourselves. The new option system, now in its second year, is running smoothly. The people in charge all know what we're doing but don't interfere. In three months, when inevitable fatigue sets in, we might not be so upbeat, but for now we share a welcome sense of optimism. It's one of those rare times for teachers when what we want and what the school wants coincide. We are flying in formation.

Even though it's the first day, I know most of the students. Rick is the younger brother of a former student. Many of these kids have come to propaganda seminars after school or film nights on weekends. Before class I learned that one girl's parents are named Sam and Ella, and one boy's father runs a restaurant in Highwood. I learned that a boy from Fort Sheridan mowed greens at the fort golf course last summer. Suzie, the girl on the floor, spent the summer at Interlochen Music Camp.

Suzie whistles softly to herself while Rick

constructs a rectangular structure with turrets. It could be a power plant—an unstable power plant because a sneeze or a moved desk could send the whole thing crashing down. Nevertheless, this is what he has built. "Done," he announces proudly and rubs his hands together. She, of course, has no idea what he has built.

I repeat the instructions. "Rick is going to tell Suzie what to build. If he gives precise enough instructions, and if she listens well enough, she will build exactly what he has in front of him. Remember, this is all one-way verbal communication. Suzie can't say anything. She can't even ask Rick to repeat himself. I want the rest of you to watch carefully. What does this prove about communication? How does it work? Why does it fail sometimes?"

A girl in the back raises her hand. "Aren't you going to tell us about the whole course?"

"Don't worry. In 45 minutes, you'll know what I'm up to." I hope this is a true statement.

Rick stares down at the blocks. "Ready, Suzie?"

"You can't do that," several people shout. They've got the idea.

Rick shrugs and continues. "Pick up the red block and put it down in front of you." Suzie stares helplessly at the several red blocks—one square, one triangle, one cylinder. And even if she knew which block to use, she doesn't know where to place it—on the edge or bottom? Facing which way? She starts to ask a question, but we all shout her down.

"Are you done?" Rick asks, but of course he can't ask, so we tell him, once again, to keep his yap shut. But that hurries Suzie anyway, and she snatches the red rectangle and places it on its broadest side; she has guessed the right piece, but it should be on its end.

Rick keeps talking, and Suzie follows the best she can, but she never knows which block to pick up or where exactly to place it. She can't ask questions, but she can tell from the laughing that all is not going well. From off to the side I hear the hoarse male whisper: "I love watching other people fuck up."

Rick finishes, stands up, turns around and gawks at Suzie's structure, which looks much more like a medieval castle than it does a power plant. He's incredulous. "Why did you do that?" He points to a red block on its side. "Why? Why? Why?" He throws his arms out and looks up pleadingly at the fluorescent lights in the ceiling.

"Because you told me to." She adds a dramatic tremor to her voice and then starts to laugh. My mouth is open to make a teacher-like comment, but Suzie beats me to it. "You can't assume that I know exactly what you mean." She fakes a frown and shakes her finger at him adult-style. "You must think of others."

I jump in. "This game really shows me how easy it is to be imprecise. Think of all the instructions you have to give to get it right. Who's next?"

Ari and Nancy hit the floor. He's a math whiz and looks like one—short, slightly stooped, and bespectacled. Nancy, who might be Ari's girlfriend, has been watching Rick and Suzie carefully. What Ari builds is something flatter and more spread out than Rick's structure, and it's less balanced. While he builds, Nancy fiddles with the blocks. She jokes, "I've got to get my moves back. I've got to get my moves back." It's interesting what people do when they know they're being watched. I have done this exercise many times. The listener will always slip into some little role to get through the moment.

Hazel, whose room we're using, comes in to retrieve a book, but instead of leaving, she stands next to me. "Is this your idea?" she whispers. I tell her that I stole it from a communications book someone sent me. I seem to recall that we did something like this back in 5th grade. My teacher, whose husband ran the hardware store, had a thing for exact measurements.

Ari does a much better job. ("Place the red cylinder on its end just to the left but not quite touching the orange arch.") Only once does he fail to tell Nancy exactly where to place the block. He uses a loud voice and short sentences. The words seem to hang over her as she follows his orders. We all applaud.

"Teacher time!" someone in the back shouts. I move to the floor. Hazel snags a cushion from her closet and sits behind me. She's dressed informally, like me. Teachers don't dress up any more. Once more I am struck by the thought that this would look strange—mighty strange—to an outsider. ("Look, Wilbur, there's that teacher on the floor with all those kids around him, and it looks like he's got Playskool Blocks in front of him. Why aren't they studying gerunds?") Very precisely, Hazel gives me instructions on how to build a small battleship. She doesn't miss a detail. The only breakdown results from my confusion about what she means by "in front of." We get a big hand for our efforts. She leaves after telling my class that she hopes they enjoy playing with blocks.

"Next," I say, "the builder can't use any shape or color words. You'll have to find other ways to communicate that information." David and Shosh take the floor. She builds, and he fiddles. Her description works perfectly. The rectangular orange piece is "cheese," the long triangle is the wedge, the cylinder is the tower, the square is a giant ice cube.

I ask the kids for other ways of limiting the exchange, and they come up with good ideas: No words beginning with letters *a* through *m* in the alphabet; no words of more than one syllable, no words beginning with vowels. The final one is to make up words that sound like the blocks. (The square is a "grunk," the cylinder is a "sloove.")

With ten minutes to go, I call a halt to blocks. Just enough time for an overview of the course. "I know you know pretty much about the course, but here's a way to think about it." On the board I have drawn a simple diagram: sender-message-receiver. "Something like this," I point to the board, "gives us a model for talking about communication. English classes, as you know, usually deal with messages in language. You are either the sender or the receiver of language messages. The messages are in accepted language forms like novels and poems. You write essays and reviews and maybe your own stories. But it's all language. Maybe you give speeches. But it's all language."

In this class, I tell them, we'll consider additional ways that people communicate—by gesture, through film and TV. And they'll consider forms like ads and cartoons. "You'll also—and this is what we're doing today—think about the whole process of communication in a very general way. You've read the class description, and you've probably talked with people who have taken the class. That's the whole idea. It's simple, but I'm simple-minded."

"Here's what we're going to cover." I can tell I'm talking too fast, but that's the way I talk. "We'll cover communication theory, non-verbal communication, visual imagery, films, TV, advertising, semantics and logic. It's a huge territory. You'll just touch on a little. It's what colleges call a survey course." They're listening well. "But you should have plenty of opportunity to try some of these other languages. You might learn something about yourself that you didn't know. Any questions so far?"

"Can we make a film?"

"Yes, or a slide show, or a radio play, or a series of original ads."

"Can we bring in guests?"

"If they can teach us something. Last year we had two filmmakers visit the class. We also had Coach Troy talk about baseball signals."

"Is there a final project?"

"A big one, and you should think about it now."
I explain that I want them to keep track of what they learn because it might be useful later on for their project. "I'll give you a list of some of the things people have done in this class for projects."
A few minutes left. We have come to the "So what?" part of the class. "Write down what this block exercise shows about the whole process of communication—how does it work, how can it fail? Don't be afraid to be obvious." I like the sound of that. "Don't be afraid to be obvious or wrong. I'll collect your answers, and we can build on them." They work with purpose until the bell rings and then drop off what they have written on my desk.

I take a look at the comments before heading to the teachers' room for a smoke. "We communicate in words." "It helps to know if the other person is getting the message." "It's hard to know what to do when others are laughing." "One mistake can lead to many." "Body language can help." "Some words have many meanings." "Sometimes breakdowns are the fault of listeners." One girl writes that she "realllllllly liked" sitting there and watching communication break down. "It was exciting." "People can do what they have to do to get a message across." I will make a list of these and pass it out tomorrow before we play charades.

That afternoon, I stay around school for two hours. My desk is in the corner of a not-so-large room with ten other desks and no windows. The same jacket has been hanging on a hook in the closet as long as I have been at HPHS. I have no idea whose jacket it is or was. I prepare for tomorrow's classes. After charades tomorrow, we'll play a game based on "The Blind Men and the Elephant" fable. I send a note to the office to be on tomorrow's school bulletin: "Teachers, bowling starts next Wednesday. Be at Strike and Spare by 4:00. Make sure you know your handicap. If you have any questions, talk to Bob

Boone or Ken Miller." I walk out to the athletic field and watch my homeroom lose to Dick Bilky's homeroom in a touch football game. I call a parent whose kid is in college and needs one of his papers from last year. I write a note to Jerry, my department chairman, telling him I can have lunch tomorrow. Lunch means walking to the fruit market for two oranges. Jerry is also in the Ph.D. program at NU. Like me, he was astounded and delighted by Evelyn's plan to restructure the senior program. He has made the whole thing work well. From time to time, he and I talk about writing a book together. I write a note to another colleague, Marc, telling him I will be in the faculty band, but to PLEASE realize I can't sing or dance. "I'll fill space but that's it. I can't even keep time to music. Believe me."

Finally, I write a note to Wally asking if I can use my communications class as the subject of my dissertation.

A few days later, kids are on the floor again. But this time there are four students—all blindfolded. They are playing "The Blind Men and the Elephant." Each will touch a different part of the same object, and then as a group they will try to figure out what they have touched. I start with an LP record jacket. I grab the finger of one blindfolded person ("Relax") and touch it to the sharp corner of the album. I touch the next person's finger to the edge, the next person's to the front and the next person's to the inside. "Blindfolds off. Can you figure out what you touched? Remember you touched all the essential parts. I didn't hold anything back."

They throw out impressions: It was kind of sharp. It was kind of smooth. It felt like paper or cardboard; it was room temperature; it had an inside like a little pocket.

Pause. "What couldn't it have been?" I ask. A tennis racket. A can of soup, a watch.

Another pause. "What could it have been?"

Someone takes over and collects the information. They all agree it could be made of paper or cardboard. They seem confused by the inside part. Finally Dede asks if it is an envelope, and then Ted figures it out.

We do this for the rest of the period with a small typewriter, a shoe, a desk, a board eraser, and finally with Matt, the smallest kid in the class. ("Watch where you touch him now.") Rick holds him like a log. My job is to grab the hand of each blindfolded person and put it in contact with a separate part of Matt. One touches his tooth, another his cheek, another the back of his shoe, another his hair. They get it right away.

Then it's "So what?" time. Most see the obvious point that we often assume part of something is like the whole of something. They can think of examples where this could happen. Several are even more interested in the group process. Who contributes what? Who takes over? Who makes the big guess?

Remember your final project, I remind them on the way out. "Maybe you could try this with little kids. Maybe you could write a short story in which the characters only know part of the truth. Maybe you could make up other games that make this point. And don't forget tomorrow's short paper." At the beginning of class I asked them to write a two- to three-page paper describing a communications breakdown that they have experienced or witnessed. I want them to be sure that this breakdown caused something unfortunate to happen. It doesn't have to be tragic. Think about sports, I suggested.

I continue to feel good about this class—if "feeling good" means not having any worries. The kids like it; the other teachers seem to like what I'm doing. No complaints from the administration. Nobody's asking me to prove that all this works. For most teachers in most situations, it sums up to an unqualified success.

The next day we share some of the "Communication Breakdown" papers. Some students read them aloud. Others paraphrase what they have written. Rick adds a point: "We've got these ideas of what people are supposed to be like. And these get in the way." His paper is all about the ways that suburban Jews stereotype city Jews. A boy describes getting caught stealing second base in a baseball game because he had misread the coach's signs. A girl tells of not getting a ride hitchhiking in Europe because she held out her thumb "the American way." Another boy got in trouble because he gave his father the finger before he knew what it meant. "But my dad did."

A day later, I have brought five LPs. On the board I write four questions: What color is it? What texture is it? How does it smell? How does it taste?

"Today," I tell them, "I'm going to play five pieces of music. Answer the questions on the board for each piece. Then we're going to share the responses to see what happens." I play each for at least a minute. The first is "Grizzly Bear" by the Alabama Work Farm singers; next is the theme song from "Black Orpheus," followed by "Miles Ahead" by Miles Davis, "Peer Gynt," and "Rock Around the Clock,"

I play, and they write seriously. Some cross out and rewrite. Clearly they must think this is worth doing, though I doubt if they have ever done anything like this before.

I collect the writing and ask them to get out more paper. "Now I'm going to read some of the responses. Write down which piece you think I'm describing." For "Grizzly Bear" the most common color was brown, the texture was rough, the flavor was soup, and so on. For Miles Davis, the color was soft blue, the texture was something smooth, the taste dry white wine. How do they know what dry white wine tastes like? It's a rich school.

111

In almost every case, the kids know what song is described even though it is not named. The room is quite upbeat. I am delighted to have come up with this idea, especially since my knowledge of music is nonexistent.

Now it's "So what?" time:

Paula: "You could do the same thing with literature, or you could do this to start a poem."

Chris: "It shows that music communicates the same feelings to most of the people in the room."

Rick: "Even though I saw 'Black Orpheus' as black, soft, and sweaty, I can see why someone might see it as red, harsh, and sticky."

Fred: "You need all of these together. One by itself wouldn't communicate the song, but together you can get the idea."

The class just ends. Several want to bring in their own music. "Remember," I call out, "to add this to your list of final project possibilities. What would happen if you tried this with different groups of people and then studied the results?"

ACCESSORY TO FELONY

One of the most popular senior options at Highland Park High School is Interviewing and Investigating taught by Joe. He has found ingenious ways to combine old-fashioned book research with on-the-spot fact gathering. His students spend much of their class time out in the "field" interviewing, taping, and taking pictures. He brings reporters to class to discuss their work. Last week a man from the *Chicago Sun Times* talked about asking good questions. Joe's kids have written profiles of local business people and family histories. One of his students made a film about the man in charge of the lions at Lincoln Park Zoo.

A lot of the success has to do with Joe, the person. He's a small man, always well dressed. From a distance he looks like the adult incarnate, but he has exceptional rapport with young people, who can tell how greatly he respects them. He is universally liked by his colleagues—a teacher's teacher.

Joe's other class, English Literature, has not been as popular. The real problem is that it is filled with seniors who have given up. They are a good-natured bunch, but they don't do anything—not an unusual circumstance. So last week Joe decided to try something new. If his other classes could go so well, why couldn't this one? What he needed to do was get these mopes out of the classroom and start them learning on their own. But how to do this in English literature? He came up with an idea.

His class was reading *The Loneliness of the Long Distance Runner*, a British novel about a young man who commits a crime. Joe thought it would be important for his kids to understand—really understand—what it felt like to break the law. His plan was a simple one: His kids were to spend the entire

113

class period out in the building stealing everything they could get their hands on. Whatever they took they would bring back to their classroom. Then it would all be returned. What better way to learn than by doing?

Joe should have known better. The instant he completed the instructions, his students were out the door, and right then he knew he has done something really stupid. "Even the nerds—especially the nerds—had this crazed look. I kept saying to myself, What have I done?"

A few minutes later one of his students, a big kid named Stan, came racing back down the hall. He was carrying a file drawer. The whole cabinet must have been too heavy. Closing in behind him was Doris Hayes, the school nurse. Within a half-hour, Joe's room looked like a warehouse piled high with clothes, plants, briefcases, cameras, lunch bags—anything that wasn't tied down when the students noticed it. The "thieves" usually went into empty classrooms, but they also invaded occupied ones, picking the place clean while students and teachers looked on astonished. Some of his people reached the far corners of the building, returning with tools from the shop, art equipment from the studios, instruments from the band room. Someone snatched a harp. Joe sent out an announcement for this to stop, but it took a while, and by the end of the melee, purloined goods were piled in the hall in front of his class because there was no more room inside. The haul included a wrestling mat, basketballs, lunchroom trays, and bicycles. Some items, like the wrestling mat, could not have been delivered to Joe's room without concerted teamwork—impromptu "criminal gangs" must have formed.

I had been out at a meeting that morning. By the time I returned, order had been restored, but I could still tell something big had occurred. The first people I questioned had no idea what had happened or why. An older teacher thought that the kids had suddenly decided to take over. One of the students thought the whole mess had been some kind of bet. A few teachers thought Joe was getting even with the school for some unknown slight. I found him in his room writing an apology "to everyone on earth." His hair was messed up and his tie hung loose. This was not the Joe I knew. He told me what had happened. He was shaken by his own bad judgment, but even more by the terrifying energy he had released in these middle-class kids. He said he felt like the character in *Heart of Darkness* momentarily looking into the real nature of human beings.

I told him that might be overstating things a little. I also told him that I could imagine myself doing something like this.

"But you didn't."

"No, I didn't."

"Aren't you glad?"

"You bet I am."

DECISION MAKING

Things are humming along. My new communications class continues to be a big hit with the seniors. I am also starting to help dropouts prepare for the GED and beginning to make plans to write a book about Hack Wilson, a great baseball player for the Chicago Cubs. And best of all, Sue and I have a new child—a son named Charlie.

I am even enjoying something called FOP—Freshman Orientation Program. This is a 40-minute homeroom held in the middle of the day where freshmen can hear the bulletin, study, and get their bearings. It's a chance for them to get to know each other and for me to do a little counseling. After the first few months, we all agree that FOP is going well, but that we should add something to it to make it more than just "social time." This is, after all, the era of Vietnam and the growing Women's Liberation movement and Black Power. Shouldn't we come up with ways to make FOP more relevant? Approximately 100 FOP classes are still scheduled to occur before June. We can do a lot of teaching in that time. We figure the parents, many of whom are liberal professionals, would like us to seize this opportunity, as would the parents who owned stores and those from the military base.

A math teacher with sideburns and bell-bottoms tells us at a FOP teachers' meeting about a program called "Decision Making." He has never used it, but he has heard it worked well with some kids from Iowa. He passes around the promotional material, which features smiling kids who obviously have learned to make decisions. In one picture, four grinning adolescents—a white boy in shorts, a white boy wearing a yarmulke, a light-skinned black girl, and an East Asian girl—sit in a circle on a lawn. They all look decisive to me and everyone else.

A week later two salesmen show up and present the material to our group. They are sharp-looking young guys with suits and razor-cut hair and ready answers. They give us shiny folders that hold a workbook and other study materials. The workbook is brimming with activities to help our young people learn how to make the right choices. There is even a decision-making chart so that our students can trace their progress from wishy-washy to decisive. The material includes dozens of true stories about good and not-so-good decisions. It has interviews with astronauts, bank presidents, nuclear scientists, and NFL quarterbacks—all of who acknowledge the positive value of being a good decision-maker. At a certain point one salesman begins to refer to Decision Making as "DM." The other claims to have been a philosophy minor in college. "A little Kant never hurt anyone" he stage whispers to the male teachers in the back row. No one cracks a smile.

The very next day we decide to go with it. How could we not? Certainly no one wants to be against decision-making. "We don't want too many Hamlets out there," one of the older teachers remarks sagely. "Well, then," one of the meekest teachers speaks up, "let us make a decision to start this in two weeks. How about that?" And then we all applaud.

Six days later, I stand in front of my homeroom, which meets in a biology lab, and tell thirty high school freshmen that we will begin a study unit in one week. I hold up the blue folder and tell them about the program, lacing my chatter with motivational words like "fun," "relevant," "enjoyable," and "important."

Had I looked more closely at Rachel, I might have sensed trouble. She is a mellow little person who always sits nearby and reads *Mad* magazine or talks with me about movies. Today Rachel glares as she fingers a Bunsen burner. Most of the others in the room stare back just as fiercely. A few yawn and shrug with a "Just try it" look about them. When I stop talking, they all return to what they do best in homeroom—gossip—but today the gossip is louder and has a sort of mean-spirited tone. When the bell rings, they slouch out sullenly. No one—not even Marc, who talks Chicago sports with me every day—says goodbye.

Other teachers get the same arctic response, but we agree that once the kids "get their hands on the material," they'll see what a good idea this is. I am looking forward to some of the group activities, which will complement the open-classroom ideas that I have embraced and have been using in my English classes. I regard myself as a teacher who likes to keep his class busy making discoveries for themselves. I want my kids to develop their individual powers. Decision Making should fit right in.

The following week, I pass out the materials along with a schedule and explain the first exercise, which calls for the kids to list big decisions they will have to make in their lives and explain what process they will follow to make the decisions. This is all to be done on special sheets with special grids surrounded by little cartoon figures. This strikes me as a perfectly legitimate class activity. I am starting to do the work myself along with them (Should I buy a new ten-speed bike?), when I notice that no one—absolutely no one other than me—is doing the assignment. Not one of them. They are staring at me as if I have asked them to eat a car or roll in goat dung. They look utterly betrayed. And angry. They look dangerous. I suddenly fear for the lab equipment—the slides, the bottles of fluids, the dried frogs, the neat stacks of lab books, the plastic skeleton, the heart, the dissecting tools.

I encourage the students to get going. They poke at the material the way my daughter Fanny pokes at food she distrusts and despises. The bell rings, and they vacate the room in a fury.

The reaction in other rooms has been just as hostile. One astonished veteran teacher reports that her favorite girl—someone already active in social service though just in her first year of high school—had snarled "asshole" under her breath as she stalked out the door. From a freshman! All day long I spot mutilated blue folders in the trash cans or on the floor or blowing through the parking lot. Rocco, the head custodian, asks me if he should save them in a special can. I tell him no. Some books have been mangled beyond recognition. Other books have been seriously modified. In one book the smiling blond youth on page three now has a penis thrusting out of his forehead!

Just twenty-four hours later the response is even more ominous. By now, of course, most of the kids no longer have the workbooks. I try to make do with extra copies and some photocopied material, but they are not going to do the lesson, which involves "Mapping the Future." Unified by rage, they openly challenge me. The big word, naturally, is "Why?" Why do we have to do this? Why don't we do this in a real class? Why can't we just talk and relax? Why? Why? Why? I nod and act like I am taking notes and say that we are "rethinking the program."

That afternoon, we FOP teachers meet in the classroom of one of the French teachers. I sit next to a poster of *Jules and Jim* and announce that we'd better cut our losses. This is not going to work. The kids are not going to back down. Everyone looks relieved. A history teacher sighs loudly. She says that she misses the relaxed good feeling of homeroom. Ben, whose idea it was in the first place, says he will write a note that we will read to our classes. It will explain that Decision Making is now a "voluntary" activity that will meet after school in the back of the cafeteria. I wonder if we should draw straws to see who will sit in the empty cafeteria after school. We are all content with instant capitulation.

The kids accept their victory gracefully. Homeroom for me is once again a place to argue about football, do crossword puzzles, and snare pieces of gossip (I learn that a boy was beaten up because he had been selling nude pictures of his attacker's girlfriend). In my regular classes, I experiment with different approaches to open education. At night I read books by my heroes among the new educators. I take my students to the movie *Slaughterhouse Five* and the musical *Grease*. My wife and I invite students to our house to plan a film. I referee intramural basketball and bowl in a faculty league. The other teachers jump back into their teaching just as enthusiastically.

Several weeks later I have a conversation with an English teacher who was not part of FOP. "What went wrong?" he wants to know.

"We were just stupid, I guess. Wrong time. It seemed like a good idea, but it wasn't."

"These are serious kids. They think about their futures. You'd think they'd like something like this."

"That's what we figured."

"I guess they don't really know what's good for them."

"That's where you're wrong. They know perfectly well what's good for them."

"Well, anyway, this is something you'll soon forget."

"Maybe not." I know a little better what Joe felt like.

HACK INTERVIEW

"Why would you want to write a book about a baseball player that no one has ever heard about or cares about?" Ruth asks. She's a student in Lyn's sophomore English class. I am there to be interviewed by her and a boy named David. They are asking me questions about the book I am writing with another teacher about Hack Wilson. I am the fourth guest writer in four days. Yesterday, the guest was a history teacher who is writing a book about progressive education. The day before a World Book editor was here. Lyn hopes these interviews with real writers will stimulate his sophomores to write inspired research projects of their own.

Ruth, David, and I are surrounded by circle of agreeable-looking students, whose job it will be to listen. It has the look of a TV panel show. Lyn leans against the back wall, arms folded. He's my height with long hair and an immense smile. He has a black belt in karate and teaches evening classes in self-defense to our students and parents. He is also an accomplished sketch artist. On Monday nights in the fall when we all sit in some teacher's basement, shouting at a TV screen full of football players, Lyn lurks in the back quietly capturing the scene in charcoal.

It seems like everyone at Highland Park High School is into interviewing and investigating. Along with my communications classes for upper classmen, I am also teaching a research class. My class has spent the day at the airport and another day at a brand-new shopping mall to gather information. We have taken a morning field trip to Chicago food markets. I have introduced my students to the writing of Tom Wolfe, George Plimpton, and the other new journalists. Maybe Woodward and Bernstein's books on Watergate have something to do with all this digging.

Before I can answer Ruth's opening question, she starts talking again. "I mean, old baseball players are not exactly a fascinating subject to most of us." Lyn has picked her for her honesty. She's going to ask questions that she wants answered, not just questions that should be asked.

My chance to talk. "Jerry and I were both finishing our dissertations and felt like writing something that wasn't academic. We wanted something we cared about. It was that simple."

"Why Hack Wilson?" asks David, who happens to be the third baseman on the sophomore baseball team. He obviously does not agree with Ruth's view that Hack is an obscure subject. He's wearing a blue Highland Park sweatshirt.

"I can remember when I was just starting to follow the Cubs, I noticed that there was this player Hack Wilson who had the major league record for RBIs and the national league record for home runs. I've always been curious about him." Ruth is taking notes feverishly.

"So, one day I mentioned Hack to Jerry Grunska in his office after school. Jerry called the library and found out no one had ever written a book about him. We also learned that Hack had supposedly been kept out of the Hall of Fame because he was a drunk. That was it. We decided right then and there to write the biography of Hack Wilson."

"I still can't believe you couldn't have found something more interesting," Ruth will not back down. "Anyway, how much longer do you have to go?" When she stops writing, she bites on her pen. She wearing jeans and a "Let's Boogie" T-shirt. She lives in a big house on the lake. Her older brother, one of my former students, once wrote a paper about smelt fishing.

"We have done tons of research. We have a good plan to follow. Each of us is responsible for certain chapters. We go through them together to try to get a single voice. We're hoping by next year to have the book done."

Lyn speaks up from the back. "I want to say something." He sounds a trifle apologetic. Like the rest of us, he hopes the kids will draw the right conclusions, but he can't resist making a point that needs to be made. "People, notice what happens when you care about the subject you're writing about. Bob and Jerry love the subject so much that they can go back to it over and over and over again. Now, as a great baseball hater, I can't imagine spending time on a ball player, but they can."

From off to the side, a tall kid speaks up "That's easy for you to say, but what if we have to write about characters in books and people in history that we don't care about? Mr. Philyaw, you let us write about people like Camus or Vonnegut. And we can investigate cults and things like that, but what if we still don't care?"

Lyn lowers his voice into a Zen-like chant. "Make yourself care, Matt. Make yourself care. But obviously you can't pick everything you write about. But that doesn't mean you can't find a good reason to write about it."

A great answer. I'll have to use it.

From that point on David and Ruth fire away, and I answer as quickly as I can. I tell them that Hack was born in western Pennsylvania in 1900, an illegitimate child. He moved to the Philadelphia area and then to West Virginia, where he started playing baseball. He played ball until he was in his mid-thirties. He went back to West Virginia where he drank and got a divorce. Later he moved to Baltimore and died there in 1948.

From the beginning, I tell them, Jerry and I have seen his life as a quick rise and a sharp fall—a meteor. I told them about the sports writers we met, the telephone interviews we did with legends like Joe McCarthy, one of baseball's most famous managers. I describe the trip we took to Martinsburg, West Virginia, to meet Wilson's son and some of his old buddies. One of his best friends was named Dubber Brumbaugh, and another was called Snipey Kaiser. I figure the kids will get a kick out of these colorful names.

"What I'll never forget," I went on, "was a trip that my wife Sue and I took to a mental hospital to visit his second wife, who had not had a visitor for 25 years." Ruth puts her notebook on the floor and moves to Lyn's desk and sits on it. "We drove into this parking lot and walked through a check point. I had called ahead, so they knew about us coming. The yard was filled with people in white gowns looking just like mental patients in *One Flew Over the Cuckoo's Nest*. When they saw us, several charged over to say hello. One took her lighted cigarette and waved it in my wife's face and kept saying 'Look I can smoke! Look, they let me smoke!'" I go on. "A nurse met us inside and led us upstairs to a room in a locked ward, and there was Hack's wife. We went into the room, but the other patients tried to get in, so I put my chair against the door to keep them out. His wife's name was Hazel. She had stringy gray hair and a crooked smile, and all she could say about her husband was that he was so nice. She stared at the pictures we showed her but didn't have anything at all to say about them. Finally we left and drove back to our motel."

Time is running short. Ruth asks if I have anything to show them. I hold up a list of all the articles Jerry and I have collected. I read part of a sports story about a time Hack charged into the stands to beat up a milkman who had been taunting him. I also show a picture of Art "The Great One" Shires, a White Sox player who had challenged Hack to a boxing match, and another picture of Hack's son sitting on Al Capone's lap. I show them his autopsy report and his obituary, and I read the words of the minister at his funeral: "I've come to pay my respects to one of the most courageous spirits who ever graced this land. It's a long way from a steel mill to a quarter-million dollars and back again. If you can travel that road, you have a commendable spirit."

Lyn asks a few more questions. "You said people called him a drunk, but he wasn't."

"He drank. He drank a lot," I answer, "but not as much as people said. People all claimed to have seen him sip from a bottle during games, but that was garbage. He was actually called a 'lovable drunk,' but that wasn't true either."

The bell is about to ring. I have been repeating stories I have told before. But after hearing Lyn's question, I feel something new I have to say. "I think what gives Jerry and me energy is that we want to prove that this theory is wrong. We're almost on a mission to tell the real story. And that's really what research can be. When you guys pick a subject, figure out what the popular view is. Then find out if the popular view is the correct view. The chances are that it isn't."

PLAGIARISM

I have decided to leave full-time high school teaching. Next fall I will teach night school. During the day, I want to finish the Hack Wilson book and look into other, less traditional teaching possibilities. People admire my courage, but it's not the gutsy risk-taking it appears to be. In fact, if it doesn't work, I can always come back to Highland Park High School. But I don't think that will happen. I want to see where this book takes me. I want to find out what's happening in the city.

It's a hot afternoon in June—the final day of school. I am in my classroom removing posters from the wall, stacking up books and waiting for seniors to arrive with their final projects—"The Spring Biggy," as we call it. Outside cars full of screaming kids circle the building. A few blocks away at the beach, a party is raging. I feel the familiar end-of-the-year excitement. Ahead for me lie three months of travel, golf, writing and sloth. And then what?

It is also a casual day for teachers, and I am sporting a yellow T-shirt with a fat dancer with giant shoes. A teacher down the hall is wearing a referee's shirt; another is in his track outfit from before WWII.

Into the room hurries Betsy wearing shorts and an Indiana University T-shirt. She hands me a large notebook filled with poetry and artwork. She smells faintly of beer. She obviously wants to get into one of those cars outside and head for the beach.

"We could discuss this at length, Betsy," I say as she heads for the door with a smile spreading across her face.

"This summer, Mr. Boone. I'll make an appointment to discuss this in the summer. Great class."

She is off, and that leaves Paula, the one senior who has yet to turn in The Biggy. I have no idea if she has poetry, a long short story or a portfolio. Unlike the others, Paula has not shared her progress with the class. She has never attended a field trip or come to one of our dinner classes. In fact, I have only seen a few pieces of her writing, but she has promised me this will be worth the wait.

Finally she arrives. She is a blond girl with bad posture and fair skin. I hate the word "waif," but because she is always by herself and never smiles, the word seems to fit. Today, Paula wears slacks and a sweater even though it's hot outside. She certainly isn't going to the beach party.

She smiles weakly as she hands me a thick folder with what looks like a short story inside. She yawns and looks at her feet. I suppose she has been up all night. It suddenly hits me that I have been given something significant. This quiet, struggling child so totally alienated from her suburban classmates has been quietly creating her masterpiece.

"Would you like to talk?" I ask, pushing the papers to the side of my desk. "We can go down to the teachers' room for a coke."

"Not really," she mutterers and hurries out the door. I had to read it. I even consider calling a friend from down the hall to share it. This is going to be good. What could this sullen little creature have to say?

I sit at a school desk, light a cigarette and start to read. It seems familiar. I read some more, and then my eye catches "Winesburg." This sensitive young child, this future Joyce Carol Oates, has copied a story straight from Sherwood Anderson.

She gets an F, but she already had enough credits to graduate. When I confront her, she says she thought she was supposed to copy her favorite story. When I told her that couldn't be true, she shrugs and says she thought I wouldn't notice.

Now, that hurt.

OUT OF THE SCHOOLS

NIGHT SCHOOL

The night-school classroom is an island cut off from the rest of the school by a gate that separates it from the main building. The only door out—a heavy steel one, at that—is to the parking lot. Unlike the day-school classrooms I am used to, this one has no bookshelves, no inspiring or even interesting posters, no plants. In the rear of the room is a locked closet. But I don't have the key. There is one eraser and a single piece of chalk smaller than a wad of chewed gum. The desk has no blotter. During the day this room hosts driver's education and health classes. A poster is Duct-Taped to the wall next to the chalkboard. It reads: "Good Things to Do Instead of Having Sex." One of these good things is a "Study Date." Beneath this suggestion, someone has written in pen, "with blow jobs." The joke was either added very recently or the printing is small enough that no one in a position of authority has noticed it yet.

I am sitting at the desk waiting for my first night school English class to start. As I always do before I start a new class, I have arrived early. On the desk are several small piles. One is a stack of unread articles about Hack Wilson. Most are descriptions of events in 1929. When the students are writing, I can read some of the articles and dig out quotes and other treasures. Wherever I go these days, I carry Hack Wilson with me. I have started to send letters to agents and publishers.

In another stack is my plan for this course. Each class will include something to write, something to read, and something to see, such as a film or a video. I hope to use many of the games and activities from my communications class. Let's hope they work as well with these kids.

This is a different bunch of students. For one reason or another, all have been kicked out of school, but they all want high school diplomas. I've been told that only a few will be going on to college. Last week the assistant principal, the guy responsible for removing kids from day school and dooming them to my care in night school, gave me the keys and some advice: "Teach them whatever you want. No fighting, no booze or drugs, no humping in the parking lot. And watch out for the fire extinguisher." The assistant principal called me "Dr. Boone" because I have received my Ph.D. from Northwestern. What a delicious irony! I get to be called "doctor" in this dumping ground for miscreants and misfits.

Also on the desk is my note to Wally. He has asked me more than once why, after I was having such a great time in day school, I had quit. The official answer is that I need the days to finish the baseball book. But I have an idea that I would like to teach independently. I'm tutoring English, and I've begun a little SAT tutoring. I like being on my own. I again glance at the note.

Dear Wally,

This feels different. No doubt about it. I am about to become an unpublished author and a part-time, freelance teacher with no mailbox and no health insurance. This will start with night school teaching at Highland Park and some tutoring, but where it is heading I have no idea. I want to keep teaching, but I want enough time to write. I want to find a way to teach in the city. I could return to full-time public school teaching in a few years, but my instincts tell me that this is not going to happen. I have cashed in my teacher retirement money, and I have taken a loan from the bank. Let's see what happens.

Bob

As class time closes in, I am growing excited. I always get the same adrenaline boost before meeting a new class. What is going to happen? Will my ideas work? How much will this be like my old teaching experiences? Will I like these kids? Will they like me?

In strolls a tall, blond, scruffy youth. I know him from day school, where he dropped out of two of my classes. Later he was kicked out of school for good for truancy. Back then he had seemed bright but gloomy. He would sit in the back and mutter. His friends were mostly older guys who worked with him at an auto upholstery shop. He has a scar on his neck and walks with a slight limp. "How are you doing, Kenny?" I ask, and the year has begun. He nods and smiles and heads for the back of the room where he slides into a desk and tips backwards.

A girl in a leather jacket follows him. I have forgotten why she was kicked out of day school, but I remember her name. "How are you doing, Liz?" In fact, I am already familiar with the names of practically all of these kids either by reputation or because of some actual contact. "How are you doing, Mike?" "How are you doing, Rosie?" This, of course, is an adult way to get things going. But, then again, one of them might actually answer me. "How am I doing, Mr. Boone?" someone just might say. "Just great. I've been kicked out of day school. I work at a job where they treat me like shit. I don't make any money. The only thing I have to look forward to is a beer after class, and that won't be for another four hours. When I get home—if I'm not stopped for drunken driving—my parents will be passed out in front of the tube. I have fucked up my past. My present is a nightmare. I have no future. But thanks for asking."

Several more appear, many in uniforms from local service stations. One wears a Marine Corps jacket. One guy sports a McDonald's outfit, another is wearing overalls, and a third a coat and tie. Generally, their hair is long and scraggly. They all looked tired.

Most smell of cigarettes and beer.

A skinny kid with a ferret face, pimples, and a torn T-shirt saunters in and stands by the desk. I look up. "How are you doing, Johnny?"

He looks down at me. "You knew my brother, didn't you?"

"I certainly did."

"Were you at the basketball game when he slugged Mr. Bilkey?"

"I was right there." Actually, I had been in the bathroom when someone shouted "Fight!" and half the fans poured out of the building and into the parking lot. When we got there, Johnny's brother had just "accidentally" slugged a teacher who was breaking up a fight. "I helped hold him down until the police came. He's a strong guy."

Johnny smiles and nods and looks away. This same brother is now in "Statesville" penitentiary in Joliet for kicking to death a sailor from Great Lakes, the Naval station not too far north along the Lake Michigan shore.

A few more stumble in, and once again it's time for me to play teacher. I move from behind the desk. "I'm Mr. Boone. I'll be your English teacher this year." From somewhere in the back I hear muttered, "Big fucking deal." It doesn't trouble me. Even though the night-school kids are in a sort of halfway house, with a final chance to graduate from high school, just the same I figured there would be the usual resentful, angrily defiant attitude. It simply goes with the territory.

I mention things like English credit and the chances for extra credit. I find myself repeating the same sentence: "I want you to find out what you can do." I talk, and they nod and then look away. They don't talk to each other, but I can tell my words are making no serious impact. No one's nodding enthusiastically. No one is scribbling down notes. Over the years, these people have learned to hate and distrust teachers—young and old. Why should they listen to me now? But still I feel comfortable. I go on to say that I am writing a book about Hack Wilson. "Maybe I'll read some of the chapters to you later in the year." No response except for a slight shrug from Liz. My interests are a matter of indifference.

Then a shout from Rick, a serious chair-tipper in the back row. "How long are the classes?" He is wearing some kind of uniform. He looks both bewildered and outraged.

"Four hours. Just like all the other night-school classes. We meet one day each week."

A shout from someone else, "You knew that, Ori."

"Screw you, asshole."

I raise my voice to intervene. "You're going to see some films too." I hold up a film container to show that we will watch one tonight.

"It looks kind of short," William, a black kid in the front row, calls out. "I need something long so I can sleep." Loud guffaws.

"What movie are we going to see?"

"*Occurrence at Owl Creek Bridge.*"

"Is that the one where the guy gets his pecker shot off?"

"You're thinking of *All Quiet on the Western Front*. But first I want you to write something."

They groan as I pass out the blue Bics and yellow pads. Start quickly, I'm thinking. Learning is doing. Doing is learning. Let them discover for themselves. Find out what they can do. "In the next forty minutes, I want you to tell me a true, funny story. You could have been in the middle of the action, or you could have been an observer. But you were there. When you think back, it still seems funny. Try to make it funny for the reader."

"Why?" several shout.

"Why can't we do something else?" Liz whines.

Already this has a very foreign feel, almost a

complete opposite from day school. Day school kids tend to be subtler when they don't like something. They might frown and ask questions, but they would never just scream out "*Why* are we doing this?" If they did, they would apologize and probably expect to be scolded. Night-school kids will not have any of these hang-ups. I'm surprised I haven't yet heard some variation on "fuck yourself." Maybe I have.

I keep talking. "I want you to write about yourselves. I know you have seen some funny things. I know you can tell stories. So show me what you can do. I start all my classes like this. Give it a try. If you're thinking about college, you could use this for your application essay." Very few in this group will be going to college. But why not treat them as if they are?

Once they start to write, I sit back down and pick up an article about Art "The Great One" Shires, a baseball player on the White Sox who once challenged Hack Wilson to a boxing match. I don't look up. I want the students to know that I expect them to write the paper. I don't want to hover over them. And when I do peek a few minutes later, every student—every single one of them—is writing away. But when they see me looking at them, they start to shout out. "How do you spell marijuana?" We'll worry about that later, I tell them. "How do you spell ether?" Later. "What if it's not funny?" That's your problem. "Are you going to show these to people?" Only the FBI. "How do you spell carburetor?" Look it up. "Should I capitalize Southern Comfort?" You'd better. "Do we have to read these out loud?" Only if you don't want to.

I return to the article and learn that the prize fight between Hack and "The Great One" was canceled at the last minute. The kids keep writing and shouting. It feels OK. I enjoy this controlled chaos. Some day, though, it's bound to go too far.

Then they are done. First Johnny and then the rest. They drop their pens and stretch their fingers and pant as if they have just completed a race. I'm pleased. Better still, they appear to be as well.

Instead of their reading the entire papers, I ask them to summarize what they've written. More loud griping, but they agree and actually seem to enjoy sharing these snippets.

Mike: "I wrote about party where guys brought a hose inside and sprayed the place."

Liz: "My mother caught her best friend shoplifting."

William: "I got kicked out of a softball game and the team had to forfeit."

Johnny: "My brother took a swing at a priest."

Kenny: "I got locked in the park district garage for the whole night." And then without asking permission, he reads the whole paper. It seems that one night while he was working at the park district, he decided to have a smoke in the bus garage. While he was in there "some moron shut the door." He pounded on the door for a long time but never got anyone's attention. He wasn't released until they opened up the garage again the next morning.

"Were you scared?" Liz asks.

"You'd better fucking believe it. There's rats in there."

I tell him I like the paper. It is a good subject—both funny and scary. He tells the story in a clear voice. He has lots of details. I tell the whole class that I like what I've heard and that I'm anxious to read the completed pieces.

Time for the break. "We can smoke in the parking lot," I tell them. "We have to be back inside here in 15 minutes. That's what they want us to do." A few minutes later, we are all puffing away. I talk to Kenny about his job. Johnny tells me another story about his brother. Terry wants to know if we can use the library. Several look at the engine of Mike's new car. It is a warm, clear Midwestern night. I feel right now as if I can get along with these kids. They seem to enjoy each other's company. They hate most adults, but for the moment they tolerate me.

After our nicotine fix, we return to our windowless classroom to watch *An Occurrence at Owl Creek Bridge.* It's about a captured Confederate officer who thinks he has survived an execution, but in the end we learn he has been hanged anyway. Most watch curiously. They seem to like the surprise at the end. But the highlight is when I play the film backwards. Instead of dropping into the water with a rope around his neck, the hero flies back out of the water to safety. Good stuff. This draws the best response I have ever had to running a film backwards. Are high school dropouts more likely to laugh at a film run backwards? It sounds like a good subject for a Masters thesis.

Near the end of class, I add some parting advice. "Think about other true stories you might want to write. We'll do this for the next few weeks. If you have movies you'd like to see, we can probably arrange that."

"How about *Deep Throat?*"

"We'll save that for the Christmas party. See you all next week."

Several actually smile on the way out. Johnny shakes my hand.

Driving home I feel tired. But not defeated.

One week later, Liz is the first to arrive, but barely. She staggers to the back of the room and drops down into a desk. "How you doing, Mr. Brown?" she slurs.

"Boone, Liz. My name is Mr. Boone." By now I am standing in front of her desk.

She looks up at me with bloodshot eyes. "What's wrong?"

"You're drunk." She shrugs and smiles and doesn't even try to act surprised.

"I just had one beer after work." She looks down at her hands.

"You're drunk, Liz. Believe me, I know when someone is drunk. I can't teach a class when you're drunk. And, if one of the administrators finds out, we're all in trouble."

"Pigs. What do those fuckers know?"

"Go home. OK?"

She stands and reels toward the door. Two guys who have just arrived pay no attention to her.

Then, at the door, she pauses and squints back. "You know, Mr. Brown, boys from around here can really be rude. Last week I was walking with my friend Rosie, and this car passed, and a guy stuck his head out the window and yelled, Hey, Rosie you fat shit, why don't you suck my cock?" Liz pauses panting with outrage and then continues. "You know, if you think about it, that's a pretty rude thing to say."

"Only if you think about it, Liz," I respond, but by now she has staggered out of the room for good.

Liz somehow set the tone, and the rest of the class goes badly. Several kids arrive late. A new student named Rich shows up, and I don't have him on the list. I ask them to write a paper about a time they were scared. Almost none take it seriously. The few who do actually start writing give up while the others ask questions or daydream. I wonder how many other students might be drunk or high. I can keep them reasonably quiet, but I still don't enjoy the bantering as much as the week before. It's raining, so we can't smoke in the parking lot. The sound system on the movie projector barely works. I let the class out early and drive home depressed. I stop for a beer in Highwood and listen to the bartender tell me why Jerry Ford is going to crush Jimmy Carter in the election.

The third week we read "Shooting an Elephant" by George Orwell. We read it aloud together, and they like this. "It's just like 3rd grade," a now-sober Liz comments. In this essay Orwell describes a time when he was working as a British colonial official in Burma. As the guy in charge, he's expected to shoot an elephant that has done some damage, even though this is not necessary. But because the crowd expected him to shoot, he ended up killing the beast. The class loves the story. "What do you recall the most vividly? Would you have done it?" I ask. "What else could he have done? Have you ever been in a situation like that?" Because many of these kids have had scrapes with the law, their feelings are not particularly sympathetic toward a cop who found himself in a tough spot. The discussion continues for more than an hour.

Not much happens in the fourth class. No one has written an assigned follow-up piece to "Shooting an Elephant." We read a story by Ray Bradbury. They write descriptions of their first jobs. No one seems interested. After everyone else has left, Rich, the smallest person in the class, comes back into the room and strides right up to me. Earlier he had been mad because he thought I was making fun of him while he was sleeping in the back. I had poked him awake, but that was all. "You'd better watch it, Mr. Boone." He punches his stiff finger into my chest. "You'd better watch it." I can't believe this is happening. I push his hand away and tell him that if he threatens me again, I'll call the police. He actually looks astonished. What does he expect me to say? Then he hurries out the door. Rich is not big and physically threatening, so I am not really scared, but I'm not happy. The furious aggression behind the jabbing finger disturbs me. With the night school kids, I should have expected something like this to happen. But still...

Later in the week, I decide to have a meeting with Rich and his parents, but before I can make any calls, I learn that he was killed while trying to break into a building in Waukegan, a lakefront town to the north, closer to the Wisconsin border. Rich was electrocuted when the ladder he was standing on fell back against a power line. I send a note to his dad.

When I get to class that next week, Mike shouts out, "That'll teach him to fuck with you, Mr. Boone." Apparently someone had heard about the threat. Probably, Rich had announced it or bragged about it. I ignore the shouts and ask how well they knew Rich. Predictably, it turns out they didn't know him at all. He was the kid who came in late, who threatened me, and then got killed. I say how sorry I am for the parents. "The worst thing I can imagine is losing a child." The class is quiet for a while, perhaps in deference to my sorrow, and then the shouting resumes.

Incidents that are almost completely alien to day-school teaching continue to occur, almost as if the differences between focused, purposeful day students and the disaffected kids in my night-school classes need somehow to be emphasized. Once I kick Phil out of class for sneaking in a bottle of rum. Another time I get called away to help break up a fight in another night-school class. When I get back to my room, I can tell someone has been smoking pot, but no one admits it. A new girl joins the class and then hangs herself a few weeks later.

Even despite this horrific interlude, I find that the classes are generally OK. I cannot build anything as I could with the ambitious day students, but I can create learning opportunities. The kids like the block game. They like playing charades. We play word games like "categories." I read several chapters from *Hack*. They like the chapters but can't imagine how I can spend so much time reading about the subject. In this, they aren't much different from the day students.

I talk a lot about college. I want them to see that what we are now doing could matter later on. "I don't care what kind of job you're heading for," I keep repeating. "Why not try college for a couple of years? Discover what else you can do? Have some fun." They listen when I say this. They believe me, I think. They know that I wouldn't say this unless I meant it, but I am quite sure that few will take me up on it.

This can be discouraging, but I have other reasons to feel optimistic. I'm excited about finishing the book. I have sold several articles to local papers. I have started tutoring. I am working with other dropouts to prepare them for the GED. In addition, several night-school kids have asked me about the GED. It's going to take them a long time to graduate if they stay in night school. Suddenly a GED is looking better. I agree to help them if they decide to drop out and go for the GED. I have started to think about a little school of my own where I can work with dropouts. Instead of having to build a curriculum, I can use the GED as the basis for my program. I am gradually developing a feeling for these kids, who, as far as I can tell, have no one speaking for them. The school wants them gone. Their parents may as well, at least, those who have any remaining relationship with their parents. They will no doubt end up in reasonably low-paying jobs, but why not give them one more chance to discover what they can do? By assuming they have something to say and by showing an interest in whatever it is that they do say, I have given them something positive. I'm not doing anything new or fancy, but at least I am doing something.

In the fall of my second year, as a favor to my brother-in-law, who runs an ad agency, I agree to model mechanic's clothes for an ad campaign. This calls for posing at a local gas station—too local, as it turns out. Throughout the preparation for the shoot, I am terrified that someone will recognize me, and on cue, when my brother-in-law is taking the last shot of me under the hood, five of my night-school students stroll by. "Hey, Mr. Boone, you don't know shit about cars, do you? What are you doing under the hood?" I feel small and silly as they crowd around and pull at my blue and yellow hat and scarf. But it is funny moment: Here's some teacher type pretending to be a blue-collar type while real blue-collar types look on in delight.

In this second year, just as the first year, the kids tolerate me. I am probably friendlier and more positive than what they are used to. Also, I enjoy their company, and they know it. They have come to my house for dinner and then stayed to watch television. They like stories by Ray Bradbury, especially "The Sound of Thunder." They like to play word games. They enjoy many of the movies I show, especially some from the American Short Stories series. More and more, I use many of my communication class activities. Some work quite well, but they serve more as diversion rather than as part of a larger curriculum. Just the same, it's always a pleasure to watch these grubby kids sitting on the floor playing with blocks.

What is constant is that these kids can write good stories about themselves. They can describe their bosses and their friends; they can describe auto shops and locker rooms. They can explain how to change a tire and how to sneak into Comiskey Park. They tell me all about beer parties and trips to the Wisconsin Dells. At the same time, it's quite clear to me that these kids do not see that this writing skill has any place in their future. Day-school kids recognized the value of writing in their high school and college education and, presumably, in whatever job they would eventually be seeking. They also valued it in their personal lives. Night-school kids value writing as an escape, and that's it. Not a bad reason to value it.

I have concentrated on content and form and paid less attention to grammar and usage than I did in day-school writing. But one day in the spring I decide to bring up the matter of grammar more directly. I have been looking at GED tests and have an idea. In the first hour of the class, we watch part of *Cool Hand Luke*. After a smoke in the parking lot and one inning of softball, we come back.

"I want you to think about something," I begin when they're all back in their seats. "I know that many of you will be taking the GED. As you know, it has a section that tests what you know about punctuation and usage." I pause, waiting for a groan or at least a scowl. But most are listening. Perhaps they have been waiting for this for two years—"Now Boone is finally going to talk about that shit."

I go on to say that, for the most part, they write correctly. "You know where to put periods and commas." But I want them understand all of the rules they're expected to know on a GED or a college-placement test. "You don't want to be stuck in some remedial class if you don't belong there." Johnny helps me out by saying a cousin of his did poorly on a community college placement test and ended up with "a bunch of morons who could barely talk."

I tell them that I want to see if they can learn the essentials in just a few days. "I believe something can be learned better quickly. Let's not drag this out." I am aware that they are aware that I am aware that this is not the kind of thing I do. But I can also sense that they want to go along with this. I'm sure that the GED has been eating at them. Now here I am promising a quick solution to all of their problems.

I start by reminding them that this is "something you know already. It's like writing. I'm not teaching you something new. You had this stuff in school. Plus, you should be able to hear most of these mistakes." I make a list of what I call the "Ten Problem Areas." For each I stop and explain briefly.

Avoid fragments and run-ons.
Use the correct verb.
Make your subjects and verbs agree.
Use the correct pronoun.
Make the pronoun agree with the noun.
Use the correct modifier.
Don't confuse similar words.
Punctuate correctly.
Keep your sentences balanced and parallel.
Capitalize correctly.

If they don't know the terms, at least they—or at least some in the group—recognize the errors. This is nothing more than simplified version of what can be found in any language handbook. But it represents the most typical mistakes found on the GED. When the list is complete, I step back and announce, "This is it, folks. You cannot make a mistake that does not fall under one of these error categories." They are strangely silent. It seems that they are genuinely stunned that I have made this stuff instantly comprehensible. We spend the rest of the day going through old GED tests and ACT tests. Most of the kids can spot and correct most of the mistakes planted in the tests most of the time. When they don't spot a mistake, they usually recognize their error.

I continue to work on English correctness for the rest of the year. I always start by asking them to write the list over again. I repeat that this list represents the "whole story." I repeat that there are several "good, practical reasons for learning this stuff once and for all." Along with correcting mistakes, I want them to identify the kind of mistake they have corrected. I keep making the point that this is something they "know already." I like the approach. I believe it gives the kids a feeling of greater control. So much of school for them—especially dreary subjects like grammar—often has been made to look utterly incomprehensible.

As the end of the second year approaches, I am struck once again at how astonishingly uncertain the whole night-school experience has been. Perhaps because I am alone in the building, I am especially conscious of how I feel. I am always a little bit on edge because these kids fight so much. And if they don't actually fight, they almost fight. The awareness of the possibility of violence is always with me. And I'm mad a lot because these kids make me mad: They break things. They take things. They lie. And I get angrier with myself because with no parents or administrators looking over my shoulder, it's too simple just to lower my standards and slide through class. And because I am alone in the building, I feel lonely at times with no fellow teacher down the hall to share stories. But when the kids are writing well and responding honestly to a story or film or playing charades, I feel better than I have ever felt as a teacher.

As my second year ends, I decide it's time to move on. I need more time to start my own learning center. As I figured, many of my first students will be night-school kids or friends of night-school kids who have decided to pursue a GED. Many of them will be recommended to me by other local high schools. In some cases the schools will pay me. In others I will charge the kids a fee. I also plan to tutor kids who need special help. I have run ads in local papers. I have made some contacts with organizations in the city. I have borrowed more money from the bank. I will not go back to Highland Park, but I may teach part-time in the city. *Hack* is finished, and now I want to write more articles.

In my very last day of night school, we read "Flight" by John Steinbeck. I ask the kids to write a true story that involves a chase. We take an extra-long cigarette break. Instead of going back inside, we play softball. I hit into a double play to end the game.

GED CHAT

It's 10:00 AM, and I'm returning to work after a coffee break. I've spent the last few hours writing. I'll spend the rest of the day teaching here at my own tiny school, which I call the Glencoe Study Center. It is on the second floor of a building across the street from the railroad station. An express train traveling south can reach Chicago in thirty minutes. Highland Park is a few stops to the north. Evanston, home of Northwestern University, is several stops south. Winnetka, Kenilworth, and Wilmette—very wealthy North Shore Suburbs—are all close by. This seems like an unlikely place to start a GED program, but business is good.

The office features a small waiting room with a couch and a table that can be pulled out and used for tutoring. Inside is a pair of even smaller offices—one a cramped writing space for me and a tight "administrative" office—plus a teaching room just large enough for a class of fifteen. The place is cozy and quiet and by any definition "non-traditional."

Joey, my newest GED student, is waiting for me in the teaching room. He's standing up and gazing at one of the many school pictures that cover the walls. Most are of old buildings and old classrooms. "I've started a collection," I tell him. He likes a large 1904 photo that Sue and I bought at the Museum of the City of London. It is of 24 orphans staring back at the camera. No one is smiling. One kid, no doubt suffering from a toothache, has a bandage around his head. Another has his arms folded and his chin raised in a pugnacious way. "He's my guy," Joey says.

Joey was kicked out of school for fighting. I've heard that he loves to fight the way that some people love to garden or play tennis. Nothing delights him

147

more than to jump into the middle of a brawl. After his suspension, he tried my night-school class, but that didn't work, so now he's going for a GED.

After we look at a few more school pictures, we sit down. Joey digs into his pocket and gives me a wrinkled check for $200. It's made out to "Mr. Boon." I take the check and then begin to explain what the test entails. After working with dozens of GED candidates in the past year, I have learned that nothing matters more than to make clear immediately what the GED is all about. Failure follows from confusion, and people like Joey are often deeply confused about the nature of the test and what they must do to pass it. Why not eliminate confusion right away? These kids deserve the big picture, and I will give it to them.

We look at the whole test—English, social studies, science and math. For English he needs to understand ten basic rules of correctness. Social studies and science are basically reading tests. I know already that Joey is a good reader, so I have confidence about these portions. Math is basic. I explain how many questions he needs to get right to pass. I explain how he can retake individual parts if he happens to fail certain sections. I give him the phone number of Nelly Nova, the woman in Waukegan who will schedule his test. I talk fast, but I make sure he's following. I have learned that people don't always listen, especially when I am talking a mile a minute. I'm not going to slow down for people, but I have trained myself to pause more to make sure they are following me.

I wait while he finishes writing all of this down in his notebook. From where I am sitting he looks a little like John Belushi or Joe Cocker. He smells of grease. He works two jobs, one for a company that assembles playground equipment and another for a company that puts up tents for parties. I know he's a good softball player. He plays for team that features several of my other GED graduates.

This young man had been rude, uncooperative, mean and dangerous all through school. He once hit a teacher with a desk. He once took a swing at a janitor. He poured sugar into a teacher's gas tank. Now it's as if his past has evaporated. Nothing matters but passing the GED. With that, he can go to college and create a life for himself. My job will be to push him along. And it shouldn't be hard because, I am convinced, he probably knows most of this already. It's in there, and I will have to help him release it.

Next we go to Big Al's for lunch. It's small and crowded and reeks of frying food. Joey has a double cheeseburger and a double order of fries. I opt for the taco. He asks about my family. While he chews, I tell him about my wife and my three kids. He tells me something I already know, that he plays on a softball team. "Make sure you bring your kids to see us play. We kick ass." I have no reason to doubt him.

After we eat, we go back to the Glencoe Study Center. I give him a programmed English book and a copy *A Separate Peace*. I ask him to write a true story about a time he was surprised. I give him a math practice book and a schedule to follow. We'll meet twice weekly for ten weeks. "Then you'll take the test. No matter what."

"Will this work?" He's standing up about to leave. Now he really looks like John Belushi.

"Joey, it will work. Trust me." It has worked before. It will work for Joey.

A WINTER DAY

The snow is so deep that village workers have attached little red flags with long thin shafts to the fire hydrants so the plow operators will know where not to go. It's so deep that Sue is afraid that our son Charlie, who's now five years old, will "fall in" and not be found until spring. A neighbor is shoveling off his roof so his house won't collapse. Last night the temperature dropped to fifteen below, and pipes are freezing. People in the city leave lawn chairs to "reserve" places beside the curbs that they have shoveled out for their cars. If you park in a place that you didn't shovel, watch out. A man operating a plow on the South Side went berserk and started ramming cars. No one will be teaching night school because the school is closed. I won't go to Waukegan because the secretarial school where I offer GED classes is shut down. I won't tutor anyone today. I was supposed to interview a retired bike-racing champion named Torchy Pedan for an article I am writing about six-day bike racing, but Torchy can't get out of his driveway.

This morning at 7:00, I walked west to the Skokie Lagoons to cross-country ski. During the Depression, these lagoons were dug out by the Civilian Conservation Corps to drain a large chunk of the land north of Chicago. This huge effort created vast acres of forest preserves. The trail through the Lagoons rises enough to offer stunning views of the Chicago Botanical Garden, opened only relatively recently. Today I saw two small herds of deer. The expressway to the city is nearby, but the Lagoons still feel isolated.

I'm no pro at cross-country skiing, but I still love it. Nothing athletic I have ever done makes me feel so good so fast. After ten minutes of bending and pulling and gliding, I feel totally purged of anything that might have been bothering me. I have become less-than-expert but knowledgeable about all of the waxes (blue for normal, white for very cold, and clisters for melting snow). Like a true aficionado, last week I bought a blowtorch to remove the excess wax from the skis.

In the afternoon, I catch an empty bus to Evanston and take the local El to Howard Street, where I transfer to another El into the city. In the 1950s my friend Hugh and I would take the same El to Cubs games. After the game, we'd wait in back of Wrigley Field for the players to emerge from the locker room in their street clothes. Their hair was always wet and slicked down from their recent showers. Usually they would give us autographs. I first learned about Hack Wilson from a person standing next to me waiting for the Cubs to appear. He claimed to have been in the crowd the day that Hack jumped into the stands and beat up a guy who'd been yelling at him. ("He was hung-over, kid. That's why the guy was getting on his nerves.") Today I ride the El past Wrigley Field and all the way downtown to meet with some students from Columbia College, where I have been teaching part time since September.

Columbia College is a school of 7,000 students located in the South Loop. Anyone with a high school diploma or a GED can get in, but the school is by no means easy. Several departments have excellent reputations, especially the English department, which is run by a man named John Schultz. The department publishes many magazines. Last year, one magazine won a national contest. Columbia's writing program is interesting. Instead of writing papers about works of literature or explanations of contemporary issues, students in the introductory course work with basic writing forms, starting with "how-to" papers and moving on to narratives. For material the students reach into their memories and imaginations. Higher-level classes—and there are many—take the students into more sophisticated writing forms. It's creative writing, but a thoroughly structured program in which the desks in the classrooms must be arranged in a horseshoe shape. To prepare for the classes, I reviewed the basic forms and studied the literature that provides models for them. When I started here last fall, I had no idea what I was getting into.

I was supposed to have a conference with a group of students at school, but school is closed. We'll meet in the bar across the street. This is not far from the downtown intersections where the police ran amok in their clashes with the antiwar crowds at the 1968 Democratic Convention. It's a far cry from the Pub, the Varsity Bar, The Kollege Klub, Chesties, and the other giant beer bars I knew at the University of Wisconsin. Except for a few pathetic pennants hanging on the wall behind the bartender, this smoky little place doesn't look at all like a college bar. But that's what it is.

Sitting with me are four students from my first-semester class. On my right is Carlos, a Vietnam vet. He writes about the war, about living in Korea and about being gay. Next to him is Judy, who attended New Trier High School, where I also went to school in the 1950s. She enrolled at Columbia College after dropping out of the University of Illinois. Andre is beside her. He's a black kid from the far South Side. He likes to write about his family. In one of his most powerful stories, he described a family reunion near Jackson, Mississippi, where everything was going well until the family collie took bite out of a hornet's nest. Next to him is Colin. He attended several suburban public and Catholic schools. He flunked out of the University of Illinois, worked for a while at Arby's ("I still have the plastic gloves") and now is back in school. Last fall he wrote a paper describing how he and his suburban buddies used to sneak into private swimming pools. ("We'd park the car in some rich, quiet neighborhood. We'd take off all off our clothes and then climb over the fence and jump into swimming pool.") To the utter delight of the city kids, he read this "Pool Hopping" piece aloud to the class, adding all the irony it deserved. He knew perfectly well what the inner-city kids must have been thinking about his suburban "crime," and, as far as I could tell, they actually respected him for his self-deprecating sense of comedy.

I return papers. I answer questions. I tell the students about upcoming classes. It goes well. They know each other's writing, so I can refer to familiar pieces to make a point. Many of my remarks are of the "Now what?" variety. How are you going to improve this? What else could you do with this? What if you told this from a different point of view?

Later I try to convince Judy to major in writing. "You're good at this, and you obviously like it. Keep doing it. You're not going to find another program like this in the country." I remind her of how perceptively she writes about people, how well she adapts to the different forms and how enthusiastically she attacks the reading.

She knows I'm right, but she doesn't like the lock-step nature of the Columbia program. "It's like all of you guys are following a script." The others at the table feel the same way. They like the writing and the classes, but the program feels a little too controlled from the top. They wonder if this bothers me.

I give them the best answer I can. "Not yet. I'm learning to be a creative writing teacher, and this is a good place to start. So I'm not going anywhere."

Later I walk over to the offices of Athletes for a Better Education (AFBE), an organization founded by a former basketball player named Chick Sherrer and a priest named Stanrod Carmichael. The mission of AFBE is to help inner-city basketball players develop academic skills so that after they're through shooting hoops, they have something else to do with their lives.

"Use basketball," states one of the slogans. "Don't let it use you." Last year I wrote an article about the summer camp AFBE conducts at Lake Forest College. Since September I have been teaching study-skills classes for this group on Saturdays. I'm here tonight to pick up a paycheck and to sign a contract to teach at the camp this coming summer.

It's an office full of boxes. There are boxes of applications for various programs, boxes of basketballs, boxes of whistles for referees, boxes of clipboards, boxes of basketball magazines—one with a feature article entitled "Deny the Flash." There are boxes of basketball shoes and boxes of shirts—red ones and blue ones. The shirts have AFBE written across the front. The words straddle an image of a basketball sitting next to some books. Cards are pasted on the wall. Each card has the name of a local high school player who has yet to sign with a major university. Next month these players will take part in a special scrimmage for coaches of small colleges. This may be their last chance to get some kind of scholarship.

Sitting in the middle of all of this is Harry, who has worked for AFBE for several years. Along with helping out at AFBE, he's also a timer at games and helps referees find jobs. He is a stocky black man in his middle-thirties. He's a native of Chicago, but for some reason he speaks with a British accent. He asks me to fill out some forms. One form asks for my profession. I scribble down "Freelance teacher." Harry raises an eyebrow. "'Freelance teacher.' I didn't know such a job existed."

I assume this is a question. "I don't know what else to call myself." I tell him that, in the past few weeks, I have made some choices that will make going back to the old classroom practically impossible. Along with signing another contract with Columbia College and agreeing to work for AFBE, I called the editors of two magazines where I have sold articles and asked them to send me more assignments. I asked all of the local high schools to keep sending me their dropouts for my GED program. I renewed my office lease and sent out a schedule of SAT and ACT classes for the spring term. I made an informal agreement with a friend to work with me in the SAT and tutoring business. I called parents I have worked with to say they could count on my tutoring their sons and daughters next year. I filled out a form for a bulk-mailing permit. I made an appointment to set up a personal retirement fund.

Harry was not expecting such a big answer, but he listens patiently and actually seems interested. He's a bit of a freelancer himself.

On the train that night I think some more about why I like the idea of freelance teaching. For one thing, to my astonishment, I truly enjoy running my own business. This wasn't supposed to happen. Don't people go into teaching to avoid business? But oddly I like looking for customers, designing ads, making brochures, doing mailings, and even borrowing money. And, incredibly enough, my little business is doing quite well.

I like teaching creative writing at Columbia College, and I like helping city basketball players at AFBE. I like tutoring kids from the suburbs. But, most of all, I don't want to go back into the schools because I don't want to stop working with GED kids. More than 80 students have completed my class, and almost all have passed the test. Quite a few have started college. The majority of my GED students are recent high school dropouts, but I get calls from older people like Mary, a 65-year-old retiree from a candy factory who needs a GED to qualify for her pension, and Vince, a mechanic from Waukegan in his forties who brought his pet snake to our first class. I find the work exciting even though it appears to be anything but. These students have failed badly enough to leave school, or they gave up on school decades ago, but they have not dropped down so far that they don't want a GED.

I like helping the students understand exactly what they have to do, making them believe that they can do it, and keeping after them if they revert to their old habits. I like finding ways to smuggle creative writing into the mix—Columbia College is giving me plenty of new ideas. Most of all I like talking with these people because—with very few exceptions—they are great storytellers. They share stories about cops and fights and road trips. They boast and lie and gossip and rant. They describe their jobs in magnificent detail. I like to listen, and I like to ask a few questions to help them bring out even more of the stories. As I tell a skeptical Wally, my main job is to discover, identify, and bring out what my students already possess. Business as usual.

I enjoy the SAT classes almost as much. A few years ago I would have regarded test prep as a poor excuse for teaching—a kind of academic whoring. Now I see it as an extension of my regular teaching. It gives me a great opportunity to help kids develop their vocabularies, to improve their reading. It gives me a chance to show kids that they are capable of doing much better than they thought they could do. Creative writing and test prep make an odd couple, but I think they'll survive and maybe benefit from each other's differences.

And then there's writing. I left teaching, in part, to finish *Hack* and to try my hand at other freelance projects. Has it worked? In a way. I certainly know by now that I am not good enough to support myself as a writer. But I have been able to sell some articles. Much more importantly, I enjoy longer writing projects—especially the research. After I finish my article about the bike racer, I plan to do a piece about a wrestling match that took place in Chicago in 1911. I want to do something about a ball player who got kicked out of baseball in 1925. Writing gives me something to do besides teaching, but it also helps my teaching. And I'm beginning to see a connection between a writer's voice and a teacher's voice. Like writers, teachers need to find their true voice. If I find myself using a phony intellectual voice or a tough guy's voice or a bored voice or an overly interested voice, I am not going to be heard by my students.

If this freelance contraption I have built for myself falls apart, I'm confident I could go back to a school, which would be fine as well. I was always quite happy in the schools. I just don't think it will happen.

When I get off the train in Glencoe, it's snowing again.

ATHLETES FOR BETTER EDUCATION

Dan lowers his voice and hikes up the volume. "Bodacious." It carries into every corner of the serene dormitory lounge here at Lake Forest College. "This is the most bodacious thing I have ever heard. You have no idea how bodacious I consider this to be." All one hundred of us stare silently—the 90 high school basketball players sprawled out on the couches or the rug, and the coaches and teachers, like me, leaning against the back wall. Last night Dan smelled marijuana smoke on the second floor, and he's furious. "Whoever's smoking that stuff, whoever you are, you are risking the futures of everyone in this room." He is now standing in the middle of the players, almost all them black. His own black skin glistens with sweat. His eyes bulge. His nostrils flare. His biceps expand. He's waiting for a smirk. No one dares. "You guys make me sick," he says, and he stalks out through the door. Through the window I can see him slow down when he gets to the sidewalk and wave pleasantly to three preppy coeds who bounce by him.

Chick is next. He is a former teammate of Bill Bradley and now the head of Athletes for a Better Education, the group that sponsors this summer camp and my summer employer. "You guys are really something. Here we have a program that gives you counseling during the year. We help you find the right college. We offer this summer camp up here in Lake Forest where you can grow into student athletes. What do you do? Excuse my language, Miss Dee," he looks over at one of the female instructors. "You fuck up. That's what you do." He can't scream like Dan, but he's a 6-feet, 8-inch white wide body, and the kids are not smiling.

"Mr. Boone here," he shoots a thumb in my direction, "wrote an article about this camp last year. It made the cover of *The Reader*," he says, referring to Chicago's free alternative newspaper. "The article won an award. Mr. Boone wrote that we not only *say* that we SUCCESSFULLY combine sports and school; we DO it. Kids take advantage of their opportunities." Everyone is now looking at me. I feel skinny and white. "Mr. Boone," Chick addresses me, "what does this pot smoking say to you about these kids?"

Silence. Then in a thin voice I reply, "I guess it surprises me, Chick, and it disappoints me."

"You hear that, you scumbags? You've disappointed him. He's a teacher and a writer. He's a Ph.D. He gives his time to help you guys, and you've disappointed him. Look at all these coaches and teachers. They're from the finest schools in Chicago, and they're here to help you guys take advantage of your God-given talent. They want you to use basketball, not have it use you. Well, whoever was smoking that shit better have a long talk with himself and realize how close he came to really fucking up" (again he begs Miss Dee's pardon) "because, gentlemen, if any of our funders hear about this, they'll shut us down forever." He glares at us, and we all nod. "Now, it's 9 o'clock. You've had breakfast. You've got four hours of class, and then we'll have practice in the afternoon. Just like always. Let's kick ass."

The room is instantly transformed into a spectacular mixture of sounds. I can hear the word "bodacious" repeated over and over again, usually followed by a laugh. The kids are wearing blue basketball shirts with "AFBE" written across the front and the logo on the back. I follow them out the door and across the lawn to a nearby building. They wave and shout at the regular summer-school students who are sprawled on the grass. They know each other's names. "Go, Andre," a lounging student shouts. "I told you my name's Watusi," a player fires back. "Go,

Watusi." From what I can tell, no one at the college or in Lake Forest is alarmed by the influx of so many black kids from the inner city, though when I told people that the camp meets up here, the overwhelming response was, "Man, I bet those people will die when they see all those black kids walking down the street."

When I get to the classroom, Tommy, a point guard from Gage Park High School, is acting out his version of Dan's "bodacious" speech. The kids are loving it. Anthony, who has seen Dan in action before, tells us that he sometimes breaks up the word. "That dude'll say 'bo-fucking-dacious'."

When I go to the front and sit on a table, the kids take their seats and listen. This is schoolwork, but it's not school. They are expected to be here, but they will not graded. In my English class they are asked to write five papers. The first paper was a personal narrative. The textbook explains the papers clearly, often with examples from sports. I can add whatever I want to the explanation. I read the papers at night, write comments, and share the best papers with the class.

"Today," I begin, "you're going to write a 'How to' paper. In other words, you're going to tell someone how to do something that you know how to do. You are the teacher. You're giving orders. Any questions so far?"

I tell them to make sure the process has at least six steps. I tell them to use the 'you' voice. I suggest that they consider basketball: how to shoot a free throw, how to set a pick, how to box out. They could do another sport: how to lay down a bunt, how to block the plate, how to protect the passer. "Just make sure you have at least six steps. Make sure you let the reader know what the critical steps are." One boy asks if he can write "How to Become a Christian." Of course, I tell him. They ask a few more questions, and then they write.

I look back through the personal narratives I plan to return after the break. I select two to read to the class: "The Time I Fooled My Girlfriend" and "My Auntie's Funeral."

When the other teachers and coaches heard that I had taught in the suburbs, they smirked. "Get ready for the illiterates," was the general assumption. These people were wrong, at least about the kids in my class. They seem familiar with the forms. They pick good subjects. What they write is generally clear and correct. But when I tell this to the teachers, they act as if I don't really mean it. And when I tell these kids that they certainly write well enough to handle college assignments, they give me a "yeah, sure," nod.

In the article I wrote last year, I made the same observation: In spite of what people might think, these kids are not illiterate. Listen to them talk, I argue. Read what they have to say. No one quite believes me. The skeptics point to reading scores, or they repeat some apocryphal story they heard about some kid in some city school who can't even write his name. It seems as though everyone has a stake in believing that city kids are stupid. And by "city kids," they inevitably mean black kids who live in some archetypal ghetto or housing project. In my experience, the assumption is nonsense.

During the break, there's a fight. For the entire session the kids have been teasing a boy named Robert because on the basketball court he shouts "Wahoo" at every opportunity. When he brings the ball down, he urges himself on with "Wahoo." When he goes for a rebound, he shouts "Wahoo." When he makes a basket, he leaps in the air with his fist extended and shouts "Wahoo, Wahoo." It never seemed to bother him that the kids call him "Wahoo Man" and tease him relentlessly. But today, during the break, Jerome apparently got too close and too personal, and Wahoo Man took a wild swing connecting on the cheek of a boy standing nearby. It happened in the crowded hallway, so for a few seconds there was lots of shoving and shouting, but the kids pulled the combatants apart, and that was the end of the incident.

Later, back in the classroom, I explain the ACT test to the kids. Marc asks me if it's true that city kids are in the bottom one percent of all those who take the test.

"Why do you say that?" I ask.

"My teacher told us. It's in the newspaper."

I grab the chance to make a point. "Marc, at your school, the average ACT score is 16. Right?" He nods. "That means that the average student is in the 35th percentile. Out of one hundred, 35 are below and 65 are above. That's what it means. It's not great, but it's not the basement. Now, if they lined up all the school's scores, your school would be near the bottom. Ninety-nine percent of the schools have higher overall averages. But the individuals at your school are not in the bottom one percent." What I'm saying is important and true, but I can almost hear the eyes glazing over. Just like the coaches and the journalists, they will continue to think of themselves in the bottom one percent. I could point out that of all the students who are accepted into Harvard, someone is in the "bottom one percent," but they don't care about the nature of percentages. They buy the received wisdom about themselves.

That afternoon Marc and I drive eight miles to Glencoe, the town where I live and where he will spend the afternoon in the library. He's enrolled in a summer school class back in the city. To gain permission to attend the AFBE camp here in Lake Forest, he agreed to complete his summer school requirements on his own. These include a short term paper. Instead of playing ball this afternoon, he'll work at the Glencoe library to gather up sources for a paper on "The Trail of Tears."

Marc goes by the name "Mr. Magic." He misses girls. ("I'm sick of all these hard bodies.") He will not be a major college player, but the camp should help him gain a Division II scholarship. He's bright and friendly and intrigued by the Lake Forest mansions that we are passing. "You mean one family lives in these houses?" This has been a typical reaction. Instead of outrage at the lifestyle of Lake Forest, the kids are simply stupefied. They were aware of concentrated wealth; now they have seen it.

"Would you like to live in that place?" I slow down next to a three-story mansion with a monstrous lawn and a greenhouse. A landscaping crew of Mexican workers is mowing and digging and planting.

"I guess so. I don't know. What kind of house did you grow up in?" He's talking to me, but he's staring up at a turret at the top of the house.

"My parents have a big house, but not this big. I'll show it to you." He smiles and leans back.

Fifteen minutes later we are in the driveway of my parents' red brick Winnetka house. We walk out onto the lawn. "This is where my brother and I used to play catch. Our basset hound had a big fight over there. We used to have a basket on the garage, but it came down in a storm." I point to the garage. "We called that Boone Memorial Hall." Marc smiles. He's probably imagining a group of white suburban kids leaping around awkwardly.

"Are your parents still alive?" Marc is squinting up at the roof.

"Yes, they're in their seventies. I'd like you to meet them, but they're up in Michigan." We walk around to the back, and I point to a second-floor window. "In high school my sister used to sneak out of that window at night and go to parties. She kept the ladder hidden in the bushes."

In the car on the way to the library, Marc talks basketball. He knows the coaches have him pegged for a smaller school, but did they see him score twenty points the other night? Do they know he's made the honor role? He's expecting to have a great senior year and then who knows? Illinois? Indiana? DePaul? "I'm going to grow another two inches."

Later that night we are sitting on the porch of my own house in Glencoe. Marc is at a table with note cards and photocopied sheets stacked in front of him. He has what he needs to write the paper. I'm sure he's noticed that Sue and I live in a much smaller place than my parents do. He likes the garden in our backyard. He tells each of my kids that they'll have to watch him when he's a pro. He doesn't like Hack, our neurotic mutt who jumps all over him.

"Why did you name him 'Hack'?"

"He's named after Hack Wilson. A friend and I wrote a book about him. The book was published a few months ago." Ever since our book was finally published, Jerry and I have heard people say, "Gee, that must have been a great experience. It must really make you proud." But Marc doesn't say much.

"Maybe I'll write a book some time. You know what I'll call it?"

"You'll call it *Mr. Magic.*"

"That's right. Was it hard to write a book?"

"Not really. It felt good to find out I could do it. If I can do it, anyone can. Let's take look at your notes."

On the way back to Lake Forest, we talk more about basketball—not about big houses and not about Hack Wilson. He tells me again why the coaches would be crazy not to help him find a Division I school. "I'm the real thing. Mister Magic is here to stay."

Later that night, after we return to Lake Forest, I'm reading on my bed when there's a pounding on my door. It's Chick. He fills the doorway, the way he must have filled space when he set picks for Bill Bradley at Princeton. The basketball camp is conducted at a variety of suburban gyms, and apparently the bus forgot to take all of the kids back from one of the other gyms. A few kids are stranded and need a ride back to the dorm. Could I drive out and get them? I hop in my beat-up old brown Matador and drive west.

The gym is at the high school on the outside of town. It is surrounded by land—lots and lots of land. When I pull into the driveway, I notice three large black kids cowering by the door. They are actually holding on to one another. One is Wahoo Man.

"Mr. Boone!" he screams. "Man, I have never been so scared in my life. We came out and the bus had gone and it's so empty here. Man, was I scared."

They pile into the back of my car, and as we pull away, Robert rolls down the window and shouts, "Wahoo!" And then the others roll down their windows and shout, "Wahoo," and before long, I roll down my window and start shouting.

TUTORING WILLIAM

Into the office lumbers William—15 years old, 6 feet, 2 inches tall, well over 200 pounds. He's a giant and terrifically clumsy. A miracle of clumsiness. Last week he knocked over a bookshelf. Teachers call him rude, irresponsible, disorganized, unmotivated, and even dangerous. He is the male student every teacher dreads. I met him first when he was a 6th grader and needed help making up work. We hit it off, and he has been "coming to me" for the past four years. I help him prepare for tests, proofread his compositions. I often talk to teachers about his work, and because he attends Highland Park, I know most of his teachers.

When his mom made the long-term tutoring arrangements four years ago, she could not have been more candid. "You're much cheaper than a shrink. Plus he hates shrinks."

"You mean he likes me." We were standing on the sidewalk in front of my office. William was sitting in the car polishing off a cheeseburger and listening to Twisted Sister.

"He thinks you're funny."

"Funny? How?"

"In both ways. You make him laugh and you're a little odd. Anyway, we'd like William to see you every Thursday for help. If he needs more, schedule more tutoring. We trust your judgement."

"Even though I'm odd."

"Even though you're odd." She got in her car and drove off as William rolled down the window and threw out a yellow wrapper.

More and more I seem to be attracting students like William. People have often thought of me—not always correctly—as someone who can work with troublemakers. My night school work and my GED experience certainly helped build that reputation. Plus, anyone who tutors will end up with kids who for some reason or other are "not functioning within the system," as the overly polite saying goes. And I have not discouraged this impression. This extends into the SAT classes where my partner Jay and I have keep the fees low in order to encourage kids who normally would not bother to plan this hard for their futures.

I met Jay at Northwestern, where I supervised his student teaching. A few years later he joined the English department at Highland Park High School. Kids like him because he's smart, funny, and serious. I like him because he's smart, funny, and serious. He plans to stay teaching in the schools, but he likes the idea of working with kids on the outside. I have a feeling he'll be a great partner.

But lately kids like William have become the rule. One of my new students got caught dropping a fetal pig from a window on the fourth floor of his school. Another boy arrived covered with political buttons. His latest was, "The moral majority is neither." I had a boy who was covered with tattoos. How someone his age managed to acquire that many tattoos, I have no idea. Another boy talked to an invisible person. I continued to tutor kids who wanted individual instruction for the SAT and ACT exams, but the number of William-types is definitely on the rise.

They tend to be male, loud, disrespectful. They hate school, but they are not social outcasts. As Jay says, "They tend to be remembered." They are probably going to college, but not to Yale or Duke. They know all about what goes on at the wild weekend parties.

My job is to be there when they really screw up. I make sure they will somehow stagger out of high school. I want them to see what they have to do to be respectable students. I would like them to feel the pleasure of learning for its own sake. Maybe by college they will have matured enough to come out all right.

Today William's wearing a bright blue sweatshirt emblazoned with the slogan, "I only swear when it slips out." He's mad at his teachers. ("That bitch Johnson gave us a pop quiz.") He has some tests coming up. He shows me the math. His assignments are up to date. Currently the class is coming to the end of congruent triangles. He seems to know what he's doing, though his homework is full of scratched-out sections. I review some science terms with him. Then he shows me English. "That asshole O'Donnell wants us to write a description of a place. It's supposed to have a lot of tension."

"Like a bar right before a fight or a football game just before kickoff."

"Why don't you write it?" He's on his feet looking at a photograph on the wall of a one-room schoolhouse.

"No, you'll write it, but I want to try an experiment. I've been thinking of something for a few days, and you, Willie, will be the first to try it."

"What if I die trying?" He's back from the window sitting at the table. He eyes me suspiciously.

"We'll donate your body to the Hell's Angels. Here's some paper and a pen. I'm going to ask you questions. Answer them quickly, and then I'll give you time to put all these into a paragraph. Then you'll be done and indebted to me for the rest of your life. A new chapter will begin as you head down the road to stardom."

He reaches for a Clark Bar, and we begin the lesson. "I want you to imagine that you are walking across the barnyard of a farm. It's early in the morning."

"I've never been on a farm," he interrupts me. "I'm a Jewish boy from Highland Park. Remember?"

"It doesn't matter. Shut up and listen. You get to the barn and pull open the door a crack. Inside in the far corner you can see a cat that has cornered a mouse. It's a frozen moment. Now scribble down answers to these questions: How is the cat standing?"

William frowns, makes a spitting noise, but then bends over and writes. I try to peek but he covers up what he has written and waves a clenched fist at me. So I continue, and William follows along.

How is the mouse standing?
What do the cat's claws look like?
What about the mouse's tail?
What other sounds can you hear in the barn?
What thoughts are in the mouse's head?
What is the cat thinking?
What are the smells?
Where is the light coming from?
What about the shadows?

For each question he has written something. He looks pleased, but he still won't show me. "OK," I continue, "now your job is to tie all of these ideas together into a unified paragraph. Use the present tense. Try to build the suspense. You can add any other details you would like." With that, I go to my small office to make few calls and leave William alone to finish what he has started.

Sooner than I expected, he is pounding on my door. "Boone, get out here and earn your money. You got to read this masterpiece." He tries to make light of what has happened, but I can see he's pleased.

We return to the big room. He shows me where to sit, but he remains standing to read.

"One morning I walk over to this barn and go inside, and there's my cat Alex about to have breakfast with an adorable little mouse. She's in the corner with no place to go. Alex is crouched over. She has her back to the wall. His claws are sticking out and his eyes are bulging. She has a little tail that's all curled up. Alex is thinking to himself, 'Man, this is going to be a great meal.' The cat is thinking, 'Holy shit.' I can hear the noises in the barn of a horse moving around. The place smells of manure. The light from the door is shining all over the place. The cat's shadow is huge and must be really scary for the mouse. I like Alex, but I feel sorry for the little mouse so I make a noise and it runs off. Alex doesn't get a meal after all."

I applaud. He applauds. He reads it over again. We both applaud some more. "Do you realize, William," I finally say, "how good this is? You have put together an excellent piece of writing. This must make you feel good."

He's not going to admit to that, but he is smiling as he leaves and even picks up a book he knocks off the table in the waiting room.

That night I go home and make lists and lists and more lists. I have hit on something that really works. I found a way to lock kids into a moment and then to use their creativity to get out. I set the stage, but they make things happen. I come up with some other scenes:

a messy hotel room

a city street corner on a hot day

a country roadhouse

a packed stadium on the last day of the baseball season

I can see how this could be used to focus on a small action: *a bum picking up a cigarette butt.* I could see how this would work for developing a character. What does he have in his pocket? What is his favorite book? What does he dream of at night?"

This little strategy should take me a long way. It works for creative exercises like the cat and mouse, but I could use it to get kids started writing about anything. I ask the questions. They answer. They make their answers the meat of what they are writing. It keeps me in the process, but it takes me out. The challenge for me is to ask questions that maybe they

170

would not consider. These questions require the kids to move down to the level of detail. I feel armed and ready.

The next time I see William, he's mad at his counselor. "That motherfucker wants me to apologize to the librarian. Hey, fuck him! I wasn't the only one with a cigar!"

I ignore him. "I got a call from O'Donnell this week. He said you read the paper to the class and everyone liked it."

William is up at the window, scowling down at the cars, checking out the people waiting for trains, thinking about God knows what.

"They loved it, but he's still an asshole, and so are you." He comes back to his place and pulls out paper and gets ready for me to ask some more questions.

AVALON PARK

He's a chubby fellow, so it takes him a while to climb the tree and work his way out on the branch that overhangs the basketball court. He checks to see if his backwards-facing cap is still on. He spots me on the lawn and salutes. I can hear him panting. Then he grunts to a girl looking up at him from the ground. Like the other kids on this outdoor court, she is black and also wearing a cap facing backwards. They could be 8th graders. She flips him the basketball. He checks his balance again and squints at the bare basketball rim, which is hanging loosely from a rotting backboard. With a grunt, he pushed a two-handed shot toward the target. Bang. Flop. The ball careens away into some bushes. In the next second, he's on the ground. Had he made the shot, one of the others would have had to do the same thing. That's how to play "horse."

As I lie on the lawn behind Avalon Park on the south side of Chicago, I remember places where I've played horse. As a kid, I played with friends in our driveway in an area we called Boone Memorial Hall. At the University of Wisconsin, my friends and I competed for beers shooting a deflated ball at a basket nailed to a tree outside the fraternity house. In Staten Island, teachers played in the new gym with a glass backboard and a swish net. The very first time there, Martin beat me with a preposterous hook shot from center court. It was particularly galling because he had a cast on his leg. The basketball hoop in Germany was in the parking lot of the school next to the ranks of Mercedes buses. The pavement, like everything else in Frankfurt, was slippery from the incessant rain. Instead of "horse," we played "pferd" in Germany. At Northwestern we played in a parking lot near a building that was later blown up by protesters. Recently the venue has been a neighbor's back yard, which features a tree stump. One time—after several gin and tonics—I sank eight in a row from the stump and won $45. That earned me the title "Stump Guy."

These Avalon Park kids keep trying the classic horse shots—the bounce shot, the reverse over-the-head shot, the behind-the-backboard shot—and I can see that these kids are all quite flabby. I am not looking at a future Connie Hawkins or a Herman "Helicopter" Knowings, the New York schoolyard legend who was supposedly the greatest player ever. Except for the nod from the tree shooter, no one pays any attention to me, even though, as far as I can tell, I'm the only white person in the area. No one shouts, "Hey, honky, get your white ass and ugly socks out of here."

Actually, I am not far from one strand of my own roots. In 1903, my father's dad moved from Hillsdale, Michigan, to the south side of Chicago to play football for Coach Amos Alonzo Stagg on the powerhouse University of Chicago team that was known as the "Monsters of the Midway." My father was born and raised on the South Side. He lived near Bobby Franks, the boy who was murdered by Nathan Leopold and Richard Loeb. He played touch football in Washington Park. He went to high school in Hyde Park. He hit golf balls at Jackson Park, and he met my mother at the International House where she was living while a student at the University of Chicago. Avalon Park is old home for me, in a way.

I am looking at my notes. In a few minutes I'll be addressing a room full of basketball coaches whose teams will be playing all summer in a tournament here at Avalon Park. I want to convince these guys that it would be a great idea to add a creative writing component to this summer's basketball program. I have rehearsed the speech in the car, and I have looked at my notes here on the lawn, but my stomach is still jumping. I can picture myself stammering as fifty men scowl at me in unison. I believe the person who told me that speaking in public is man's most basic fear—even stronger than the fear of death.

We meet in the Social Room, between the Craft Room and Wood Shop. On the wall is a schedule of classes in sewing, square dancing, and bridge. Also displayed on the wall are pictures of elderly black couples getting on a bus. The men are in suits and ties. The women wear dresses and big hats and carry large purses. The caption reads "Off to the Race Track."

When the group is assembled, Forrest Harris, the director of the tournament, walks to the front of the room. He's a tall, light-skinned black man who starred at Phillips High School in the early 1950s and then went on to the University of New Mexico. He has worked with young people and athletes all of his adult life. He was the first black referee in the NBA. I met him the summer I taught English at the basketball camp in Lake Forest, and we have continued to work together in the city. Like all of the other coaches, he calls me "Doc."

"Doc here and I wanted to add something to this basketball tournament," he announces. "Instead of your guys just coming here and playing basketball twice a week and reviewing rules of grammar, they'll do some school work just like they used to when we held this thing in Lake Forest. Doc wants your players to write creative papers. He'll read them and evaluate them. He'll have other teachers help him. Your guys can use these in school. We'll have some kind of magazine. Anyway, Doc will explain more, and then you can ask questions. After that we'll go over the schedule of games."

I move to the front, and Forrest walks to the back and sits with the coaches. I have known many of them quite well. I have played golf with two of them and eaten lunch with several others. But now, as I fiddle with my notes, I look out and see only what they have in common: large forearms, thick necks, short hair. They all are chewing gum and grasping clipboards. They squint and frown. They know me from various basketball camps. I'm the guy who's written some sports articles. I'm the guy with the terrible jump shot. I overheard one coach say that I was a "teacher sort of person."

"My attitude about your players," I begin, "is very much like your attitude. You believe they can be better basketball players. I believe they can be better writers. You want them to learn by playing. I want them to learn to write by writing. What's holding them back is thinking they can't do it. They get this idea from the newspapers and maybe from their teachers. I want them to find out for themselves what they can do."

A coach from a small Catholic school raises his hand. "Doc, this isn't a new idea, is it?"

"An old idea. Look, people like me have been around for a long time. Sometimes there might be too many of us, but I think now what the kids here need is a chance to show what they have in them. And I believe they have a lot in them. It's that simple."

I'm speaking faster than I should, but the words are coming out right, and no one's leaving. "Your students will write one paper each week of this summer tournament. The papers are what real writers produce. Descriptions, stories, arguments, profiles. No exercises. I want these kids to feel that what they're writing has a place in their world. At the end of the time, we'll put together a magazine." I go on to describe each assignment in more detail. I tell them that my experience at the basketball camps has convinced me that these young people know how to express themselves, and they want to express themselves.

No snores. No guffaws. No raised eyebrows.

Many nod encouragingly. Leo, the Harlan High School coach, tells me he's a social studies teacher and would be glad to help out. "My kids will write." Floyd wants to know if these papers can count for credit immediately. I tell him not exactly, but maybe the kids can use them next year. I'll be glad to talk with the teachers at their schools.

"Do you care what they write about?" Leo is talking again. "Can they pick any subjects they want?" Others nod.

"Of course, I naturally expect them to write about basketball and sports. They'll write about their lives. They can write what they know and what they imagine. That's the idea."

"You might get some strong stuff," Leo says.

"I hope so. I want the kids to feel they can write what they want. But," and I pause because I want to make sure the next point is clear, "I'm not here to look into their lives."

"You're not some white guy from the suburbs who finds all of this titillating." Leo's smiling broadly, but he has his head tipped in a way to tell me he wants an answer.

"I hope I'm not that kind of guy."

I pass out the schedule of assignments. The kids will turn in papers on the days that they have games. "Should I make them do it?" one coach asks. "I can just say: If you don't write, you can't play."

This is, of course, the big question. "I'd prefer that you keep reminding them, but that you don't make them write. I want this finally to be their choice. If we can get them to see what this all means, they're going to do it." A coach from a far South Side school is smiling skeptically. I look right at him. "Tell them it will make them better people." A pause and a few guffaws.

"Even better people," Leo calls out.

"Yes," I say. "It will make them even better people."

They agree to do it. They'll encourage the kids. They'll show them the assignments. These are competitive guys. No one wants his school to be the one that didn't do it. And they are teachers. They believe in what we are all doing.

Instead of heading directly back to the highway, I drive east all the way to Jeffrey Boulevard and then head north. I pass the Bryn Mawr School. The fence around the school was my grandmother's idea. In 1919, one of my father's friends chased a ball out onto Jeffrey and was hit by a car. My grandmother led the crusade to get a fence around the playground. I turn east again and drive a few blocks to Paxton and then drive south and pass the little house where my dad grew up. The kids sitting on the stoop stare curiously at me, probably wondering what the white guy in the station wagon is doing in their neighborhood.

I feel great driving home. It looks like I'll have good support for this program. But I also feel nervous, for the obvious reason that the idea may fail. Flat-out fail. I recall the play I tried so incompetently to direct back in Staten Island. Maybe no one will write. Maybe the coaches, who seemed so interested today, will forget about this. After all, they are coaches. And if one team forgets about it, the rest will forget about it. My arguments make enough sense for the people to nod. But will they work? I will make the schedule clear. The kids will know what each assignment is. They will know when it's due and when it will be returned to them. I'll have phone numbers and extra conference times. But what if they just don't do it? Would I have done it in high school? In the summer?

I drive past Comiskey Park just as the fireworks are erupting. Someone has hit a homer. The Cubs, who last year won the division, are off in Cincinnati disgracing themselves.

Ten days later, the card table is as shaky as my confidence. "I hope it doesn't collapse under the weight of all the papers," laughs John, who is sitting with me in the Avalon Park lobby outside the gym. John, a youth worker and teacher, has been my friend for several years. I was delighted when he offered to help. He likes being around kids. He recognizes good writing. He loves basketball. "You just want me here," he said last week, "so if no one turns in anything, you can say it was the black guy's fault."

I have been here for hours. I bought two tangerines from the Muslim lady who has a food trailer in front of the park. I took a walk. I talked to several cops who stopped by. They welcomed me and said they would be following the progress of the program. One of them played basketball at Hirsch High School. The other had read Joseph Wambaugh. The director of the park is a lady who knows what she wants. She has several assistants, including the pool supervisor. She introduced me to the others as a member of her "team."

I've never been in a situation where so much rides on one thing. If the kids start turning in papers, it's working. If they don't, it's failing. We'll still have time to keep asking, but I know this first submission is key. I have called the coaches and their assistants and even some of the kids. Do you remember the assignments? Do you understand what I mean by a personal narrative? Do you see why that piece by Richard Wright is a good example? I have hung around the park to talk to them afterwards. I wonder why the fear of failure is so much greater in this situation than in other episodes in my teaching career?

Several vans pull up in the circle driveway in front of the park. These will be the players from Chicago Vocational and Dunbar. Players jump out, and soon the lobby is full of shouting kids. Many are dressed to play. Others carry bags.

No papers are in sight.

The first player to pass by me is David Gordon,

a junior at Vocational. He's wearing a blue sweat suit. In the last week he has talked to me several times about the papers. "Anything for me?" I ask weakly as he reaches the table. "What? What? What are you talking about, Mr. Boone?" But he's holding back a smile, and he has actually stopped, as have all the players behind him. "Papers, my man. True stories. Your assignments." John is raising his voice. "And remove your hat, please." An oversized youth in the back takes off his baseball cap and nods an apology.

I sit stupidly looking up at these young giants. I have a bad taste in my mouth, the acrid taste of failure. Then like a conjurer, David reaches into his gym bag, gropes around for a second, feigns a look of panic, and pulls out a paper—a typed paper! "My, my! Look what I have found." With both hands he gently places it in the box in front of me. I have labeled the box, "Assignment #1 - True Story." Then the other players do the same. To my delight, the box is soon overflowing. John is on his feet slapping their hands and laughing in a way I have never heard him laugh before. Then off they start for the locker room.

"Wait." I'm standing up. "Stay here for a second." I don't always have a good sense of occasion, but this time I feel we must do something. "David, you're the first. I'd like you to read your paper aloud. This will give us all something to remember."

He holds out his hands and shakes his head, but I'm determined to have him read, and he does. By now others have arrived. Several college scouts carrying clipboards lean against the side wall next to two referees already wearing their zebra shirts. The park people have come out from the back office. Forrest is standing in the back with some of the other coaches. The two cops have reappeared. David puts down his sports bag and moves to the center. He dramatizes an oversized bow, grins and starts to read.

179

"I went through an experience that I thought I would never get over. It was about two years ago, when I found out that my mother and father were being divorced. It was a hard thing to go through for me. When I noticed what was happening it was May 18, on my father's birthday. Everyone was in the front room (living room) presenting to my father his birthday presents. I gave him a gold watch. My sister gave him a pair of dress shoes, and then my mother served him with papers to appear in court.

"After then, things were never the same. They were arguing a lot, and even minor fights flared up. The part that really bothered me was when my sister and I had to choose who we were going to stay with. I never heard the words 'I love you' said so much until that time came up. I remember one night when my father was telling me and my sister what to expect. My mother walked in the door and swore that my father was trying to turn us against her. That started yet another argument to deal with. I was very close with my father. When I found out that the judge told my father he would have to be out of the house by November, I felt real bad about it. I cried, I could not eat, sleep, or enjoy myself. When I had to decide who I wanted to stay with, I thought a lot about it and chose to stay with my father. My sister wanted to stay with my mother.

"The next day I was leaving with my father, and my mother was going completely nuts. She did not want me to leave because I am the youngest. She would yell and pout about it. After the family was split up, the house was to be sold. That night I was sitting in my grandmother's kitchen (my new place of residence) doing my homework. I was thinking that it would not be right for me to grow up not really knowing my sister. I got up from the table and walked into my uncle's room where my father and Grandmother were talking. I told them what I was thinking about, and they told me they were talking about the same thing. The same night we decided I should go back home.

"When we arrived there, I had a very cold feeling inside of me. We all talked again, and after a while my father had to leave. I hated to see him go. But I was thinking, 'It must have been a long ride back to my grandmother's house.' One of the choices the judge said was 'if both of the children chose the mother or father, that person would keep the house.' I just thought all night about how my father felt going on his way back to his new house."

Pause, then applause. Real applause. David hurries off and probably doesn't hear what John and I have to say. "Not bad," one of the cops says before he leaves to make another ride through the neighborhood.

After the game I talk with David outside in front of the park building. The steps are filled with fans. We walk over near the trailer where the Muslim lady sold me the tangerines. I tell him that, for me, his story worked exceptionally well. The subject was powerful. He wrote in a clear and honest voice. The opening paragraph with its description of the birthday party worked superbly. "It was just so sad and funny that you had your mother serve papers to your dad on his birthday." The last part showed how much he understood the situation. "You really showed how much you cared for your dad, and you decided this was important to put into the story." David tells me he wants to be a journalist. We shake hands and he leaves. I look to my left, and there's John talking to David's coach. They are both laughing.

Two days later, more papers arrive. John

especially likes one from Vincell, which tells of a time on a farm in the South when he decided to "borrow" a baby chick from its mother.

"As I glanced over my shoulder, the mother hen was gaining ground fast. And even though I had been running forever, I still had ninety yards to run, and all this time my mother was standing at the door yelling at me to drop the chick, but I ignored her until the mother hen was too close and looked as though she was about to attack. I dropped the chick. The mother hen ceased her chase and I made it safely to my mother who was waiting patiently at the door with a hug and a smile, and that was the last day I bothered chickens."

Vincell leaves right after his game so we don't have a chance to talk to him. But I write a note telling him how expertly he had described the action. "We were right there with you." I liked the ending, which pulled it together. It worked so well too because his mom was right there watching. "This is really a story about two mothers isn't it?"

This is truly teaching from a distance. I have set up the system, which seems to be working because the players are turning out strong stuff. But I am not "teaching" in the traditional sense. On the contrary, I assume they have already learned how to write correctly. I assume they know what I mean when I ask them to write a personal narrative or a description or a profile. I assume that they will find our comments useful. I would like to assume that when the summer ends, they will keep on writing.

The coaches and other adults are impressed by how clear and correct the writing is. More important, the writing is fun to read. It is not unusual to look up and spot some oversized coach leaning against the wall with his nose buried in a paper.

Several tell me that this proves that kids like to have their stuff read and responded to right away. They like writing papers that are likely to be published. They like the fact that this isn't school. One day Forrest told me that he saw the kids writing in the park.

I wonder sometimes if the atmosphere of basketball encourages writing. The game seems to invite language. On the front steps after these summer games, the fans tell stories about someone's buzzer-beating jumper from the corner or in-your-face stuff. Instead of saying that someone got in the way of a player cutting to the basket, they say, "He denied the flash." Doug Bruno, a local coach, told me a wonderful story in astonishing detail, about a state tournament game in which the star player for each team scored fifty points. "They shot and shot and shot and never missed. One fan had a stroke. There's a picture of him being carried out." One of the players became an All-American in college and later played in the pros. The other player is a referee at Avalon Park.

By the third week, we have already collected more than one hundred papers. Several teachers and friends are writing responses. The players read our comments carefully, and some have written extra assignments. Some have telephoned me at home with questions. A teacher from one of the schools sent me a note. She wants to know what's going on at Avalon Park. The coaches continue to stop by the table, to ask about particular kids, to wonder if maybe the players could submit these papers to their teachers.

The next week, we receive descriptions. These are shorter but just as readable. Almost all of the descriptions begin with a clear statement.

"My front room has a special comfort to it."

"My grandmother's house has a special image of paradise."

"Home is where the heart is. Well, that's where my heart is going to stay."

"The kitchen holds the key to all my free time."

"My room at home reflects my personality."

"My favorite place is in the back room of my basement, for it gives me great privacy. It's a place all to my own."

Some are highly detailed, like Tony's description of the family bathroom: "The washroom on the upper floor of my family's house shows you just how artistic my mother is. When you open the door, you are immediately blinded by the luminous pink walls and silver wallpapering. In the corner sits a blue-green commode with a bright pink seat cover. The floor is covered with a pink carpet, and the distant odor of perfume is in the air."

Some, like Darryl, try extra hard to communicate the feeling they experience from a certain place: "There peace is found. One day when I was at the park the kids were playing and all good things were being done. At that moment I found out what makes that park a special place. There was no need, no need for a car or anything of value. There is only one thing that could cause trouble: PEOPLE."

Dwayne describes his neighborhood in a piece called "Being Afraid." "Sometimes I walk down the street knowing that I could catch someone's bullet. It's a problem at night but also in the day. This type of scariness runs in a circle. It never begins and never ends. It's just something that's there. You can almost say it was put there. It continues over a period of time. It's always there."

The next week they produce profiles of people. George begins with physical features of the person: "My new neighbor was five feet four and had long straight black hair. Her fingernails were as long as an eagle's claws. The sight of her frightened me so much I closed the curtains."

Keith writes about his grandmother, but he also writes about himself: "She be tired when she get home from work. I go over to the house on weekdays and clean up for her. All of her children are grown and there is no one there to help her. She usually be happy when I'm there to give her a hand. "I will never turn my back on someone who raise me. She raised her children all by herself. Sometimes I try to cheer her up by bringing her flowers. I feel that I owe her and my mother something. I love them both and will do anything for them. I wish people would start helping each other."

It's late July, and I'm sitting on the stairs in front of Avalon Park talking to a reporter from *The Chicago Sun-Times*. He's impressed that the kids write about so many things that have nothing to do with basketball. His favorite is a story about a family picnic in Mississippi in which a dog is attacked by bees. He has interviewed several kids. Now, he wants a few final quotes. He seems like a good guy. He's an old Southsider whose brother coaches. "Have you been surprised?" he wants to know.

"Not really. I have worked with the kids at basketball camp. Many of my students at other schools, who weren't supposed to be good writers, could write if I gave them a chance."

"What's that mean?" He's scribbling on his pad.

I explain that I ask for real writing, the kind they find in magazines and newspapers. I don't want to do exercises. "I also give them choices. I might assign a profile or a true story, but after that it's up to them. And I show them some good writing. They read Wright, Orwell, Plimpton, Ellison, and lots of others."

It's the last day. I have made up "Certificates of Achievement" for all the participants, their coaches, and the people who work in the park. The only papers turned in that day are a few more of the "How to" assignments from the week before. Terry gives me a long piece titled "How I Became Athletically Inclined." Alonzo writes about running a fast break, Andre about shooting a free throw, Nick about fixing a flat tire, and Kelvin about taking the "El." Danny's paper is called

"Eight Steps to Making Yourself a Person." (Number 8: "Take chances. Always try to do something which will not hurt you mentally, physically or emotionally.") Jerry calls his paper "The Process of Clean White Teeth and Fresh Breath." ("...now after making sure your gums are clean, you have to brush your tongue.")

In the fall, fifty of us are at the Press Club in Chicago to announce the publication of the magazine we put together collecting the writing from the summer Avalon Park program. The room is comfortably filled with teachers, coaches, parents, and players. Each carries a copy of the magazine, which has a basketball shoe filled with pencils on the cover. Forrest Harris starts it off: "Welcome coaches, parents, friends and players, and authors. We want you to be here for the release of our publication, *Hardwood.*"

Now it's my turn. I thank coaches, park people, friends, Forrest Harris, John Zeigler. I especially thank the kids for proving that they could do something like this. But I don't want to act astounded. I want them to think that they could always do it, that I believed they could do it. Three players read their pieces from the magazine.

Leverne describes almost drowning: "When I finally came to myself, the ambulance was there and someone was pumping water out of me. People were standing around. My father rushed over and then took me home and lectured me for about three hours."

Willie describes getting mugged: "He went into my coat pocket and took out forty dollars. He took a piece of rope and tied my hands together and then he tied my hands and feet together. Then he told me to roll on my stomach and not move. I was sure the man with the gun was going to shoot me, but the only thing I heard was footsteps running away."

Jerry tells about winning a race: "I went over to Steve, who placed second, and congratulated him on a great race. This is the truth—before I walked away, he said 'Jerry, next year that number one trophy is mine.' We smiled and walked away. Until we meet again, Steve."

I sit down afterward with a *Chicago Tribune* reporter who is writing a long feature about this summer program. He asks if the kids wrote a lot about gangs and violence. Yes and no, I tell him. I tell him there were many like the mugging paper. "But they write about lots of things. City kids have lots to say that isn't just about the city."

One parent stays behind to meet with me afterwards. Her son had written the paper about getting chased by the mother chicken. "You know," she says, "Vincell spent a lot of time on those papers. He didn't mind us knowing he liked doing that. One night he asked me to help him remember some of those things he wrote about. That made me feel good. How does it make you feel?"

"How do you think?" I smile.

That day I drive to see Wally, my advisor from Northwestern. He's retired now and even grumpier, but he has liked what he's heard about this program. We sit in his apartment in Evanston. Next to him is a pile of mystery novels. He looks old and frail. We look at some of the stories in *Hardwood*. I tell him once again how we set up the program. He grumbles because it's too structured for his tastes, but he can't keep back a small smile and a nod.

"Don't forget," I tell him, "you have a lot to do with this. You filled my head with all this creative nonsense."

"Simple stuff, isn't it?"

"Maybe that's why people don't do it enough." I disappear into the kitchen to make him a martini as he struggles to hold back the gloat.

Chicago, Illinois, Winter 1988

SCHOOL STREAKER

It's 7:00 AM, and I'm climbing the stairs of a high school on the South Side. To the right, traffic speeds along a major boulevard. Beyond the traffic hover public-housing apartments. This is a neighborhood as gritty and unforgiving as the bitter January wind. Crowded inside the door of the school will be my ACT students, waiting for me to lead them past the security guard and into the building. But today when I reach the top of the stairs, no kids are waiting. Instead, the doors are wide open. Small groups of students stand whispering in the rotunda. I hear a few giggles, but not many. Off to the side three janitors stand facing down the middle of the hallway. I have never seen them together before. Two secretaries huddle by the door of the front office. One is wiping tears from her face. Near them two uniformed police officers are talking with the principal. He is frowning and shaking his head.

I ask a girl standing nearby what has happened. She tells me that a homeless man had been living in the basement of the school. Early this morning he took off all of his clothes, came upstairs, and ran around the building shouting for God to punish all the sinners. A teacher on her way back from the ladies' room had seen him and called the police.

Just as the student finishes telling me about the naked man, I look down the hall and see a large, red-faced Chicago cop striding toward me. Walking with him is a young black female police officer. She is clutching the arm of an older black man walking between them. The man is wearing a long blue topcoat and no shoes. The coat is buttoned to the neck. The sleeves are too short. The man, who has a scraggly beard and gray hair, is looking down at his

188

bare feet and moving his lips. The lady cop is smiling up at him and talking. When they pass by me, I can hear her voice. "It's all right, William. It's all right. You'll be safe now."

The three of them walk out the door, down the stairs, and to the back seat of a police car that has pulled up on the lawn. The lady officer gets in last and straightens William's collar before pulling the door closed.

FROM SOUP TO COPS

It's gray and cold outside. I am drinking a cup of coffee and looking out of the window of a soup kitchen on Paulina Street one block south of Howard Street. I am waiting for my students to arrive. This is as far north as one can be and still be in the city of Chicago. Across the street people are lined up in front of the Howard Area Community Center. Inside they can get medical advice, information about jobs, day care, and GED instruction. They can also find a warm place to sit and chat. There are young African-American mothers, American Indians, blacks from the Caribbean, Hispanics, and old Russian Jews. For lunch, many will come across the street to the soup kitchen.

The local elementary school is so crowded that kids are released for three-week interim periods to make room for other students. During these periodic breaks, the students take classes, such as the creative writing class I am teaching here at the soup kitchen. If they don't take my class, they can take dance at a local studio, photography at a church, acting at a nearby theater, art at the park district facility, or cosmetology from the Pivot Point School of Cosmetology down the street.

The soup kitchen is dark. A lady who works in the back and who keeps my coffee mug full tells me that "dark is better. It don't look so nice all lighted up." A few weeks ago I was sitting in the back with the staff when a desperately glaring man in a torn red shirt and sweat pants strode into the soup kitchen. His arm was bleeding, and a giant scab covered his forehead. He hurried to the back, grabbed a tray full of sandwiches and headed out. We stayed where we were. Finally, one of the staff called out halfheartedly, "Hey, what are you doing?" but the guy just walked on out. "That'll teach us to leave the food out too early," one of the ladies commented as she got up to make more sandwiches.

I get ready for class today by putting materials on the first table the kids pass on their way into the large room. The younger ones will grab large sheets and crayons; the older ones will take a legal pad and a pen. They're supposed to pick up a copy of a story written by a girl named Lauralee. It's about a trip she took last year, back to the town where she was born in Belize. The highlight for her was when the car broke down and she had to sleep outside "right near a jungle."

Before I started these classes, I was told all the kids would be junior high school age, but I later learned that the group would include 1st and 2nd graders. So I was forced to come up with new strategies. Sometimes they all do the same things: make up riddles, respond to music. Sometimes the older kids work with the younger kids. Sometimes they work on something separate. Once I have them sitting down and spread out, they almost always write the entire time. ("On task," as we teachers call it.) Except for being too dark, the space is perfect for a writing class. The kids can write and draw. I have room to move around and see how they are doing.

Today is the final class for this group. They'll write for the first hour and have a party the second hour. We start with riddles. A 6th grader named Tasha stands up and reads while all the others try to guess what she is describing. Even the people who work for the soup kitchen slide their chairs closer to hear Tasha, who stands behind a rusty music stand. "I can be bent," she begins in a loud voice with an accent I cannot quite identify. "I can also be used as a tooth pick or a back-scratcher for a gerbil. Without me things can come apart. But I can be dangerous; I can put out your eye. You don't want to sit on me. I come in many sizes and shapes. I can even be colored plastic. When people need me, they need me badly, and they get mad if they can't find me." The kids all shout out answers, many of which, like "gorilla," don't make any sense at all. Finally Beth Anne shouts "paper clip." Tasha nods, and we all applaud. I remind Tasha that this little riddle can become a poem. Tasha is followed by one of the little girls who does "cloud" ("I carry rain.") and an 8th grader named Frances who is a bomb. ("You'd better not touch me.") I then ask Lauralee to read her Belize story. After that I pass back notebooks with their writings. A 7th grader named Patrice has written so much that she gets two folders. "Please," I tell them, "give these to your teachers. They will be impressed."

All of the kids are black. Some are from Jamaica or, like Lauralee, from Belize. Almost all live with a single mother who is on welfare. Some have to walk here by roundabout routes because of the gangs in the neighborhood. Two little girls go to the Bahai Church and happen to know our next-door neighbor in Glencoe.

In an hour my daughter Fanny arrives accompanied by Griffin, her black Labrador retriever. She is now married and working part-time with me for the Glencoe Study Center. Fanny is loaded down with pizza, cokes and cupcakes. Even though the class meets in the soup kitchen, we have to supply our own food. Some people from the school come over with the director of the Interim Program. There is also a journalist and a photographer. I have brought along samples of writing and drawing, and the kids hold up what they have made. A 5th grader named Tyrone reads his story, which is called "Calvin the Loser." It's about a little boy who loses everything he owns until he gets a dog named Michael Jordan who helps him find things. He has little drawings that go along with the story.

The reporter asks me how the class has gone.

I tell her that it started slowly because I didn't know what to do with the little kids. But now that I've come up with things they can all do, it's gone well. "I look forward to the class." The reporter used to be a teacher. She can understand how this has all the "good stuff" about teaching without the hassles of meetings and paper grading. The photographer takes a group shot of the kids and me and the cooking staff, who are getting edgy because they have to get the place ready for the crowd of people already lining up outside.

I call the kids together at the end. "We'll see each other again," I say. "Keep writing. Maybe we can make a magazine out of this later on." I give each one of them a pen and a notebook. "Don't forget that what you can remember and what you can imagine is important. Write it down because you never know what might happen to it."

My next stop is a formidable stone mansion near the lake on the Northwestern University campus. This was obviously built to be some rich person's home before it was taken over by the university. Now it is the home of the Traffic Institute where I teach a class to police officers. I started the class a month ago at the request of the Traffic Institute's director, who was looking for someone to teach a six-week writing class to officers involved in a nine-month graduate course that will give them an advanced degree in Police Science. Most come from Chicago, while others come from the East Coast, California, and even as far away as Australia.

"Part of what they need," the director had told me, "is to learn how to write a staff report." This report includes the definition of a problem, a summary of possible solutions to the problem, and a description of the best solution. "But what they really need," he went on, "is just to practice writing. Too much of what they write is just jargon. They need to learn to sound like people." He had heard about the program I had used at Avalon Park and wanted me to do the same thing with his cops.

We meet in a classroom in an annex behind the mansion. The officers sit at long tables. They always sit in the same seats. They do not slouch. They are never absent. They listen carefully and do exactly what I ask them to do. They are smart and insightful. From what I can tell so far, they have enjoyed writing descriptions, personal narratives and profiles. They seem to be taking pleasure in their break from police work. Many have their families with them. When they're not studying, they're doing something together. Last month Sue and I went to a Halloween party hosted by one of the officers from the city.

Today is the last day for the cops, just as it was for the soup kitchen kids. I begin by returning the final staff reports. I have included lots of comments, but I talk about a few. One paper raised the question, "Should officers be allowed to carry three-foot long flashlights?"

Today the class will be devoted to sharing. I've asked them to bring in some of their favorite pieces to read aloud on our last day. We begin with some of the descriptions. Bob reads his piece about the Chicago Housing Authority elevators: "Your initial reaction is to ride the elevator without actually having to stand on the floor." Roy's tries to capture Newark: "No shore. No mountains. No verdant environment—just noise, temperature, and black sticky asphalt. Blah!" The other descriptions range from ordinary classrooms to miners' shacks.

I then switch to true stories. Homer reads his piece about discovering a corpse in the water: "He entered the world in the fetal position and left in the fetal position." David tells of finding his first body. The older cops knew where it was, but he, as part of his rite of passage, had to find it himself. The veterans "gleefully explained that the smell of a dead body sticks to your clothes for several days." Robert reads his account of explaining to some kids that their parents had been murdered. Dianne tells of a watching a woman who had just killed her husband "calmly preparing for her small children to be taken in by relatives... she failed to blink an eye even when she learned she had taken the life of someone she loved enough to marry." Others read about non-police events—the birth of a child, playing in the Ohio State band, fishing in Wisconsin. Alan shares his piece about going back to the house of his recently deceased grandfather, who had also been a police officer. The room had "the stale odor of cigar smoke." There was an "old hickory billy club with a rawhide strap strung through the ribbed end."

With fifteen minutes to go, we play the block game. I had used this as an icebreaker the first week, but I return to it because the students like it so much. I have used this activity dozens—maybe hundreds—of times since I started it with my first communications class. Beyond question, these cops are the best at precise communication.

Finally I give them a journal for their writing. I tell them that this has been one of the most gratifying teaching experiences of my life. The class president, the officer from Australia, stands up and "on behalf of the others" thanks me and then gives me a gift certificate for an Evanston restaurant.

As I am putting on my coat, I tell them again how much I admire their work. "You have a great sense of subject. You always follow some kind of a plan. You have vivid imaginations. And you have a great sense of detail. You're all very observant. But I guess cops are supposed to be observant."

"That's why we're here," says Homer. "And not in the ground."

On the way home I detour away from the campus to see Wally, who is now living in a retirement home in south Evanston. He's reading a John Dickson

Carr mystery novel when I walk in. After complaining about all the old people ("This one old gal is driving me crazy!"), he listens to me talk about the soup kitchen kids and the cops. He gives me a "see, what did I tell you?" look.

He enjoys hearing about my classes, but he has something else he wants to talk about. What really puzzles him is how my business partner, Jay, and I can teach creative writing and then turn around and teach SAT classes. I've been waiting for this. I've known for a long time that he cannot fathom how or why two Ph.D.s from Northwestern would end up competing with Stanley Kaplan.

I look over at an old lady in a pink bathrobe standing by the door. Wally waves her off. "Jay and I talk about this a lot." I try not to sound defensive. "Students seem to enjoy these classes, and I think I know why. We teach the same way as we teach anywhere else."

Wally grunts, raises his eyebrows and delivers one of his classic smirks.

"You won't really believe me," I plow on, "but think about it. We assume the kids can do the work; we build the class around discovery exercises; we emphasize that what they learn has value beyond the classroom. And we try to make it fun."

"Fun!"

"Sort of fun. You know what I mean. The kids aren't being graded. They come from all these different high schools. They are all together learning something they have decided is important."

"Fun?"

"Funnish."

"And then there's the money."

"Yes the money. There's that too."

UMBRELLAS OF CABRINI

Until recently, I always skirted Cabrini Green. In the 1950s my high school friends and I passed by the complex of low-income housing towers on our way from the suburbs to the Red Star Inn, only a few blocks away from the projects. Wearing sport coats and neckties, we'd climb the creaky wooden stairs and find ourselves inside a huge dining room with chandeliers. We'd sit at giant round tables and be served apple pancakes and dark beer by silver-haired German waiters in shiny black tuxedos. If the Black Hawks were playing hockey on one of those nights, we'd drive back past Cabrini on the way to the Chicago Stadium to watch Bobby Hull and Stan Mikita.

Later, in college in the early 1960s, we'd pass Cabrini on our way to the Old Town Pub, where we'd argue about Sartre and Camus. I was out of the city for most of the '60s, but soon after I returned in 1969, I drove down to a studio near Cabrini Green to watch Abby Hoffman and his Conspiracy Seven buddies rehearse a film produced by a friend of mine.

In the 1970s I taught in Chicago's northern suburbs and had no reason to go to Cabrini or, for that matter, any other city neighborhood. In the 1980s I began to teach in the city—little kids on the South Side, basketball players on the west side and teachers in Rogers Park—but never anyone in Cabrini Green. While I drove by occasionally, I never went in. The projects remained for me what they were for most people in Chicago, black or white—places you didn't want to be. Other projects administered by the Chicago Housing Authority were bigger and more dangerous, but Cabrini Green came to symbolize urban danger probably because it is so close to downtown and because it is so densely concentrated. The fact that a Chicago police officer was assassinated by rifle shots from one of the towers may have had something to do with it. To the city's journalists, it was a "War Zone." I played golf one time with an elevator repairman who had worked at Cabrini Green. He said he was known as the "Vator Man" and was treated very well there, but he would never forget the urine stink of the elevators and the dark halls. Once, a dog attacked him. Another time he interrupted a drug deal.

Then last summer I started to teach classes in Cabrini Green, and that's where I'm going tonight. I drive past clusters of men openly drinking. Some glower, but most just stand around semi-dazed. Kids are chasing each other in the glass-infested lawns in front of the big buildings. Standing nearby are three young hookers and a dog with three legs. When I first came here, I expected to see things like this, but I was still surprised and frightened to see them up close. In the second week here I almost bailed out after one of my students was stabbed to death by his girlfriend. She had used scissors.

My class tonight will meet in a community center on the edge of the projects. The center is known by an acronym: CYCLE. I can never remember what it stands for. Along with several youth agencies, the facility is home to a Legal Aid service, a gym used by an AAU basketball team called the Demons, and several counselors. This building once was a health clinic. The halls and stairways are wide. Some rooms are large and some tiny. The temperature is usually too hot or too cold. It has a seedy, third world feel to it, but it is not depressing—not with so much activity.

The room where I will teach is jammed with at least thirty 8th graders. Some sit in desks, some in regular chairs, and a few slouch on a couch in the corner. The boys all wear shorts and T-shirts. Hats are not allowed. The couch has a missing leg and is supported by a stack of old World Book encyclopedias, once red but now turned a sickly purple from the sun's rays. Unlike a regular school classroom, watched over by an individual teacher, this room is shared by dozens of people, so no one takes much responsibility for keeping it in shape. This is where my students write stories and poems and play charades and other games.

These kids, all from the neighborhood, are part of something called the College Opportunity Program. For the past several years they have received tutoring, counseling and special classes here at CYCLE. Next year, as high school students, they will get additional support. I am a "support person." Part of the summer I have held creative writing classes. I have also helped them with grammar and math. I have taken them on a field trip to Taste of Chicago and to the Chicago Historical Society. We have gone to the North Avenue Beach. Our new magazine just came out and has made quite a hit. It includes writings from the 8th graders and from the older kids who take my other classes.

A few weeks before, in this same room, I discussed the magazine with three board members of the College Opportunity Program. Two were astonished that the kids had so much to say and that they could find so many clever ways to express themselves. "Great stuff," one said. "I'm going to have to read all of this." The third board member, a former teacher and youth worker, was not surprised at all. She knew how well kids can write if you give them a chance. But whether the board members were surprised or not by what they found, they all liked the poem on the cover. It's called "Maybe."

MAYBE

Often when I look in the mirror,
I feel as if I have been cheated.

Maybe God made a mistake
when he made me black with an eager mind.
Maybe I was meant to be part of a different race.
I feel the same as a rickety car with
a brand new engine inside.
People see only the outside of me
and never bother to find out what's inside.

Or, maybe I was meant to be black.
Maybe God created me to prove people wrong.
Maybe I was created for God's special purpose.
Maybe God created me to bring together
the sparse population of the
black race.
Maybe God is black.
Perhaps I was blessed
to be the color of God.
Maybe being black
is not bad at all.

Jermaine, a high school freshman, wrote this in class on a "Free Writing Day" earlier in the summer. He had asked me for a title. I said "Some Day." He changed that to "Maybe," and 40 minutes later he was reading his new poem to the class.

Even though we will not be writing tonight, I ask for two volunteers from the class to read something from our new magazine. I read through some of the titles: "The Girl Who Should Have Obeyed," "The Black Cinderella of the 80s," "The Lawn Mower Adventure," "How to Recognize a Phony," "How to Be Cool," "The Talking Fish," "Why We Have Rain," "My Room."

Gerald volunteers to read his poem, "How to Be Cool." He's a little guy with big eyes. Tonight he's wearing blue shorts and a white T-shirt. He stands on a table so everyone can see him. 8th grade boys can be tiny while the girls are in all ways more developed.

You've got to go to cool street.
You've got to dress cool.
You've got to be popular.
You've got to walk cool—start with your right foot
and bounce off of it.
You've got to have had at least 50 women.
You got to have gold chains.
You've got to have cool in your heart.
That means you've got to be born cool.
And finally, you've got to be like Gerald the Great.

He and I then go through a routine we have followed ever since he first read the poem several months ago. I ask him if I can be cool. He hops down to the floor and looks down at my brown socks and sneers. I tell him that I have cool in my heart. He smiles but stays silent. And then he shakes his head. Do you have to be born cool, I ask him? He shakes his head harder. Can't I ever learn to be cool? I plead. More shaking of the head. "I guess I'll get used to it," I say to no one in particular, and we all laugh.

Before we start the class, I pass out a list of poetry starters. There are first lines and last lines and photographs. There are short poems and quotes. If enough writing comes in during the final weeks, we can have one more magazine. Then I repeat an announcement I have been making for the past few weeks about a new idea I have, one that really appeals to me: "I am thinking of starting a scholarship program just for high school kids from the city who like to write." I tell them that the program will begin sophomore year and run through the rest of high school. The classes will meet on Saturdays. The kids will write stories and plays and take part in writing activities with other young writers. The kids will come from all over the city, not just Cabrini Green. Several nod and look interested. Tenaya, one of the most avid writers, says she would like to help plan the program.

Tonight, I have been asked to teach something

more basic than creative writing. The people in charge want me to introduce these 8th graders to the ACT exam. That way, when they start high school, they will at least know what's waiting for them. This seems quite reasonable, but who says kids like what's reasonable?

I pass out sample ACTs. I explain that in just a few years they will have to take this test. I try to sound upbeat. I tell the kids that after tonight they will have a better idea of what's expected of them. They frown and moan, but I continue with teacher-like arguments. "It may seem boring but . . ." "Give it a chance . . ." "You want people to know how well you can do . . ." "What you learn here, you'll need to know in school anyway . . ." "If you don't want to do it, you can leave." But they stay because they like to be here.

Plus tonight, the students—especially the boys—are deeply absorbed in what is developing among three of the girls. Two girls sitting in the back row are taunting a third girl who is sitting near the front. They quiet down when I ask them to keep quiet, but then—to the delight of the boys—they start up again. The only words I can identify are "garden instrument."

The taunters are cousins; their target is one of the class leaders named Yasheeka. She's big and forceful, and usually she can use her size, humor and her temper to take over a group. But tonight the cousins are getting to her. I keep asking them to quiet down, and they stop for a second or two but then resume their quiet taunting. The boys make a sleepy effort to finish the ACT, but they gleefully follow the taunting as if they were watching a tension-filled tennis match. Only Anthony, a boy who has always liked me, is not sharing the excitement. Instead he glances at me with a worried look. I look back and shrug—an honest shrug because I don't know what the hell is happening. The other boys whisper excitedly to each other. And I keep hearing, "Garden

instrument, garden instrument, garden instrument."
Finally I just give up. "Let's get out of here. You win." The van will be downstairs to drive the kids back into the projects. I will drive a few others who live in the row houses that surround the towers. We'll have one more writing class next week. "You can finish the ACTs at home," I add hopefully. I remind them again about the writing scholarship program, which I have decided to call Young Chicago Authors. "Think about it. OK?"

On the way out, Antevia, one of the most eager writers in the group, tells me she would like to be part of the writing program I have described. I tell her that she would be perfect. (She once wrote a story about the hooker who got fired for working too hard.) Then I ask her what's going on with Yasheeka and the cousins. "What's all this stuff about 'garden instruments'?"

She looks up at me in mock surprise with her hands on her hips and her eyebrows arched. "You don't know anything."

I remind her that I am not cool and nod down at my socks.

"A garden instrument," she lectures to me, "is a hoe. Get it, a hoe. They're calling Yasheeka a hoe!"

Now I get it, but before I have a chance to claim that I knew all along, I hear some bad noise on the stairwell, and off I sprint. Yasheeka and the cousins are face-to-face, shrieking at each other. "Downstairs," I shout. "Let's get out of here."

Outside on the street it is even more chaotic. For one thing, it has started to pour. And the van is not there. Just when I am about to tell the kids to wait back inside, I hear a swooshing noise, and to my left I see the two cousins going after Yasheeka with small folded umbrellas. One umbrella is red. The other is blue. The cousins look like midget Samurai warriors as they wade in and flail away while Yasheeka kicks at them karate-style screaming at the top of her lungs.

"I'll tear your fucking heads off!!" And then it starts to rain even harder. All the boys, except for Anthony, are cheering and hooting.

All I can say is "Hey! Come on, girls. Stop it!" But I can barely hear my own voice because the shouting and the rain swallow it up. I push my way through the crowd and arrive at the backs of the umbrella-wielding cousins, the shorter of whom has just been kicked in the stomach. I reach out and grab the umbrellas, which slide out of their wet hands. And then, while people jeer and howl from the windows of the surrounding buildings, I sprint across the street to my car as the cousins chase after me leaping up to get their weapons back. I am too tall for them. When I get to the car, I open the trunk and flip the umbrellas inside right next to my golf clubs.

When I get back to the action, I find Yasheeka screaming even louder because her glasses have fallen off. Anthony is stretched out under a car where they have somehow landed. Finally the van pulls up, and most of the kids—including the cousins—pile in. Yasheeka and a few others stay with me. I tell the driver what has happened and that I will write a report tomorrow. One of the cousins starts to argue, but I tell her to be quiet and hurry her into the van.

The others squeeze into my car. We drop Yasheeka off first. I ask her if she wants me to come along and talk to her mother. She says no. Amazingly, she sounds calm. She even jokes about how funny it must have looked from the buildings to see the two small girls jumping up to get their umbrellas back from me.

After she's gone, I ask the others in the car what happened, but they don't really know. There had been name-calling. There had been a similar incident last week. I asked if they would all stay friends. Of course. Why not?

At that moment, I suddenly feel oddly calm. Earlier I had been frustrated and angry and then but terrified, now I feel relaxed. Who would have guessed that after witnessing an umbrella attack in Cabrini Green I would feel so mellow? Of course, I am relieved that it's over and that no one is hurt. I'm pleased that I handled the problem somewhat effectively. I'm actually rather smug about the car-trunk idea.

But that's not why I suddenly feel as I do. I feel this way, I think, because the kids in the car, even the boys, seem so concerned for me. They sit silently and watch as I drive to the south end of the projects where I will drop them off. When Erica gets out, she asks how I feel and pats me on the knee. "Are you going to be all right?" Others nod and thank me for the ride. Anthony, the last to get out, shakes my hand and tells me I can call him if I'd like.

Two days later I'm back at Cabrini for a meeting about the incident. I tell the director of the program what happened. Yasheeka and the cousins—the two who were beating her with umbrellas—are there sitting next to each other! They agree with my version of events. They all look at me with the same little smiles. I wonder if they're slightly pleased at what happened. Have they taught me a little lesson? Certainly they couldn't have planned it that way, but maybe now that it's over, they might take some pleasure in having treated me to this experience. They say they are sorry. They say it will not happen again. They're all friends, and this was just a misunderstanding.

They leave together, and I talk some more to the director, a lady named Pat who grew up in Cabrini Green. Pat tells me she is really sorry I was put in that position. She's embarrassed. She takes great pride in things like this not happening here at CYCLE. I tell her that I've been here for two years. I have met with hundreds of kids at all times of the day or night. In spite of what people might think, this has never happened before. This has not changed my opinion of anything.

I ask Pat if she understands what happened. She doesn't. I mention the garden instrument, and we laugh and agree that was key. But still, why did it happen? I'm not sure if the girls know why they got so mad at that moment. They called her a hoe, and she got mad. The boys kept the incident going.

Then Pat mentions Young Chicago Authors. We talked about it briefly last week. She says she's thought about it, and she tells me how much she likes the idea. It will be good to have kids from all over the city come together to write. She hopes a lot of the Cabrini kids get involved. Then she asks, with a laugh, if I still want to go through with it.

"Absolutely," I say. "Why not?" But I know what she's thinking.

"I don't know, Bob. You're fifty years old. Your children are practically grown up. You might have better things to do."

I tell her that this is the best thing to do. I am just the right age—old enough and young enough to pull it off. I'm also smart enough and dumb enough. I have had enough experiences to feel confident, but not enough to taint my vision. I know people who can help me out. And I bet there are lots of others out there that I'll meet. I am convinced that this is a good idea.

"All right. All right. I believe you." She holds out her hands to get me to shut up. And if she hadn't stopped me, I would have kept right on. I could have said that this "umbrella incident" was another of many of my experiences that combine stupidity and bad luck. I could have said that experiences like this have helped shape me into a certain kind of teacher. I could have said that every teacher I know has experiences like this and that this is what makes teaching such a unique profession. I could have said that one day I might write a book about all of this.

On the way out, I run into Tenaya, the girl who

offered to help me plan the program. She tells me how funny I looked with the umbrellas over my head while the cousins were jumping up to get them. Had I noticed the people in the windows cheering? I tell her I'm getting sick of hearing how funny I looked. Now she's really laughing.

FIRST YEAR

Fall 1992—In the early 1960s, as a college student, I spent two summers as an intern at Erwin Wasey Ruthrauff & Ryan, an advertising agency across the river from the Wrigley Building. Every morning I'd ride the Chicago & Northwestern train down from the suburbs and, following the curve of the Chicago River, hike over to the office. One of the other interns had flown planes for the Israeli Air Force. Another intern, a Californian named Sandy, described almost everything he liked as "bitchin." Our boss collected postcards featuring girls with gigantic breasts. ("Look at this one, Bob. Don't you love that Scandahoovian pussy?") Some days, I'd meet my father for lunch at a place below Michigan Avenue called Quincy Number Nine. After work on Fridays, I'd go with friends to the Berghoff Restaurant on Adams Street and drink beer brewed on the premises.

By that time in my life I had pretty much decided to become an English teacher, but I also thought I might want to become a businessman. After all, most of the people in my family were in business, and all of my friends planned to wear ties and carry briefcases as they made their daily trek to the office. I half-expected that working in the Loop might redirect me toward business. But it didn't. I liked going downtown, but teaching was what I wanted to do.

Almost thirty years later, I am back downtown. But now I'm in the Monadnock Building in the South Loop. It is an awesome structure partially held up by its own load-bearing masonry walls. It is a frequent stop on architectural tours.

The conference room on the eighth floor easily accommodates a table large enough for me and the fifteen high school sophomores who are about to become the very first Young Chicago Authors class. In just a few minutes they will start showing up down on the street, where Sue is waiting to greet them and show them which elevator to board.

It's taken fifteen months to get here—a grueling but highly pleasurable fifteen months. I've had to assemble a board of directors, establish not-for-profit status, raise money and recruit kids. I've worn my suit and run meetings. I've written letters asking people to give me money. I paid a former GED student to design a logo, which features a Chicago skyline and a pen. This logo now sits atop our own stationery, which has the names of our board of directors and supporting organizations. I have developed sales pitches and slogans: "These are ideas that we have already tested." "Let's give talented kids a chance to develop their talent." "Creativity must be acknowledged." "Creativity is power." "Creative people can make the world a better place."

I am a little surprised by how much I enjoy this administrative side of the program. Maybe these are business talents that I have picked up from running the study center. Maybe they come from my middle class suburban background. Maybe I acquired them as a child, through osmosis from my father.

I especially like going to schools to recruit kids for the program. It's fun to walk into a strange school, meet the department chairmen, and talk to kids about this opportunity. If I didn't like doing this, I'd be in big trouble, because YCA (as we already call it) will require lots of good planning and execution.

But all of this administrating is not necessarily good training for teaching creative writing, and I have a long way to go to be an accomplished creative writing teacher. I've succeeded with basketball players at Avalon Park and with little kids at Cabrini Green, but I don't always feel like a creative writing teacher. For one thing, I don't write fiction or poetry myself, so

I am not teaching from experience. But in a few minutes I will be eyeball to eyeball with fifteen young people who are willing to spend 128 Saturday mornings over the next three years writing stories, plays, and poems. When it was still little more than an idea, with this first class signed up but not yet giving up their time, an article in Chicago's free newspaper, *The Reader,* called Young Chicago Authors the "only program of its kind in the United States." That's something to think about.

Tenaya and Antevia, both of whom I know from Cabrini Green, walk through the door together and sit directly across from me. "I can see my reflection on the table," Antevia says. She looks down and sticks out her tongue. She's little and dark and eager. They stare at the giant photographs of Chicago hanging on the polished wood walls. They eye the thick green carpeting. This is nothing like the cluttered classroom where I have spent so much time with them at Cabrini. They ask if I still remember the umbrella night. I groan inwardly.

Leon comes in next. He lives in a Puerto Rican neighborhood on the Near West Side. He wants to be a cartoonist. Right behind him is Michael, a hayseedy-looking kid whose dad teaches existentialism and other philosophy classes at De Paul University. Carol, a short light-skinned black girl, hurries in. Her handwriting is so tiny that I almost needed a magnifying glass to read her application. Christine, a tall girl with a big smile, referred to herself in the application as a "mother figure." She sits next to me. She looks around smiling and says, "Hi, everyone." The others smile a bit awkwardly but don't say anything. It feels a little bit like a first dance.

Vivek, Carlos, and Mike stroll in together and sit together. They are all in an International Baccalaureate program at their high school. Mike is a rabid Chicago sports fan. When I interviewed him in June, the Bulls had just won their second championship. He said he was so nervous watching the Trailblazers build a big lead in the final game that he almost threw up, and when the Bulls caught up and won, he ran outside and screamed, "YES! YES! YES!" I told him that my son and I get so anxious watching the Bulls that sometimes we have to turn off the TV set. Today, I ask Mike how he feels about the Bulls' chances this year. "No sweat," he grins and then shakes his hands in mock anxiety. I ask others how school is going. I get a few "OKs." I ask how they spent the summer. No one says much except Christine, who took care of kids during the day and worked at a restaurant in the evening. The rest answer politely in a few words.

Sue arrives with the last few students, one of whom attends a special math academy. Just in case they haven't figured out who Sue is, I tell them. "This person happens to be my wife. She'll be very involved in the program. She's an artist, so Leon and others who like to draw might have a chance to work with her." She says hello, waves good-bye, and leaves.

I go over the usual stuff. We'll meet here every Saturday. Each class will have a specific purpose. They are free to bring in whatever they are writing. Professional writers will come to class. We'll go to plays and movies and readings. Michael thinks his dad knows professors who could come in. I ask if they understand how the $2,000 college scholarship works. They all nod. And then, before moving on to some writing, I tell them to call me by my first name. "I'm not always in favor of this teacher-buddy thing, but we're going to be together for a while, so that's how I think we should do it." More nods and maybe a smile or two.

Nothing more to be said. "Well, then, let's do it." I ask them to write a description of a place they know well. "Capture both the physical and emotional reality of the place; consider all of the senses; you want the reader know what it is like to be in that place." No questions. It won't be as necessary, as it might be with some other kids, to justify what I do. They must understand that, at one time or another, a creative writer—or any writer, for that matter—must be able to describe a location. They reach for their journals and begin to write.

As I watch them ferociously scribbling, it occurs to me how often I do this sort of thing: I meet a class, say a few words and then—instead of lecturing or leading a discussion—put my students to work. Lately I have watched cops, basketball players, and SAT students write. And here I am again, gazing at fifteen kids who say they want to be writers. Michael sticks out his tongue. Carlos nods his head and moves his lips. Is he singing? Leon adds little sketches to his work. Christine chuckles. Antevia looks out the window every so often. Earnest sits on the carpet in the corner.

After forty minutes, I tell them to come to a good stopping place. Two minutes later, they are calmly looking back at me. "So, how did it go?" I ask. Nods and small smiles and shrugs, but no verbal response. "Who'd like to read?" Several volunteers. I point to Carlos. He has dark curly hair and is wearing a sport coat. He describes his room at home. ("It's typical, but sparse.") Christine chooses a fast-food place near her house. ("The smell of grease gets into your pockets," which I think is an outstanding image.) Several select classrooms. Leon describes the inside of a van. Michael's description of a park area near his house ends like this:

"Every day for two years, I came out and played with my friends. It is a concrete jungle supplied by the city for its people. Compared to a park, it is dirty and unsafe, a travesty of neighborhood renewal. But every day we gathered there. Every day we played there. It was small, dirty, and unsafe. And I loved it."

I tell Michael that I can feel the affection he

has for this park. "Your writing has a nice bounce to it." Then I ask if anyone picked the room where we are sitting right now. Liz, the student from the science and math academy, raises her hand and reads in a soft, convincing voice:
"Fifteen strangers sit uncomfortably in a large room. They sit like King Arthur's knights around a circular green and brown table. Each person is writing frantically. I wonder what they're thinking about. A soft light glows down from various lamps onto the different colored skins of the people in the room. It's like a Benetton commercial in this room eight floors up in downtown Chicago. Sophisticated brown and white photos surround us. An intricately painted radiator and a plush green rug complete the picture of luxury. Brown closets and funky Easter egg yellow metal chairs are out-of-place touches in the well-put-together room. I wonder where everyone will go later."

After class, Earnest waits around to tell me that he is finishing a long soap opera and also a book of original myths. Leon, the cartoonist, wants me to see his drawings. He'll bring them in next week. I walk down the hall with him, and we wait for the elevator together. It's Saturday, and the building feels abandoned. The intricate metalwork along the stairwells casts long spooky shadows. I have never taught in a place that resembles the Monadnock Building in any way.

Driving home, I feel good, even though my teaching was not inspired, and even though the kids didn't have much to say. My guess is that this group will stay quiet. But they obviously like to write, and what they wrote today was good. Back home I plan the next few weeks—more descriptions, an interview, and maybe a true story. I have no high school curriculum or SAT test to consider. I am definitely on my own.

January 1993—Chuck Leroux, a tall, bald and bearded friend who is also a *Chicago Tribune* feature writer, is telling the class what he does. Even though he is a journalist and my students see themselves as creative writers, I figured they would like him, and I am right. "Writing is writing is writing,"

Chuck likes to burrow into the lives of eccentric people, like the old fellow in southern Illinois with the world's largest ball of string. Chuck is attracted to medical subjects. He won several awards for his series of articles about Alzheimer's Disease. He has written about cannibals. ("They like to eat out.") He pedaled his bike across the state in search of local stories. He prefers face-to-face interviews to telephone interviews because, he explains, "When you're in the same room together, people have to keep talking. They can't just hang up." The kids respond well, warming to him and his subject. I think they can see how exciting a writing life can be.

I met Chuck in the back row of a philosophy class at the University of Wisconsin. We took several other philosophy classes together. He was a Madison resident and took me to local joints like the Italian Workmen's Club and Faith's Flame Room. The particulars of life intrigued him—not the theories he could draw from them. He was one of the first real writers I ever knew.

Chuck is our fifth guest. Our first guest was Fred Marks, who co-directed the film *Hoop Dreams*. A biographer of Jane Addams, a poet from Ghana, a writer of family histories, and finally an academic writer from Northwestern followed Fred. After Chuck, we'll have another journalist, a mystery writer, and an author of children's stories. Nick, a graduate student from UIC, has been helping me out. He knows much more than I do about opportunities for writers in the city. He's also a serious poet.

With or without guests, the YCA kids don't say much. They respond to my prompts, but in a businesslike way. Every so often, their silence gets to me, and I feel like shaking them and telling them I want noise and movement, not just writing and more writing. At these times, I wonder if this no-nonsense conference room has something to do with their no-nonsense attitudes. But in general I am quite satisfied with this quiet commitment. Now, if they weren't writing...

February 1993—Carlos is reading aloud, and the class is laughing hard for maybe the first time of the year. I have never heard them make such a collective noise. It all started with today's assignment, which was to "make up a story that makes something ridiculous seem sensible." I gave each student a card with a description of odd behavior. Antevia wrote about a man who burned all of his money. Christine described a girl who walked away from the love of her life. Carlos' story was about a guy who ate Chapstick. Here's how he began:

"My name is Chuck, and I'm a Chapaholic. It all started two years ago at a New Year's party. I was getting ready to leave when someone said, 'Hey, Chuck, it's cold outside. Here's some Chapstick.' At first I thought nothing of it. I put it on and, yeah, it felt smooth on my lips, but I never thought that I would use it again. I walked out of the room. The Chapstick felt soooo good on my lips. It felt so good that I started to laugh. My girlfriend said, 'Chuck, I think I'd better drive tonight.'"

Carlos reads in a soft confessional, slightly crazed voice—in sharp contrast to his normal serious voice. He is a studious kid, quiet even by the silent standards of the class.

Later in the week, I read Carlos' Chapstick piece to students in my SAT classes in the suburbs. They applaud. Lately I've been trying to bring together the two sides of my life. I want the suburban kids to know what I am doing in the city. If they're involved in creative writing at their own high schools, I want to know it. I want the city kids to know they can come north to take SAT classes.

One of my SAT students is writing a term paper about urban education. He knows that I teach in both the city and the suburbs and asks me to explain some of the ways city kids and suburban kids are alike. I tell him that most kids I know are suspicious of adults. They want to discover things themselves. They don't want to look silly. They have secrets they will share with only certain people. How do they differ? They differ in their views of the future. Kids from the suburbs, or at least, the wealthy North Shore suburbs, think they know what they want, and they think they know what it takes to get there. Their understanding is realistic. The inner-city kids don't always know how near or how far they are from what they want.

Along with the SAT program, I am also teaching writing workshops at Cabrini Green and other places. Last week I asked 8th grade students in a Southside school to imagine "that a very weird person sat next to you on a bus." I began with questions: Why did this person look normal at first? What was he reading? What did he say to you? What did he announce to the other passengers? What was he eating? How did he make his final exit? Next they shaped their answers into a short narrative. The teacher said she had not seen her kids work that hard all year. One girl described her character as wearing the clothes of a typical student, but behaving in all other ways like an old hippy. "Peace" and "Love" were tattooed on his hand; he called everyone "Man." These directed exercises work well with kids I see only a few times.

March 1993—As the Chicago winter grinds its slow way along, the class continues to go well—quietly well. Now, they all are working on longer projects. Every week, Earnest presents me with more chapters of his soap opera and poems filled with gods. Michael is writing a play about baseball. Christine is working on an airplane story. She is the one person in the class who has told me she would like a little more noise and chumminess. At the moment, I am more the editor than the teacher. I manage the whole operation without doing a lot of direct teaching. It's not hard to keep this group busy.

Last week most of the class submitted poems for a summer magazine. Many of these poems have addressed big philosophical questions.

Earnest made a prediction: "And there will come a time / When all of humankind / Will dance the dance of love and life."

Antevia talked about God: "God's voice is like a melody sweet / A rush of rhythm running through my soul."

Michael considered Change: "The past can't be brought back / The future must continue / The wheel has revolved / Mighty change is the only constant."

Christine and others are more specific. Hers is called "Busy Signal." ("It smirks. It laughs. It cries.") Carlos has composed a piece about a giggle in church. In "Someone Dies," Tenaya, a lifelong Cabrini resident, has more serious concerns. ("Someone dies / As hail falls from the sky / Someone dies / As shots rang out.") Liz attacks an archaic view of women by writing in the voice of someone who holds that backward view. ("Little girls should destroy the idea / That they can stand on their own two feet.")

Perhaps in an effort to identify more closely with my teaching, I've joined a fiction workshop! My teacher is a young novelist. My classmates are older people from all over. I enjoy dipping into my memories and my imagination. My first story is about a teacher in an Eastern prep school.

April 1993—Sue and I are about to take the YCA kids for a weekend trip to the University of Wisconsin in Madison. We meet at the Monadnock Building at 6:30 AM and pile into a rented van. This is the first time the class has seen me in shorts. I get the usual "nice legs" comments. Three hours later, after a quiet (what else?) drive, we pull up in front of the student/alumni center. An hour after that, we are listening to the head of the writing department describe the program. The kids ask lots of questions. (How many writing classes can you take? What if you decide to switch majors? Does the school have a good literary magazine?) Some obviously know what college is like. Others are astonished that classes meet only a few times each week.

Later in the afternoon, they explore the campus while Sue and I walk around. We pass the fraternity house where we had our first date. We walk down to Lake Mendota and see that the piers are filled with students. We drink coffee on the terrace down by the water. In the late 1960s, when we came back to visit during the anti-Vietnam days, Madison was an armed camp; now it's much more mellow. And it's spring—the first warm weekend.

Later that evening we eat at a Mexican restaurant. Old friends from Madison join us for the meal. After dinner we hear Luis Rodriguez, also visiting from Chicago, read at a bookstore. The kids have all read his book, *Always Running.* Afterwards he autographs their copies. We make plans for him to visit our class. His son, who has joined him on this trip, talks to me about doing some GED work. On the way back to the dorm, Christine tells me how happy she feels. "We should have done this before. I feel much closer to the kids." She's finally getting what she wants. The next morning we take a tour of the campus, eat pizza for lunch and drive back in the van. Twice I have to ask the kids to quiet down.

The next week after class Christine hands me a "Journal Page" detailing the highlights of our trip. Meeting the professors was OK, and it was great to hear Luis Rodriguez, but what she liked most of all was exploring the campus with the others. She describes the hippy neighborhood, the street fair, the beach, the pool hall, the student union. She recalls coming back to the dorm and finding Sue and me "waiting like nervous parents." She's grateful for the new friendships. "We now have new nicknames and new memories to share." After class, Christine hangs around, and we walk together to the elevator. She asks me how I feel about the trip.

"Great!" I say. "I've wanted the class to be a little more open and relaxed. Maybe if we met every day, we could relax a bit more. But still..."

She interrupts me because she knows what I'm going to say. "Still, we write all of the time. And we do. And that's all that really matters." The elevator arrives, and that's it for that conversation.

That afternoon I stop in to see Wally at his retirement home in south Evanston. He's sitting beside the window of his small room reading a novel by Elmore Leonard. It's hot in his room, but he's covered with a heavy red blanket. He looks gray and frail. I tell him about the trip to Madison. He's lost energy, but not his sarcastic wit. He likes what I'm doing. He's pleased that the students don't need prompts ("tricks" in his view) to get them started.

June, 1993—It's the last day of class. The Bulls are champions for the third year in a row. A few days ago, my son Charlie and I watched, terrified, as they held off the Suns to win. Today the students have brought in a favorite piece of their writing from the year. A board member has stopped in. Carol reads her personal narrative about a family experience from when she was four years old. Natoya reads a personal narrative about animals. ("Dogs always make me edgy.") Vivek has written a "semi-true" story about teachers. Earnest has put together a pantheon of original gods. Several kids have written "trialogues"— three sided arguments about the same subject. Michael has a long short story, which begins "Rend's gray bike flew smoothly over the ancient asphalt highway." Michael's play about baseball has just been named a winner in a citywide drama contest. I save Antevia's poem for last. I ask her to read, and she stands proudly.

Go 'head Girl Witcha Bad Stuff

Divine and so fine by the wisdom of time

Dressed to impress
In a red, flashy dress
Hips shakin to the east and shakin to the west
beauty dominating above the rest
   This is a Black Woman
A mighty might
   pure
Black Woman
   She's a go-getter
   She's a creator
   She's a doctor
   a doctor of motivation, liberation
   and education
Graduating with a Ph.D. of sophistication
and a masters of desperation
Is there too much "-tion" in her wisdom?
   I think not!
Cause baby she got
She got the complexion of chocolate candy
A shape so "ehm" and so dandy
She got the stride of pride
She got the hair color of sandy deserts
   in Africa

Carrying on her brown boastful eyes to her cousin
   in Jamaica
Oh yes, she's got it all and she's still smiling
   She's styling, profiling, and
prowling
I am the younger Black Woman
   Right now I'm studying for my
   bachelors in tranquility
Soon I'll have my masters in ability
Then,
   I'll have the ability to preach about
   the Black Woman—
   with versatility
—She is the Black Woman
—I am the Black Woman.

     The whole class—this quiet group of serious young writers—leaps to its feet to applaud. "Antevia, that's wonderful," Christine shouts. "Read it again." This time Antevia stands on the table.

     Before we say good-bye for the summer, I tell students where they can mail their work. Michael will be attending a summer program in the East where he will be taking writing and photography. Several others will be participating in a city-run arts program. Earnest will be working at a bank. Christine will be baby-sitting.

     We all leave together. I drive Tenaya back to Cabrini Green, and then I turn onto North Avenue and head to the expressway. Tomorrow I will be coming back downtown to interview some students who want to be the second group to enter Young Chicago Authors.

RESPONSE

José is sitting on the floor, writing a poem. He's leaning against the mailbox rack, which has enough slots for the 45 kids now in the YCA scholarship program. Today the boxes are stuffed with edited stories and poems and with issues of *Sleazy Writer*, our one-page weekly newspaper. *Sleazy* has a calendar of the future events: Next week we'll be going to a reading by Studs Terkel; in three weeks a writer from the *Chicago Sun Times* will stop in. It also has news: fifteen kids entered the Young Playwright contest; Michael will again be attending a writing workshop in the East this summer; Aja would like people to come to her school's play. It has information about other writing contests and summer workshops. It also includes random ideas for stories and poems: Write a story that begins with this sentence: "Life for us changed dramatically the day Mom took up kick boxing." And there is gossip, mostly false: "Christine was seen at the Cubby Bear with Sean Penn." "Vic's poetry to be published in *PlayGirl*." "Joseph's new tattoo to be in iambic pentameter." "Marcus arrested for wearing a thong to class."

This room and the other two that make up our workshop are quite small, but we can make the place work. When I first looked at the space, the walls were slathered in gold goo. It looked like a ghastly throne room and smelled awful. I stood gawking until I figured out that the goo was there to kill the millions of cockroaches that had colonized the place. Now the encrusted roaches have been scraped off, and the goo has been replaced by Sue's wall hangings and with samples of our students' poetry. We have posters of Alan Ginsberg and Gwendolyn Brooks and photographs taken of our juniors on a winter trip to the

University of Illinois. One picture is of the kids along with me and Sue huddled next to the university library squinting at the camera.

The YCA workshop is on Division Street in a neighborhood known as the East Ukrainian Village. Nearby is a Ukrainian Orthodox Church with golden onion domes. Louis Sullivan designed the church. Few Ukrainians live around here anymore. Not far away is Wicker Park, near where Nelson Algren lived. Mike Royko was born in a hospital up the street, not far from his family's tavern. To the west is Humboldt Park, the boyhood home of Saul Bellow. For a long time it was a Jewish neighborhood. Now it is the Puerto Rican capital of the city. To the east of us is the Russian Bath. Often when I pass the baths, I see very old men emerging from shiny new cars. Someday this neighborhood will be gentrified, but it may take awhile.

Last month some local gangbangers beat up one of our students. Since then, I've met with the police and the alderman. Hector, the man who runs the hardware store on the ground floor of our building and who claims to "know" the gangbangers, assures me that our guy was a victim of misidentification. "It will not happen again." But he doesn't want our kids to take long walks or hang around at night. After I heard about the attack, I thought about moving out and going back to Saturday classes at the Monadnock Building. Then gradually I got less scared. Now I feel relieved that the incident seems to be over.

José is working on a poem that he started in the van on the way back from Glencoe. This morning the YCA kids read some of their own stories and poems at a Glencoe junior high school, a school my own children once attended. The suburban kids liked to hear what these city kids had to say. The YCA kids enjoyed playing the role of streetwise city people, although I think they were surprised (and maybe disappointed) that this suburban school actually has a few black kids. After the performance, we drove over to my house for lunch.

José is a member of the second group of students to join YCA. In the very first class he wrote an anecdote about a time when an old man tried to pick him up at a record store. ("Hey, kid, wanna put your hand down my pants?") He writes constantly, and much of what he writes is quite raunchy. He never misses a class. He shares his reactions to the writings of others. On weekends he reads his poetry at cafes in Wicker Park and the Pilsen area further south. The gay experience is one of his favorite subjects. One of José's recent poems includes this stanza:

> He stands before Mommy in full drag
> Not knowing of words such as fairy or fag.
> She exclaims, "Baby, what's wrong with you?
> That is not something little boys do."

Joseph, a sophomore from a small Catholic school, is writing something in the back room. Unlike José, who's tall and dark, Joseph is small and white. With his tattoos and slicked-back blond hair, he resembles a 1950's greaser. He reads in a low compelling voice. The Glencoe kids found him very sexy. He insists on calling me "Sir." He sometimes brings a girlfriend to class.

Back with Joseph is Carlos, who is working on a term paper about Thomas Moore. Carlos' International Baccalaureate requires long research papers. This morning, he read his piece about Chapstick to the kids in Glencoe. The audience wanted him to read it again, but he refused, joking that he doesn't want to be "known" as a Chapstick writer. Instead he read a poem called "Innocent Giggle."

Sweet and pure.
In a church where
it ought to be
Misunderstood
Those who have grown old
Thought impure,
Chastise the church giggle
Even though
It is innocent
and benign.
Like he whom they love
And worship
The acts they commit
Are far more
Heinous than the laugh
And yet they
Stare down the young child
With fire eyes.
And communicate
Blasphemy
Blasphemy that she
Uttered with
An angel like sound
Heard in a church

Also in the back room is Lauralee who is putting the final touches on her story about a time she was in a car that broke down in her native Belize. This is a longer version of the same story she wrote several years ago at the soup kitchen in Rogers Park. Like so many of the kids who joined the program in the second and third years, and unlike the students from the first year, Lauralee is noisy and expressive. One of her short poems is on the wall.

Lies start as one.
The more you tell
The more they become.
Lies don't die.
They multiply.

Despite the gang attack, the kids seem to feel safe here. It's obviously a good place to write. They really like it in good weather when they can sit on the back porch. From there they can see the golden domes of the church, the roofs of the small houses that make up the neighborhood, and the Sears Tower.

I also use this space for other classes, and this afternoon I'm conducting a GED class for adults from the neighborhood. They arrive together and take seats at a long table in the middle room. All are Puerto Rican women in their mid-thirties. Several are wearing Bulls' sweatshirts. Two are in skirts and blouses. Most are quite short with black hair and round faces. Those who work have minimum-wage jobs and would like the GED certificate to give them a chance for something better. Except on holidays, like today, they usually don't have much contact with the YCA kids. Last week we canceled class so they could see a special Oprah show (it was O's birthday), so I haven't seen them for a while. They ask me about some of Sue's new quilts. I ask how their kids are doing in school.

Today we have a new GED student named Lizette. She tells me she has little kids at the local school. Her husband works at a box factory near Logan Square. She asks about my family, but before I can answer, Rosie, the self-appointed class busybody, fills her in. "His daughter Fanny works for him. She's married. And his other daughter has a house over there on Haddon near the Ukrainian church. She's a teacher. His son goes to school in the West. He's going to be a math teacher. His wife's the lady who's made all the quilts. She's nice."

A week ago, Lizette called to say she was

joining the class. I told her what she needed to know and then asked her to write something for me. I asked her to respond to this statement: "Things are not always what they seem." She was to write a true story that proves this point. Today, I notice that she has the essay with her. "Would you like to read it to the class?" I ask. She shrugs and looks at her hands. "Come on, Lizette," barks Rosie, "we're all buddies here." And with that Lizette starts to read, first haltingly, but soon with confidence.

"A lot of young people nowadays think is so easy to have a family, but is not and this is why.

"At the age of seventeen I became pregnant and had my first child by the age of eighteen. Two more kids followed after that. People might assume that I had it made. I had a man and my own apartment fully furnished, had a car and some dollars to spend. But what people don't see is that with that came responsibility and lots of bills. Raising a child is not just changing pampers and giving a baby a bottle of milk. My first child had colic. He cried all day and night for months and months always sick. My other two are in and out of the hospital. I have my kids all day every day, but they always manage to get hurt and do things they're not supposed to do like light fires.

"I had to drop out of school in my third year to raise my kids. Now I have a very low education. These were not my dreams as a child, but then what's done, it's done and there's no changing the past only making the future better.

"My husband works every day and on weekends to put clothes on our backs and food on our table. He didn't dream of these. As a young boy he wanted to become an accountant but he has no time for school seems he's always working. I enjoy my kids but looking at things how they are now a days I should of thought of getting an education and being financially stable in order to raise a family the proper way."

We all applaud, and when we stop, we

applaud all over again. Maria says the paper is "really honest." We all agree.

I decided, long before YCA, that students who have failed in school could use a heavy dose of creative writing. Lizette's classmates have written profiles of real people and descriptions of real places and imaginary places. In three weeks, when they sit down to take the GED, they should have no trouble with the essay. The GED essay might be more formal, but they'll know what to do.

Today, instead of writing, these students will read "A Kind of Murder," a story from our anthology. The story, which takes place at a military school in the 1940s, is about an old teacher named Mr. Warren who takes over for another teacher in the middle of the year. From the very first study hall, the cadets make the old fellow's life miserable. Most of the other teachers are just as cruel. The abuse doesn't let up, even after Mr. Warren saves the school dog from drowning. For a while the narrator stands up for the old guy, but finally he lets matters take care of themselves, and in the end, Mr. Warren has to leave.

Before reading the story, I make sure the women know what a military school is. I give them a list of some of the challenging words from the story. The list includes "sadist" and "menace." Then I read aloud as they follow along. I stop frequently to ask questions. "What will happen next?" "What would you do?" "How do you suppose this old fellow feels?" They answer enthusiastically. "I think the old fellow will leave." "I'd get out of there fast, man." "I'd want to slap those little brats. Don't they know he's trying to help them?"

"How'd you like it?" I ask after I finish reading the story. Without exception, they smile and nod.

"Why do you like it?"

"I like the way it makes me feel."

"I didn't know what was going to happen. I liked being surprised."

"It showed how nasty men can be." Those that don't have a particular answer simply say, "I don't know. I just liked it."

Next, I ask them to write down answers to the questions that are printed in the anthology. They grab their pens and notebooks and dig in, and while they write, they talk and laugh. Even though this story's about an all-boys prep school in the 1940s, these Latinas from the city have no problem identifying with the issues, as I learn when they share their answers. What do they think about the narrator choosing not to defend the old man any more? Jesse a thinks the narrator should have stood up for the old man. "As long as it takes. It's not right to let the old guy get ruined by those kids." Yesenia thinks the narrator did the right thing. "He's got his own stuff to think about. He doesn't need to take care of a weakling all the time."

What kind of a person is Mr. Warren? According to Rita, he's a "worm." Others like him, especially after he rescues the school dog. "He old," Ava says, "he deserves to be treated well. Those little scumbags are rotten."

Why is this story called "A Kind of Murder?" Jesse thinks she knows. "The narrator killed him. He had a chance to save the man and he didn't. He should feel guilty. Real, real guilty."

We take a break. José goes down to buy drinks at a nearby grocery store. I ask Joseph to explain the YCA program to the ladies. He tells them about the Saturday classes and the trips and the magazines. He points around the room to illustrate his points. The ladies nod and listen politely. They probably don't understand the concept completely, but at least they know a little more of what YCA all about. It's certainly possible that one of their children might want to join our scholarship program some day.

When we reach the time to practice with some actual GED readings, I pass out copies of an old test and ask the women to turn to "Test 4 – Literature." They'll read the first four selections and answer the questions that follow each. "Remember that you can underline and that you have time to read each selection twice." When possible, they should try to picture what's going on. "Before you answer," I add, "write down briefly what the passage is all about and how you feel about it. Then answer the questions. See if you can get as involved in this as you were in the story about Mr. Warren."

The first passage is a short selection from *All My Sons* by Arthur Miller. The second is taken from Beryl Markham's memoir, *West With the Night*. The third is a poem by Pablo Neruda, and the fourth is an essay about a songwriter.

Most of the students are able to read. Those who can't read at all sign up for other programs. I can expect most of the women to answer 60 percent of the questions correctly. Today, though, the majority answers at least 80 percent correctly. And two get every answer right! Not only that, but they have a lot to say about the selections. If they're wrong, they want to know why.

I'm pleased with the results, and I tell them so. "Do you think that starting with the longer story helped?"

"It did," Lizette says, as she starts to pack up. "After that I felt like reading."

I don't need to add anything to that. "See you in a few days, ladies. For Thursday, I'd like you to read 'A Kind of Murder' over again and then write a letter that Mr. Warren might have sent the cadets a few months later."

After the class leaves, the YCA kids appear and sit at the table with me. They all enjoyed listening in on the class. José tells me that there are lots of people from his neighborhood that might want to take this course. Joseph was touched by Lizette's story. "It made me cry."

WALLY'S DAY

Wally died last month. The funeral was held at a chapel on the Northwestern campus. Afterwards, several of us met for dinner. Today there will be a memorial reception for him in Milwaukee where many of his former students and friends will be attending a convention. Jay, my business partner, and I are driving up there.

Earlier in the day I had to cut short a session with a student named Ben—a kid Wally would have liked. Ben is part of something called Jump Start, a program for at-risk high school seniors who are finishing up through independent study. Jump Starters are also required to have a serious job. Ben works for a carpenter.

The high school asked me to run this program because of my GED experience. The dean figured I would be "comfortable" with this "population." I'd take the job seriously, but I could be "flexible," which meant that I could look the other way to help someone slip through. He also told me that I could "smuggle in" as much creative writing as I wished. He knew all about Young Chicago Authors.

More than 100 students have been involved in Jump Start, and no one has worked more eagerly than Ben. He arrives early and leaves late. Or, he'll just show up unannounced, flop down on the couch, and read. He writes in his journal constantly. He sees movies and plays that have some connection to what he's reading. For his Vietnam term paper, he saw *Full Metal Jacket, The Boys of Company C, Platoon* and *Apocalypse Now.*

He has read several novels, his favorite being *Lonesome Dove.* He has written a long term paper about the Leopold and Loeb thrill murder. He has completed a modern history book. Next year he will attend the University of Northern Arizona at Flagstaff. Today, we talked about *Cloud Splitter*, Russell Banks' biography of John Brown. I had asked him to select twelve passages that he considered essential to the book and then explain why. He nodded agreeably. I told him that I stole the idea from my advisor at Northwestern, "a guy named Wally."

Wally was intrigued by the kids in Jump Start and often asked about them. "Is the Polish guy still working all night at the hardware store?" "What became of the girl who got kicked out for ordering all of that pizza for her teacher?" "What about the Latvian girl whose mom is a marriage broker?" "What happened to that fellow with the snake?" "Why does that girl dress like a witch?" "Did that boy with all the tattoos keep his job at Starbucks?" "Is that little girl still writing that wonderful love poetry?"

In the car, Jay and I talk business. He teaches full time at a local high school and writes mystery books. He is also the chairman of the board for YCA, and we discuss some fund-raising ideas. He wants some more copies of *Yak Dreams*, our newest magazine. He'd like the YCA students to do a reading at his school.

The auditorium at the Convention Center holds several hundred people and is nothing at all like ivy-covered Gothic building where I had my first class with Wally. That old lecture hall at Northwestern, with its narrow windows, shadows, horrible ventilation and creaky floors, reeked of academia. This place in Milwaukee is unapologetically utilitarian. It's clean, windowless and comfortable. It's set up for elaborate audio/visual presentations. It's a place that would have set Wally's eyebrows twittering.

We all gather in the front to chat. We are dressed better than the teachers were dressed back in our Northwestern days, but we won't be confused for trial lawyers or ad men. I spot several out-of-fashion ties, and one fellow is actually wearing a leisure suit. There are English professors, education professors, high school teachers, elementary school teachers, school counselors. One man left teaching altogether to get into publishing. Several are writers. Another is a programmer for a chemical company. As far as I can tell, I am the only freelance teacher. It's a rare experience to be in a room filled with "what-I-might-have-beens." I can see myself in almost all of these roles, but I'm pleased with the choice I made.

The man running the program begins by reading letters from people who could not attend. One letter is from a professor of education at the University of Kansas. He'll always be grateful to Wally for making his profession "academically respectable." Wally had told him there was no need for education people to think of themselves as "ex-coaches who couldn't make it in the real academic world." What they were doing was far more important than what some "pretentious scholar" might be doing. There is a letter from an English professor who credits Wally with waking him up to "the real business of teaching." That theme is repeated several times in the letters: Wally made the education people feel more like legitimate scholars, and he made the scholars feel more relevant. He accomplished this by helping them find their true teaching voices.

We are invited to come up to the front to tell our own Wally stories. An English professor from Stony Brook recalls the time in the summer of 1970 when several of us moved Wally's books from one office to another. There were hundreds of books, all carefully categorized according an obscure Wally system. "It was hot—really hot. When we finally finished after the days of work, we discovered that we had moved the books to the wrong office."

I tell the story about using a coat hanger to get into a locked car on the street near the English department office. While Wally stood agape, I calmly fed the extended hanger over the window and down to the lock. "Nothing I did in the whole Ph.D. program impressed him more." I then tell the story of how Wally gave me an "A" in my Independent Study before he discussed the books with me.

One older man explains how Wally had helped him "get on" with his dissertation, which had something to do with the history of teaching English. "I wanted to quit, but Wally wouldn't let me. He got me to see that the subject was actually quite interesting. He made me ask questions that mattered." Several described classes like my first class with Wally. Like me, people felt from the beginning that this odd little man knew something important, even though he couldn't always demonstrate what he knew.

Later I find out where some of these people are teaching and what they are teaching and how they are teaching. I find out what they've been writing and reading. I tell them about Young Chicago Authors. A professor from Indiana University is fascinated. Wally must have "loved the idea," she says.

Back home, I tell Sue that we spent most of the time laughing.

"Wally would have liked that," she says.

That is true. He knew precisely what sort of character he was. He would have been moved by all of the praise, but he would not have admitted it. He certainly would have approved of all the different kinds of teachers who showed up. He would have been pleased that so many of us found the right place in education. He knew that people like Jay and me did not belong in the university world, and he knew that others, like Bruce, would thrive as professors of English.

Wally was not a role model or a father figure. He was a presence, an irascible character who gained tremendous insight into his students and, in his unusual way, motivated all of us to find what we had inside ourselves. I never thought of him directly as I made the choices that led me into a unique career, but on some level I was always confident that what I was doing was OK with him—even the SAT work. He knew enough about the teaching profession and about his students to recognize when something good was happening.

POE TO THE RESCUE

It's a warm Saturday morning in May, and as usual I'm sitting in a room full of YCA students. The constant noise of Division Street pours in through the open windows. Last week the sounds came from a Puerto Rican Independence Day parade, which, among other things, featured old men on tricycles. Today it's the sound of cars, many the SUVs of local yuppies, who are rapidly taking over the neighborhood. We're all officially appalled by the gentrification, sneering in an obligatory way at the well-heeled young adults and various developers who are improving properties left and right, but privately just about everyone is pleased that the neighborhood is now safe enough for young people to visit our office any time and stay as late as they wish.

Through the years, YCA students have come from every imaginable background. We have had Spanish-speaking kids from Puerto Rico, Mexico and Peru. Some of our black kids were born in Chicago; others were born in the South and moved here. One black girl is from Jamaica. One black boy's father lives in Ghana. The white kids are from many places besides the United States, including Poland, Bosnia and Rumania. We have three Asian kids—Korean, Chinese and Filipino. We have had two Indian students. And then we have had "mixtures" like Janelle, whose background was Asian, Jewish, and Latina. "You look like The United Colors of Benetton," a reporter said a few days ago, unknowingly repeating the joke made by Liz during the very first YCA class. "Writing obviously attracts kids from every possible background."

But it has occurred to me lately that while the variety of students makes us politically correct, these official categories of race and religion don't begin to tell the story. The kids from our program—including the ones sitting across from me today—are diverse not because they are multicolored. They're diverse because their writing is so varied—varied subjects, voices and forms. The kids write about the past, the present and the future. Some write about what they immediately know. Others rely on their imaginations— Annamaria, a girl from Rumania, is finishing a story that takes place on a Georgia plantation. They write mysteries. They write tight poems and loose ones. Visitors who study what these "city kids" choose are astonished that drugs and gangs play such a small part in their writing.

We've just read through our weekly newspaper, *Sleazy Writer*. I've reminded them that graduation is coming up ("NO THONGS"), that we have a reading at the Printer's Row Book Fair, that we still have summer jobs available at a nearby school, and that the students who traveled to Africa in April will be making a presentation at the Chopin Theater. Finally, I announce that my daughter Sarah has started a learning center down the street. She'll be teaching classes for little children and may be looking for volunteers. The YCA kids, whether they are sitting in chairs or lounging on the rug, listen with detached interest.

I am still overwhelmingly gratified that the program is working so well—both the scholarship program and the outreach programs we offer in the schools. I'm still very much involved in the teaching, but I've found some excellent people to help out. We have gained a citywide reputation. "Young Chicago Authors," according to one journalist, "has made the city safe for young creative writers."

But along with feeling a touch self-satisfied, today I also feel frustrated and annoyed and bothered. The simple fact is that these kids—these wonderfully talented young Chicago writers—have not been writing much at all lately. And what they have been writing basically stinks. This happens every spring, but for some reason this year I am much more bothered by the epidemic of indifference.

I have some prompts for today, but I'm not sure they'll work. The kids will write a little; they'll respond amiably. They'll hang around the office afterwards. They might all go off and have lunch together. But that will be it.

The least I can do is tell them what's on my mind, even though they probably know already. This doesn't call for a lecture or a rant. I'd just like them to know that I want them to wake up long enough to write something worth taking seriously. I start by reminding them how important these classes are. "This is where so much of your good writing starts." I list several recent pieces of YCA writing that began in class and ended up in a magazine or winning a contest. "I know the weather's great and that you have finals, but give yourself a chance to write something powerful. We have two more classes, and that's it. See if you can write something you're proud of." I pause. No more to say.

"So you want us to feel guilty." Alan is talking. He's a short kid who will attend Northwestern next year. He also plays in our band. He's one of the few who have not stopped writing. Now he's got a big smile.

"You bet I do!" Alan's given me an opportunity to change into a slightly ironic tone of voice. "You all SHOULD feel a little guilty for squandering your talent. Grab the moment. I mean it." I feel like really laying on the *carpe diem* angle, but I stop myself.

I'm about to describe today's prompt when Alan starts talking again. "Why don't we do something with an author? Remember all the great writing we had after you read us that story 'Haircut'?" Grunts of agreement.

He's absolutely right. The "Haircut" class was

something special, and so were the other classes that focused on a single work. I'd read a story or a poem to the class. We'd talk about it. I'd make a few suggestions. And that would be all the class needed to start writing. But lately I have been relying on my own prompts. "Fair enough. Who should we read?"

"Whom." I've been corrected by Martin, who spent last summer with his relatives in Ireland.

"Thank you, Martin. *Whom* should we read? I've got some copies of Poe stories. Do you all want to read Poe?"

There's some talk, but most feel Poe will work. Molly, who plans to be a doctor, thinks it will be fun to read someone "we haven't read since 8th grade."

Without waiting for a minority opinion, I pass out copies of "The Tell-Tale Heart." I feel a surge of energy. I ask Chris, a tall sophomore from Hyde Park, if he'd like to read. I tell the class to pay close attention to the images. "Let your senses be taken in. Look for things to borrow."

"You mean steal."

"Thank you, Martin. Remember, you'll use this story as a starting point for something original."

As Chris reads, the class smiles, laughs, groans, winces and gasps. This happy little tale about the servant who smothers his master has not lost any of its punch. The class is especially enjoying it because they're listening to it as writers, not as literature students.

When the story's over, I ask for a quick recall. Sounds? "The beating of the heart." "The squeaking floorboards." Sights? "The bulging eye." Smells? "The candle burning." I fire off several "what if" questions. "What if someone else had told the story?" "What if the murder took place right away?" "What if the author used only one-syllable words?" "What if the servant had another motive for killing his boss?" The kids shout back answers. They're awake. They want to write.

I toss out a few ideas, but not many. "You could become one of the characters. You could write a true story about revenge or guilt. You could take Poe's first sentence and use that as the first sentence of an original story." I tell them to consider using a strong narrative voice, to remember the connections between feelings and actions, and to create vivid settings. Above all, I want them to take this seriously. "This can be more than an exercise."

Off they go—some to the Duct-Taped couch, some to desks, some to the rugs, some to corners, some to the stairwell, some to the back porch. I make myself a cup of coffee. The kids are writing nonstop and barely notice me as I walk from room to room. We now occupy the entire second floor of the building that we first moved into in 1993. Along with the original space with the mailboxes and the long table and the small office, we now have several computer rooms, a kitchen, and a darkroom. The room overlooking Division Street is a large classroom. Some walls are covered with posters, samples of student writing and Sue's quilts. Other walls have large pictures of our kids in action. Visitors usually respond the same way: "This doesn't feel like a school."

I stroll through the neighborhood and run into my daughter Sarah and her dog. They're on the way to her learning center. We stand at the very spot where our student was beaten up several years ago. Now the neighborhood is known more for its sushi restaurants than its gangs.

Ninety minutes later, I am back upstairs sitting with the class in a circle on the floor ready to listen. Two of our other teachers have joined the group. First I ask what the class now thinks of the plan to use Poe. A shrug and several smiles. Their notebooks and journals look full.

"Has anyone written something in the voice of one of the characters?"

A little guy with big hair named Ben raises his

hand. "I've continued the story. The killer-servant is still talking." He waits for a second and then begins to read:

"The irritating smiles vanished from the faces of the officers, doing much to relieve the horror that had overcome me. The old man's heart continued to beat, but noticeably quieter than before. The men stared at me blankly for a moment. I slid down into my chair, as the nervousness that had been surging through my veins was replaced by an onslaught of quiet serenity. The men stood and moved toward me. Their voices grew harsh as they interrogated me. I revealed to them—and I admit that I did so with a certain amount of pleasure and pride—my flawless plan.

"Their eyes grew wide as I described what I had done with the dismembered body. The youngest of the officers pulled a pair of handcuffs from his belt and fastened them around my wrists. They asked me where I had put the crowbar that I used to pry up the floorboards, and after I told them, the officer who had handcuffed me went to get it.

"One of the remaining officers grabbed me by the collar and thrust his face up close to mine. With a great deal of anger and a small amount of fear in his voice, he questioned my motive. Ha! What did he know? He never had to endure the stares of the old man's vulture eye. Thinking of that hideous eye immediately takes away any remorse that is building up inside my conscience.

"Of course the officer, lacking the aforementioned knowledge, had little insight into the cause of my actions, and therefore had no sympathy for me. He called me mad, and spat upon my face. Before my rage could get a firm hold on me, the younger officer returned with the crowbar. It took me a minute to identify the correct floorboards, but I did so, and the men went to work. As the boards were pried up, and the mutilated body was revealed, a look of disgust and sickness came over their faces. I begged them to open an eyelid on the severed head, so that they could see the reason behind my so-called crime. Oh, how I know that if only they had done my bidding, I would certainly have gained their sympathy. However, they did not do as I asked, and the officer who had previously said and done very little pulled out his baton and slammed it into my skull. Barely conscious, I watched a trail of blood trickle onto the ground as they dragged me outside so that I could be taken to the station. I am fairly certain that I fell unconscious at this point, for the next thing I remember is waking up in this dark, dirty cell, locked up like the madman they have accused me of being."

Smiles and nods and then applause. We're all impressed that this feels so "finished." Chris likes phrases such as "lacking the aforementioned knowledge" and the other Poeisms. Rebecca thinks Ben has done a first-rate job keeping the narrator in character: "Little things still made him mad." I tell Ben I'm glad he ended with the narrator still convinced he's sane. I also tell him that I can't recall him ever using a voice like this in his writing.

Ben, along with Alan, is one of the few students who had not lost interest in writing, so I am not surprised by his strong effort. Hyo is another story. Lately, she hasn't been writing anything at all. Today she cheerfully offers to read her version of what the cops might have reported:

"Did I realize he was mad? Oh, yes, from the start, I knew something was wrong with him. As soon as he opened the door, he started making these nervous smiles. At first, I just thought he was on some kind of antidepressants. He kept smiling without any reason. He couldn't walk straight and kept looking around the house the whole time my partner and I were there. So we couldn't just leave him there, we being police officers and all, we decided to stay a little longer with him since he looked very lonesome living in that gigantic mansion all alone, without the old man. My partner and I had warm hearts.

"The second thing I noticed about his sick behavior was that as soon as we mentioned the shriek, he begged us to search the house. You know, we were there to ask him a few questions, not for investigating. My partner and I couldn't say no since our job was to serve the citizens. We searched everywhere, even all the closet in the house. Boy, were we exhausted!"

More applause. Oscar points out that Hyo's cops do "cop-like things." He's right. They ask questions. They search. They draw astute conclusions. They fear for the safety of the servant in the large mansion. Ben is amused by the phrase, "Boy, were we exhausted!" He says, "It sounds like something people say after putting up a tent."

This is the most animated the class has been in a month.

Several students have written true stories—mostly revenge pieces. Danny, who lately has been promising much and producing little, describes a fight with his older brother Juan, who just happens to be a graduate of Young Chicago Authors.

Lexe gets even with her sister "for her stupid little tricks through the years." She reads:

"I waited for what seemed like eternity until finally I heard my sister come out and climb into bed. Believing that I was sleeping, she said, 'Good night, Lexe.' I said good night from the closet and watched through the shutters as she rolled over and closed her eyes. I counted off at least a minute in my head and then I slowly started to switch the closet light on and off. I heard my sister turn to my bed and stammer, 'Le-e-x-ce?'

"Finally I couldn't hold it anymore. I started laughing hysterically because I knew I had gotten her, and I opened the closet door.

"It's funny, though, every time I remind her of this incident, she claims that she knew it was me and was just playing along—I highly doubt it."

I tell Lexe and Danny that I appreciate this peek at their darker sides. Writers should be able to show some bad qualities. Others think that Lexe had built suspense in a Poe-like way. ("I waited for what seemed like an eternity . . .") Barth thinks that the last paragraph is important because it shows her sister's character. And "It gives Lexe a reason to scare her one more time." Good comment.

Oscar, perhaps our least-angry student, writes about someone he hates.

"I'm always close. I hear all the awful things he mutters. 'Did you see what she did to her hair?' 'Why is she wearing those ugly and old-looking clothes?' 'Why is it that everyone dresses so weird?'

"What gets me even more mad is that he pretends to be a very nice friend and tells others how nice they look. What a liar!

"All I want to do is get up and tell him, 'What's the problem? Why is everybody less of a person than you are?' But I don't. I keep it to myself."

Clearly, Poe has given Oscar a voice to express something that has been bothering him for some time. Previously, he has written about his family and his teachers. He has described his father's factory job, but he has never talked about something like this.

Several students, like Alex, have started with the first sentence of Poe's story and then written their own stories in the style of Poe:

"True! Nervous—very, very nervous I had been and am; but why will you say that I am mad? I tell you now, ever so carefully, of the sinful deed, which I, so very meticulously, carried through. It was at the Corner Pantry store, a place which over the years of my childhood I had wandered into from time to time. Usually I did so for trivial, meager tasks, food, candy, and other such meaningless childhood necessities.

"It was through these adventures that I had become very well acquainted with the store's clerk, as we made a commonplace ritual of discussing our day-to-day affairs. I had even made a regular habit of purchasing a bag of chips and a can of coke every time I came into the store. It was on this particular day, however, that I had something very different in mind.

"Why I even decided to do what I did, I know not, only that once my mind grabbed hold of the idea, I could not escape it. It soon became the very object of all my thoughts, and I began finding myself staying up for hours at night as my mind began to formulate my devilish plan. For weeks on end, I planned and schemed, and when that very day came, I was ready. As I approached the store, I made sure to do it with a certain swiftness, as not to attract unwanted attention."

Naturally, we want to know more about the "devilish plan," but Alex isn't telling.

Annamaria has made up a story about a girl who must make a speech at graduation. "I like this character," Annamaria tells us. "She does the kinds of things I would like to do." Her story is in the first person:

"I took a seat in the auditorium. How dreadfully nervous I was. My hands trembled as I accepted the diploma. When the principal introduced me, I took a deep breath. Here goes nothing. I hurried to the podium so quickly that I didn't see Michael, the star athlete, who had nothing better to do than trip me.

"I lost it. I took off one of my high-heeled sandals and aimed at his head. I scored. The students, the teachers, and the parents gasped. What did I do?

"I calmly put on the sandal. I flipped my hair back with one manicured nail and stepped to the podium as if nothing had happened."

We agree that the "one manicured nail" is good stuff. She wants to keep working on his.

Time's up; they'll leave the papers here for us to type. "What should we do next week?" I ask as they are starting to leave. Several shout, "Mo Poe."

That afternoon I meet with the other teachers. Jocelyn, who has been with us for several years, tells me how the current mystery magazine is coming along. Tim tells me the plans for drama next year. He'll also help out with the summer activities. Koz, one of our graduates, is now one of our editors. I give her the Poe papers to type.

All of the other teachers are amazed by the energy of today's class. Jocelyn asks me what happened.

"I listened to them. That's what happened."

"What do you mean?"

"I was going to give them one of my prompts, but they wanted to do an author. We did Poe, and you heard the results. You saw them all smiling and alert when they left. That's what happened."

I feel like gabbing. These kids have "so much to say." They can do so much in one sitting. They can write about what they know, and they can write about what they imagine. They never stop surprising me. "Who would have guessed that Ben had such a good ear for someone else's speech patterns?"

I go on and on about what all of this "proves" until Jocelyn finally jumps into the conversation. "It also proves that we should listen to what the little sweethearts want to do."

"I've known this for 30 years," I say. "I just forget sometimes."

BACK TO CABRINI

I am at Cabrini Green again, but this time with little kids. The place is called PEP—Project Education Plus. It is a tiny agency that meets in one of the row houses that sit like satellites around the high-rise blocks. The room is too small for the twenty kids. There are tables crammed together along one side and an open area with a rug on the other. The air conditioner in the window makes a lot of noise, but it doesn't seem to work. We are on the rug. Toni, a graduate of YCA, is taking pictures. She has to push the kids away to get good pictures. ("Stand back, Nerds.") I get them in a group in front of me, and we tell a story together. "Today, it will be a story about an animal with a problem."

A few nods and shouts. They really like doing this.

"So what kind of animal is it going to be?" I ask. There's tremendous shouting, but finally elephant wins out over mouse and amoeba.

"What's the elephant's name?" More shouting and arguing, but they finally settle for Itzy.

"Now then. Think hard. What's Itzy's problem?" Silence. Uncharacteristic silence. I can hear them panting, and they are looking at their hands or off into the room frowning as they try to decide. No one says anything until Jerome stands up and hollers, "Bumps! Itzy has Bumps."

I ask more questions, and their answers become the story. Where does Itzy live? "In the jungle." Who's her friend? "Flubby." What does Itzy look like? "Big and gray and strong." Where are the bumps? "On the trunk." What does she do to take care of them? "Tries lotions. Later she goes to Dr. Feelgood." What does he do? "Looks in his doctor

248

book." What does he find? "Special stuff to make the bumps go away." How does Itzy feel now? "Happy."

Next I ask Sheronda, one of the older kids, to repeat the whole story. The class shouts when she forgets a detail. Several more try until we have the whole thing all in our heads. "OK," I announce. "Make drawings that go along with the story. This can be any scene you want." The kids go back to the tables and draw furiously.

The students range from just 4 years old to 10 years old. The older ones find it fun because it's a little silly. The younger ones like it because it's new and they're good at it. Tonight I'll take the story and drawing home. I'll give them to Sue who will make them into a book. Each kid will get one. Then we'll do another one.

I have been doing this for the past few summers. Along with "Itzy The Bump-Trunked Elephant," my classes have written "Suspicious Suzy," "Pamela the Python," "A Bad Day for Gregory Gorilla," "Where is Sweety?" "What's Wrong with Mr. Jones?" "Harry's Bad Day," "The Nerd from Bucktooth," "The Saber-Toothless Tiger," "The Case of the Missing Comb," and "Georgie the Iguana."

The kids all pile together for one last photo, and then Toni and I leave.

It's hot.

PRISON LADIES

I have never been in a room like this before. For starters, it has no windows. But that's nothing; I've been in windowless rooms before. It has more pieces of computer equipment than I have ever seen in one place. There are stacks of keyboards, monitors, circuit boards, servers, printers and modems. There is one corner with a mountain of mouses (mice?). Some stacks literally touch the ceiling. The dozen desks in the middle all are covered by piles of materials that relate to computers. One has only wires. Another desk has stacks of books that explain how to maintain and repair computer equipment. There are green plastic trays with tiny plastic boxes of even tinier nuts and screws. There are tiny screwdrivers for these tiny things.

The room, which is in a building on Milwaukee Avenue just west of Ashland in Chicago, is a classroom. The students who come here at night have recently been released from prison. They come here to become trained computer technicians. Once they have gone through the book, they take a test. If they pass the test, they get a license and charge $40 or more for an hour of their services.

The students who come here during the day are also former offenders. They are taking my GED class. Last spring a man from the Prison Action Committee called to ask if I could give several people tips on how to be GED instructors. When I showed up, there were no teachers for me to instruct. We rescheduled the meeting, but no one came that time either. When it became apparent that there would be no instructors to teach the former prisoners, I offered to teach the classes myself.

I start the day by making a few phone calls.

First I must find the phone, which today is buried under a mound of keyboards. I call a man about the web site he is creating for Young Chicago Authors. I call a printing company about the new magazine we are doing for the older kids. ("Geezer Teaser" is the working title.) I call Jay to confirm the dates for our winter SAT/ACT program. I leave a message for myself to e-mail information to the seniors about an upcoming trip to a writing conference in Wisconsin. I sit back and relax. I never would have guessed what great pleasure I would get from organizing and planning. It's almost Zen-like, sitting here in the midst of someone else's clutter as I think about all the little contacts I must make to hold this whole thing together.

This gives me an opportunity to think about the students who are about to arrive. What sets the group apart from other collections of my students, obviously, is their unfortunate past. If most of my other students are chasing some sort of dream, it seems that the students who come here are being chased by nightmares.

In our very first class, they wrote me letters. One girl lost her parents when she was young and went to live with her auntie. Everything was going well until she got into a relationship with a man. "I was eight years old when this man started to molest me. I was so scared I didn't want to tell anybody but I finally did and when I did he cut my auntie's throat so I thought it was all my fault."

Most started young: "At the age of sixteen I was on my own and it became real hard for me. I started going to jail. Back and forth. In and out. I didn't learn anything, just in and out."

Another girl described sleeping in cars, "when I didn't have to sleep in the hallway. I made my kids turn away from me. They did not want to see their mother on street corners selling drugs."

But I learned from the letters that most had

started to win back some self-respect: "I learned to start my day off in the morning instead of at noon. I learned to be responsible for what I do. I found out that not all money is not good money and that you can do more with hard-earned money than with drug money."

"I did things in the pen that I never thought I would do. I went to school and parenting classes and church. Today God's really been working with me. I am going to get my GED and change my life around today for me and my family."

"My plans are for getting my GED and A+ Certificate so I can live a better life. I want to be someone. I plan to live healthy with my kids in Mexico."

"I'm doing well for myself. I am working now, something I've never done before. But now at this point I am grateful and blessed. I've found God and a new life. I have a lot of supporting people to help me along the way. All I can say is thank God for supporting me. These 29 years of my life have been a true learning experience."

Most of the class arrives on time. First through the door is Izzie. She's wearing a silver New York Yankees jacket. Like almost all of her classmates, Izzie is a black female who lives in a group home near the United Center. She calls the home when she gets here and calls it when she leaves. Rubie, nicknamed "Fruity," is with her. She is wearing a new blue and red jogging suit that she bought on layaway from a store across the street. Patsy arrives with food. Last week she showed me the funeral program for her brother, who had been shot to death in a bar fight. While we clear the computer debris from the big table in the back, several more come in—Cassandra, Susan, Tiffany and Barbara. In this second group are Ritchie and Chris, the only males.

We are just getting ready to begin when Etta arrives. Like the others, she greets us all with a friendly hello, and then she sits down and opens up the book. "What page we at?" But before I can answer, she starts to rant, "I ain't going to take this test ever." On the floor next to her, she puts down a bag from the Bargain Tree. "I don't know enough to pass this thing and I don't know why I am trying." She looks around, then back at me and gives a friendly nod. Several others, led by Maxine, start mumbling in agreement ("no way," "I need to study for two more years," "I'm just going to fail; why bother?").

"Would you please," I say in a loud, mock-angry voice, "stop talking such crap." I clear my voice and begin to lecture. "You have nothing to worry about, and even if you do, worrying is not going to help. All you need to do is get one-half right. You have all done very well in class on the tests that I give you, and I give you real tests. You know that I give you real tests." I wave one in the air. "Pass the test, and you have all kinds of options. Plus, when you pass the test, you'll prove that you are as smart as I know you are. OK? OK?" They nod and smirk a little. They've heard this before, and they'll certainly hear it again. They know I mean it. They know I am right. But they're probably still skeptical about what they can do when it really counts.

Sometimes I tell them true stories about former GED students like the 55-year-old candy factory worker or the mother of ten or a former leader of the Latin Kings. These people needed to discover for themselves that they could do the work. Once that was accomplished, they passed the test. It was that simple. Inside they had what was needed.

Today we start with a little math, something the class truly hates. After giving them a quick overview of a sample test, I pass out a sheet reviewing fractions, decimals and percentages. It also reviews the basic operations and includes terms like *sum, product, difference,* and *quotient.* It also explains the Pythagorean Theorem. Then, it's Big Question time.

This they will solve as a group. I'll read this one time only, so they must listen carefully to pick up the pertinent pieces of information.

"Izzie is walking down the street with $500 in the pocket of her Yankees jacket. She sees Rubie, who owes her $200 but who can only pay her 1/2 of what she owes her. Izzie pockets the money and then goes to buy a turkey for Thanksgiving from Maxine's Turkey Central. Turkeys normally cost $40 but this one is on sale for 25% off. She buys some milk and gravy for $15 more and then heads home. But on the way she meets Etta, who's in a bad mood, and who asks for 0.6 of the money so that she can go to Patsy's dance performance. Then Izzie is stopped by a Wizard named Ritchie who offers to sell her a sausage pizza in the shape of a right triangle. The pizza costs $15.00 per square inch. One side is 6 inches and the hypotenuse is 10 inches. After she buys the pizza, how much money does she have left over?"

It takes a while for them to get all the information straight and to agree on what to do. But before long they have the right answer. I'm quite sure this helps with the math. How could it not? It also helps them concentrate on details and to communicate with each other.

Next on the agenda is an imaginative description. While it's not at all like the GED essay test question, which asks them to defend a position, the imaginative piece will give them practice writing down responses and then shaping them into something complete.

Once they all have paper and pens, I begin. I ask them to imagine that they have just walked into Moe's Cafe, which is the filthiest restaurant in Cook

County. I'm going to ask questions about the place. They are to scribble down answers and then compose their answers into a unified description. They listen and write as I ask them to consider the waitress, the smells, the other customers, the pictures on the wall and other details that create the atmosphere of Moe's Cafe. Before they start to write, I remind them that they can add any details they would like. When they write their papers, they should try to make their ideas into a letter to someone who would enjoy hearing all about Moe's.

The next thing I know, they are writing like crazy. Occasionally they ask me to spell a word. They might show something to the person next to them. But mostly they work purposefully and in silence. Clearly they think what they're doing is important.

Forty minutes later, a smiling Izzie is reading her paper to the class.

Dear Maxine,

I just wanted to let you know that I went to this restaurant called Moe's Cafe the other day. And it was so disgusting. The floor had big cracks in it and coffee stains from the front to the back. And the waitress was just as gross. She had on a dirty uniform, and she was wiping her nose on her apron, saying "May I take your order?" The menu was just as bad. The whole place smelled like someone had dropped their garbage in the place. The toilets must not have been working. I couldn't believe it smelled that bad. And let's not forget the owner himself. His T-shirt and apron were dirty and he was fat and nasty looking and smelled like he hadn't showered in weeks.

There was this dog in there that looked like he had fleas. A lady came in with her kids. Her hair was nappy and the kids' hair was too, and their noses kept running. So she wiped them with her T-shirt. I just couldn't believe it myself.

You couldn't really see anything because the lights were so dim and dirty. And there was no light from the outside because the windows were filled with just as much dirt as the lights. Then I saw a plate of food go by. It looked burnt. Insects were crawling around the edge. The whole place was very unsanitary, but there was one thing that I saw that was OK and seemed like it shouldn't have been there. That was me. I felt so out of place. I just want you to know: Don't stop at Moe's. It's not a good place for anyone.

LOVE, IZZIE

"What did you like?" I ask. "The toilet smell." "The dog." "The kids with the nappy hair." I tell them all that this paper is wonderfully rich in detail, that Izzie should be proud of this. I suggest that she make a story out of it some time. I repeat the details I like. I tell her not to forget that this paper has a definite form and shape to it. "It sounds like writing, doesn't it?"

The next volunteer is Aleesha, who starts off like this:

Dear Angel,

Girl, let me tell you what me and Antoine did last night. He took me to this restaurant. Girl, if you were there, you would have smacked the shit out of him. The floor was nasty. It was worse than dirty it was filthy. I swear to god. Then we had this waitress. Her name was Blanch. I was two inches away from beating her ass . . . the bathroom stank all over. The floor's got urine on it and everything. The walls are sweaty.

We read some more. In Ritchie's version, the menu is so dirty that he asks for a towel to wipe it off. The dog in Maxine's is covered with mange. Kelia's waitress sports yellow teeth and smokes and wears a dress so small "that you could see her underwear." In her story, Patsy puts roaches on the floor.

I then distribute typed copies of papers the students wrote earlier in the fall. Many of these will go into a magazine published by Young Chicago Authors. They look through the material eagerly. "Which ones grab you?" I ask. Several like Keila's true story, which begins with a rush: "My boyfriend slept with a nasty girl and I still love and care for him and act like it never went on" and ends with a simple moral: "If you stay mad it will get you nowhere."

We ask Tiffany to read her true story, which describes a friend whose boyfriend had stuck their baby into a clothes dryer and nearly killed it. "Bitch, quit playing," Tiffany had said to the girl when she admitted what had happened. When the girl then told Tiffany that she still loved her boyfriend, Tiffany shouted right in her face. "How could you love someone who hurt your child?" When the girl said her boyfriend had given his life to God, Tiffany answered, "You stupid bitch, he might as well give his life to God because he ain't got shit coming in jail. They're going to tie his ass off." Applause.

Like all my other students, these GED students like to write. They take enormous pleasure in putting together these pieces, whether they are imaginary stories about a Moe's Cafe or true stories about prison. They sense that strong writing needs sharp details and a strong voice.

Time to go. I have more teaching, and they have jobs. I distribute subway passes while they make calls to the Center to say that they are leaving the GED class. I tell them one more time not to quit, that their writing should prove to them what they are capable of accomplishing. I know that I repeat myself too much, but I can't shut up. On the way out, Maxine shouts back, "Hey, Bob, stay away from that waitress at Moe's."

My next stop is Marshall High School on the west side. The basketball coach has asked me to help

257

a few of her players who will be taking the SAT in a few days. Marshall was the first all-black Chicago school to win the boys' basketball state championship. It is one of those schools that ends up with the kids who do not get into the magnet school or the competitive Catholic schools. Reading scores are low; dropouts are high. Not too many go to college, and the ones that do often flunk out. Kids in schools like this spend far too much class time preparing for reading tests so that the principal can keep his job.

My first contact with Marshall students was in 1985 at Avalon Park where several players took part in the creative writing program. When I began to help basketball players with the ACT and SAT exams, the Marshall coaches asked me to help out. I did, gladly. Like the coaches at Avalon Park, the people at Marshall defy the stereotype: They are educators, teachers who believe in education.

Marshall High School is a big red brick building on the corner of Adams and Kedzie, down the street from a restaurant that features "Tacos Jew Town Style." It's a relatively short drive but a very long distance from the North Shore suburbs. I park in front and walk through the metal detector past two oversized security guards in yellow jackets and down the hall to the girls' gym, in a far corner of the building, where Coach Dorothy Gaters has her office. She is by far the most successful girls' basketball coach in Illinois and certainly one of the best in the nation. On the walls are pictures of several of her state-championship teams. There are trophies from tournaments in Milwaukee and Las Vegas.

When I'm in an office like this, I am always reminded how most schools have certain individuals with power and identity. They have their own phones and offices. Their reputation far exceeds the current administration's. In Germany our power figure was Bernie, who was in charge of all the buses. At Highland Park it was Ralph, who sponsored both the yearbook and the newspaper. At Marshall, it seems to be Dorothy Gaters.

Gaters and I gab some about Chicago basketball. She tells me where some of her players will be going next year. She asks about Young Chicago Authors and gives me the name of an English teacher who might have some people for our scholarship program.

Then three players arrive: Benatta, Simone and Tonika. Benatta, who is one of the top prospects in the country, will attend college next year, but if she wants to play as a freshman, she'll need to raise her test scores to qualify. We find a corner of the gym with some school desks and go to work. They have a game later that afternoon, so at best we can work for 45 minutes.

I start off by showing them the SAT and reminding them that it is like the ACT in many ways, but that the vocabulary parts make it unique. The SAT is supposed to be harder, but that's not necessarily true. They eye the verbal section and then scowl at the scoring system. They don't look convinced. But they are not hostile. They are healthy-looking young people who sit up straight and look me in the eye. They're jocks.

We start with sentence completions. These are short passages with one or two words omitted. Each question has five possible answers. "Here's how I want you to do it," I say in my best coach's voice. "Instead of looking at the possible answers right away, I want you to ignore the answers and decide what word you believe should go in the space. Find a word or words that make the sentence work. Only then check the answers. Maybe put your hand over the answers so you won't be tempted. You'll probably find your word or one like it. At least you'll know what to reject."

For this first section, I let them work as a team. They grimace and laugh self-consciously. The words must look difficult. The question format must seem odd. When do they see questions that look like this?

Some potatoes of the Andes contain _____ known as glycoalkaloids that induce stomach pains, vomiting and even death.

(A) nutrients
(B) secretions
(C) inversions
(D) toxins
(E) preservatives

At first they do just what I recommend not to do. They scream out answers ("Secretions!" "Nutrients!"). They are looking at the words on the test, not words in their own memories. I tell them again: "Put in YOUR word. Find one of YOUR words that makes the passage work. THEN look at the choices." Benatta gets the idea. "It's got to be something that isn't good because it makes you throw up." They slow down and quickly decide it must be a word like "poison." They look at the choices and recognize "toxins." Okay, I tell them, you're one for one. The second question reads like this:

The chamber orchestra refuses to identify its members; it is this insistence on _____ that sets this ensemble apart.
(A) longevity
(B) disparity
(C) anonymity
(D) mediocrity
(E) dissonance

Once again they start off by plugging in words, but when they take the time to find a word, they come

the notion of "no name." Then they look and eliminate "longevity," and "mediocrity." Then Benatta can see that "anonymity" works, and they are two for two.
The pattern continues. They look at the passage, laugh nervously and then take a stab with one of the answers. When I suggest that they look for their own word first, they get the right answer and then all say "For real?" On the SAT, the problems move from easy to hard. The next-to-last problem reads like this:

"A ____ person, he found the training almost unbearably monotonous, but he resolved to check his ____ and perform the basic tasks required."

      (A) bitter / submissiveness
      (B) reclusive / reserve
      (C) dynamic / restlessness
      (D) mercurial / constancy
      (E) vivacious / ambition

This time they start off by looking for their own words. They argue and probe and eventually get the right one. The key for them is "unbearably monotonous." They decide that "impatient" would work for the first word and "impatience" would work for the second word. They then look at the choices and come up with "dynamic" and "restlessness."
They are pleased. I give them practice working alone, and they get most of the next batch right. I tell them that at this rate they could get a score not just passing but considerably above the national average. We work on analogies and reading and math. Again they can—if I capture their attention—get most of the answers right. Gaining their attention means starting with what they know or with how they react. Start with yourself. Look inside. Make a connection.
Coach Gaters shows up with a basketball and a clipboard. Game-prep time for them, home time for me. Let's hope they pass. They'll have several more

chances, but it would be nice to have today's work pay off.

I stop into Dorothy's office to make a call and then walk out through the gym. The three girls are at a corner basket working on outside jump shots. I grab the ball and demonstrate the Boone Sky Hook and the Boone Set Shot. I go for a rebound, but Benatta rips it away. "You don't have White Man's Disease," she laughs. "You have White Man's Plague." When we stop, I get their attention one last time. "All right, ladies. Now I really know what you can do, and you know what you can do, so good luck on the SAT." They nod and smile. They agree with me, but this short experience is probably not going to shake loose the doubts they might have. But it might help.

GRADUATION

"What are *Yak Dreams*?" Christine asks. She is standing beside a table loaded with stacks of YCA publications. The wall behind the table is covered with pictures of kids from the program. Some of the pictures are of students writing. In some they are sitting in the audience for a performance; some are performing on the stage at the Chopin Theater. Christine and I are standing in the lobby of the Pritzker School, across the street from Wicker Park. In a few minutes, we'll be holding our seventh graduation. Christine, from the very first YCA class, is one of the first to arrive.

"*Yak Dreams* is what we called one of our magazines."

"I can see that. But why would you call anything *Yak Dreams*?"

"I'm not sure why we called it that. We'd been joking about yaks all year long. The teacher who put out the magazine thought she could do something with 'yak' and 'yack'—as in chatter. You know, 'yakkety-yack, don't talk back.' And so here you have it." John Zeddies, my son-in-law, walks by carrying a cooler full of drinks and heads for the back table where my daughter Fanny and Sue are laying out the food. Behind John trails my two-year-old grandson Nick carrying a paper airplane.

"What are all these kids doing?" Christine is pointing to an enlarged photo of a crowd of our kids climbing onto a bus.

"We're on the way to a writing festival in Whitewater, Wisconsin. When you guys started in 1992, I didn't know anything about stuff like that." I didn't know about the performance possibilities either. And I didn't know that we would also work in schools and youth agencies.

By now Christine is only half-listening to me. Instead she is picking up copies of the other magazines with titles like *Le Boom, One Voice, Our Voice, Dark and Story Night.* In all there are fifteen different magazines. "Look," Christine holds up a skinny orange publication. "Here's the very first one— *Young Chicago Authorings.*" She flips through the pages. "Here's my poem 'Busy Signal.' I can remember the day I wrote that at the Monadnock Building. It was raining that day. And a parade came by on Dearborn Street."

"Ten years ago," I say. Down the hall people are starting to arrive, even though the ceremony isn't for another hour. Most of the kids are dressed up. Relatives accompany many. Some pause to admire Sue's quilts that we hung on the wall for the occasion. Others are looking at the other large pictures that we have displayed. We have done what we could to make the school look less like a school.

Christine keeps talking. "I've kind of lost touch. I know that Michael is in the Peace Corps in Estonia and Carlos is teaching writing and art in California. Vic is doing graduate work at Carnegie Mellon. What else do you know?"

"Antevia is about to graduate from Howard. She spent one year on active duty in the military. Now she's in the reserves."

"Our little black rapper in a uniform. I love it!"

"Carol graduated from Northwestern. Now I think she's studying in Europe. Natoya is about to graduate. She wants to be a teacher. And Liz finished the University of Chicago early, and now she's at the Harvard Law School."

"I knew Liz would fail miserably." Christine is beaming. I'm really glad to see her. I still think of her as the mother figure from that first class. I'll never forget how much she enjoyed our trip to Madison.

I look through the side door and see one of our

families standing across the street in Wicker Park. This is where Nelson Algren and Simone de Beauvoir must have taken walks. Lately the whole neighborhood has become known as "literary," although the real story might be the middle-class families moving in. Our office is only a few blocks away. At one time it was a dangerous neighborhood. Now there are upscale restaurants with valet parking.

"How about Earnest? I hope he's still writing soap operas and mythology." Christine was always one of Earnest's biggest fans.

"Out of school. Never went too far. He used to stop by for some adult classes. He worked in our summer program, but now I've lost track of him." I reach over and grab a small sandwich from the food table.

Christine is eating a salad and sipping an iced tea. She's wearing a blue flowered dress. She looks mature and relaxed. More people have arrived and are heading for the table of drinks, salad and sandwiches. "How about Yolanda?" Christine asks through a mouthful of tuna fish.

"She tried UIC for awhile, but then she had a baby, and now she's had two more. We talk a lot on the phone. I think she'll go back to school. I really do."

"You think I'll go back?" Christine dropped out after her first semester at DePaul. We were astounded that she quit because she, of all the kids, seemed so suited for college life. For a while I badgered her about going back. I've stopped that now, but she knows how I feel. I'm just glad that she's here for graduation.

"Of course, you'll go back to college," I say. "Why not? Stranger things than that have happened. But whatever, we'd like to have you stay near."

By now I'm moving off to talk to some parents. The place has become really crowded. People are taking magazines and looking at all the pictures. Some are of the kids writing on Saturday mornings.

Others show the kids performing at the Chopin Theater. There are several pictures of the Slam Team. Suzy, who teaches our photography classes, is snapping pictures.

Old friends are hugging. Most of the younger teachers are here. They are standing at a table where chap books from this year's class are on display. One of the chap books is titled *Chocolate Covered Lovely.* My son Charlie, now teaching math to 8th graders in Oregon, has come in for the weekend. He knows several of the graduates because one year he helped me teach some of the classes. Fanny has prepared the food. By slow degrees, the lobby area clears as people move into the auditorium. I join the students on the stage.

The large auditorium is almost full, and considering all of the little children who are there, surprisingly quiet. Jay welcomes the people and then introduces the student emcees, who present Rosie Ricks, the mother of one of our graduates, with the Parent of the Year Award. Charity, Rosie's daughter, wrote a play this year that won a big award. Her play is based on the life of her grandmother, who as a young girl in Mississippi in the 1940s was forced to marry someone she did not know.

The next award is given to Anna West, one of our teachers. This is the Wallace Douglas Award. We give this every year to someone from the community who has brought out the creativity in young people. Anna has taught creative writing classes for us at a homeless shelter for high school kids, at a hospital, and at settlement houses. She also coached our Poetry Slam Team. In her acceptance speech, she describes visiting an orphanage in Mexico.

I don't want to make my comments sound like a formal speech, but I do want the graduates to know what's on my mind. Creative writing teachers don't get a chance to do things like this. "You chose YCA because you must have believed certain things about yourself and about writing. You obviously believe that at some level it's important to write creatively. You also must have believed that you had talent and interest. You are a unique minority." They seem to be listening.

"I hope that now, three years later, you feel that way even more. I hope you have discovered even more strengths, that you have found forms and voice to express yourselves and subjects to write about. I hope that you have figured out ways that writing can become a big part of your lives." They look back and smile agreeably. I think they listened.

I tell the audience about the books. "Every year we give each of the graduates a book. The book represents something about their writing. We might pick a book because of its subject or because of its form. We might want the book to serve as a reminder or maybe as a goal. You'll get the idea."

The first to receive a book is Adrienne. Adrienne is a strong girl. I was never more aware of this strength than when I listened to her speak at her grandmother's funeral. She has had her own hairstyling business for several years. She wrote her own chap book and now plans to go to a local university. "I thought that a strong, purposeful person like you would enjoy reading about another purposeful person." I hand her a biography of Rosa Parks.

Following Adrienne is Annamaria, our girl from Romania. We met at her high school, where I was conducting workshops. We talked after class, and soon she signed up for our program. She writes poetry when asked to do so, but she prefers stories. Her most recent story starts off on a porch in the southern United States. We all wondered how a girl from Bucharest would want to write a story that takes place in the South of plantation times. Annamaria has just won a Golden Apple Student Award; this award is given to high-achieving high school students who plan to become teachers. I give her book about teaching.

I then give a book to Jesus, a tall, quiet Hispanic from Pilsen. His preference is opposite to Annamaria's. We've tried to get him to write stories, but he always returns to poetry, most of which he writes in a journal that he carries with him everywhere. He wants to fly planes. I give him *Night Flight* by Antoine De Saint-Exupery and read a quote from that book: "Although human life is priceless, we always act as if something had a greater price than life . . . but what is that something?"

Next is Kelli, who happens to be Jesus' girlfriend. She's a small black girl with a bouncy walk. She's usually quiet, but when she talks, she can take over the class. Like so many of the others, Kelli wants to be a teacher. I give her a book about inner-city teaching. In her first year, she was having trouble at her high school.

Some of the books are obvious choices. Nick has been writing about zombies, so we got him a book about the supernatural. Oscar has just started to write mysteries. He gets two novels by Raymond Chandler Reader. Alvin was a member of our Slam Team. He receives a book about performance poetry in New York. Clinton has been addressing his poetry to young black males like himself. He gets Styron's *The Autobiography of Nat Turner*. Kyra, a multitalented kid, gets a photography book with essays about friends. Wayne, another artist, receives a book about cartooning. Charity, the young playwright, traveled to Africa this year. We give her *Things Fall Apart* by Chinua Achebe. Tashanda has been writing lots and lots of personal poetry. She gets Emily Dickinson.

Some were a little less obvious. Marcia has written and rewritten a story about a girl who doesn't like her name. In fact, much of what she writes has something to do with what people choose to call each other. I thought she might like *Invisible Man*, whose hero is bothered by the same things. I make a point of thanking Mandy for "finally doing what I had asked kids to do for three years." She took an idea from one form and put it somewhere else. She had written a poem about kids in the park. Later she took this scene and made it part of a short story. She's another student who wants to be a teacher. I give her a book about children by Vivian Paley. I tell her that my daughter, also a teacher, loves this book. Mark gets *Catch 22* because he always writes stories and plays filled with comic characters.

Afterwards, in the lobby, one of the fathers tells me how much his daughter enjoyed the program. "She would have done OK without you guys, but this gave her a chance to do something she really loves. And now she'll keep doing it." We talk some more about his daughter, who plans to be a teacher.

He and I shake hands, and he starts to leave, but then he stops. "You know something," he says, smiling back at me. "This was a good idea."

ABOUT THE AUTHOR

Writer, teacher, editor, Bob Boone holds a Ph.D. in English Education from Northwestern University. He currently runs a private learning resource center north of Chicago and directs Young Chicago Authors, a scholarship program for inner city high school students. He has contributed to *Writing, Current Media, The Chicago Reader, The Chicago Tribune, The Chicago Sun Times, Confluence, The Willow Review*, and other journals, magazines and newspapers.

Bob's first book, a biography of baseball star Hack Wilson, was published in 1978. Since then he has written four textbooks and numerous articles. He was a consultant for the movie *Hoop Dreams*.

Hack, by Bob Boone
is available through
The Puddin'head Press

The Puddin'head Press also carries titles from other
publishing concerns including:

OMMATION PRESS
Poems From The Body Bag by Michael Brownstein
Cheap Entertainment by Liz LeBlanc
No Mean Feet by Liz LeBlanc
Languid Love Lyrics by Effie Mihopoulos
Mooncycle by Effie Mihopoulos

THORNTREE PRESS
When the Plow Cuts by Kate Andraski
The Music of Solid Objects by John Dickson
Waving at Trains by John Dickson
Girl in the Empty Nightgown by Eloise Bradley Fink
Lincoln and the Prairie After by Eloise Bradley Fink
You Are Involved in a Fable by Barry Goodman
The Literate Person's Guide to Naming a Cat by Lawrence Jarchow
The Disappearance of Gargoyles by Mary Makofsko
Looking Across by Marcie Lee Masters
Naming the Island by Judith Neeld
What is Good by Hilda Raz

LAKE SHORE PUBLISHING
The Talking Poems: A Family Legend by Anne Brashler
Yes, No Maybe by Glen Brown
I've Been Away So Many Lives by Richard Calish
Sit by Me by Edith Freund
Next Year Country by Louise Liffengren Hullinger
From the Foxes Den by Priscilla A. Johnson
Why Horses, Mrs. K by Blanche Whitney Kloman
Times Rides the River by Robert Mills
Oils of Evening by G.E. Murray
Soundings: A Poetry Anthology by Carol Spelius
Aqueus and Other Tales by Carol Spelius
How We Got Here from There by Carol Spelius
I, Mancha by Carol Spelius

OTHER PUBLICATIONS

Mapmaker Revisited by Beatrice Badikian
The Green Ribbon by Daniel Cleary
Back Beat by Al DeGenova and Charles Rossiter
Avalance Expert by Shelia Donahue
Cook County Forest Preserves by William Eiden
Departures by Robert Klein Engler
Empty Chair by Moonlight by Robert Klein Engler
One Hundred Poems by Robert Klein Engler
Street Preachers, Hookers, and Other Martyrs by John Martinez
Bucket of Questions by Chuck Perkins
A Beating Of Wings by Gertrude Rubin
Shakespeare's Funky Love Cats by Bruce Tate
A Dozen Cold Ones by E. Donald Two-Rivers
Cinnabar by Martha Modena Vertreace
Light Caught Bending by Martha Modena Vertreace
Maafa: When Night Becomes A Lion by Martha Modena Vertreace
Oracle Bones by Martha Modena Vertreace
Second House From The Corner by Martha Modena Vertreace
Second Mourning by Martha Modena Vertreace
Smokeless Flame by Martha Modena Vertreace
Dragon Lady: Tsukimi by Martha Modena Vertreace
Rosedust by Larry Winfield

and

AFTERHOURS Magazine

THE PUDDIN'HEAD PRESS

Publisher and distributor of fine books

CURRENT TITLES

PROPHECIES by Lawrence Tyler
THROUGH MY EYES by Samuel Blechman
CONVERSATIONS WITH FRIENDLY DEMONS
AND TAINTED SAINTS by Nina Corwin
LAKE MICHIGAN SCROLLS by John Dickson
I'M NOT TONIGHT by Kris Darlington
LADY RUTHERFURD'S CAULIFLOWER by JJ Jameson
PROFESSIONAL CEMETERY by Johnny Masiulewicz
JUST A SOUTH SIDE GIRL by Rose Virgo
THE ANTI-MENSCH ANTHOLOGY
THE ANTI-MENSCH II ANTHOLOGY
STARWALLPAPER STUDENT ANTHOLOGY

Published by Puddin'head Press and Collage Press

THRESHOLDS by Jeff Helgeson
CROWDPLEASER by Marc Smith
LESSONS OF WATER AND THIRST by Richard Fammeree

For More information and a complete catalog call or write:

Puddin'head Press
P. O. Box 477889
Chicago IL 60647

(708) 656-4900

phbooks@compuserve.com